WHICH

NEW ZEALAND

INSECT?

What's covered in this book?

All insects likely to be noticed by the beginner in New Zealand have been included, as well as the larger, or more striking, of the rare species.

It isn't possible to include in one book *every* kind of insect found in New Zealand as there are about 20,000 species here. But most of the insects which have been left out are so small that they cannot be identified without a microscope and specialist knowledge.

Are the photos really life-size?

To show how big each insect is, all the photos (unless otherwise marked) are shown at exactly life-size. The precise scale of these photos is ensured with the use of a calibrated macro lens.

How is this book organised?

With the beginner's needs in mind, the most conspicuous groups (Orders) are covered first. (See QuickFind Key on page 7). And then, within each of these Orders, the most conspicuous and larger families come first.

PENGUIN BOOKS

Penguin Books (NZ) Ltd, cnr Airborne and Rosedale Roads, Albany, Auckland 1310, New Zealand
Penguin Books Ltd, 80 Strand, London, WC2R 0RL, England
Penguin Putnam Inc, 375 Hudson Street, New York, NY 10014, United States
Penguin Books Australia Ltd, 250 Camberwell Road, Camberwell, Victoria 3124, Australia
Penguin Books Canada Ltd, 10 Alcorn Avenue, Toronto, Ontario, Canada M4V 3B2
Penguin Books (South Africa) (Pty) Ltd, 24 Sturdee Avenue, Rosebank, Johannesburg 2196, South Africa
Penguin Books India (P) Ltd, 11, Community Centre, Panchsheel Park, New Delhi 110 017, India
Penguin Books Ltd, Registered Offices: Harmondsworth, Middlesex, England

First published by Penguin Books (NZ) Ltd, 2002

1 3 5 7 9 10 8 6 4 2

Copyright © Andrew Crowe (text, line art & photos) 2002

The right of Andrew Crowe to be identified as the author of this work in terms of section 96 of the Copyright Act 1994 is hereby asserted.

Photos, research, text, line art & design concept by Andrew Crowe
Mole cricket & thrips photos by Mt Albert Landcare
Typesetting by Janine Brougham
Printed in China through Bookbuilders

ISBN 0 14 100636 6
www.penguin.co.nz

WHICH
NEW ZEALAND
INSECT?

With Over 650 Life-Size Photos of New Zealand Insects

Andrew Crowe

the answer is on page 21.

dedicated to the six-year-old girl at Kaurihohore School who drew a picture of this moth for me and asked me its name. The

2x

PENGUIN BOOKS

Introduction

What is an insect?
Unlike us, insects are not held together by an internal skeleton but by a 'suit of armour' (exoskeleton) rather like a medieval knight. Their body is divided into three parts, hence the name 'insect' which means: 'in sections'. They are easy to tell from spiders, slaters and centipedes, because all insects have six legs.

In the beginning
Insects have made this planet their home for about 370 million years. They began to walk the Earth more than 100 million years before the first dinosaurs and have already thrived for more than 200 times as long as us. Without doubt, they are one of the world's most successful life-forms.

The world picture: numbers
The total number of individual insects alive in the world today is thought to be over 10,000,000,000,000,000,000. That's over 1500 million for every person.

There are also more *kinds* of insects in the world than anything else – more, even, than all the other animals and plants put together. So far, over one million species are known (and this number keeps on growing). By collecting samples from tropical trees, scientists now estimate that the complete worldwide tally could be between 15 and 30 million species. (Compared, for example, with about 300,000 known species of plants.)

A family tree
To accurately identify all these insects, entomologists (insect scientists) have found it useful to group them into a family tree. This tree is intended to show the way in which insects are related to each other – how they might have evolved. One of the useful things about this grouping is the fact that insects in the same group not only tend to look similar, but they often behave in the same way, living, for example, in the same kind of habitat, often eating the same kind of food. So this family tree also helps us to understand insect behaviour.

Like the entomologists, you can use this family tree to find out what something is. For example, if you spotted a huhu beetle for the first time, you could start at the top of the following list, first asking: Is it an arthropod? And then work your way down to learn which kind it is.

> **Phylum:** Arthropods [Arthropoda] – jointed legs, body made up of segments
> **Class:** Insects [Insecta] – six legs
> **Order:** Beetles [Coleoptera] – hard wing cases
> **Family:** Longhorn Beetles [Cerambycidae] – very long antennae
> **Genus:** Huhu group of Beetles (*Prionoplus* species)
> **Species:** Huhu Beetle (*Prionoplus reticularis*)*

The New Zealand picture
As most insect families are found worldwide, this family tree also provides fascinating insights into New Zealand's prehistoric links with the rest of the world.

For about 65 million years, New Zealand has been isolated from other land. From its unique 'basket of life' many new species evolved over this time which are not found anywhere else. This explains not only why the kiwi and kauri are unique to New Zealand, but also why at least 90 percent of New Zealand's insects are endemic (not found anywhere else in the world).

All up, about 10,000 insects have so far been named in New Zealand, although scientists currently estimate that the true total will turn out to be twice that.

---

* For the more technically minded, this basic system is then further divided into superclasses and subclasses, superorders and suborders, superfamilies and subfamilies, subgenera, cohorts, sections, divisions, series, tribes, subspecies and varieties. But for most purposes, the above summary will do.

Example: take the beetles

For fifteen years (1974 – 1989), Dr Willy Kuschel counted how many different kinds of beetles he could find in one corner of just one Auckland suburb (Lynfield).*

To everyone's surprise, he found 982 different species, most of them unique to New Zealand (endemic). Most (he discovered from his survey) needed their little patch of native forest to survive. Flightless ones were left marooned on an island of suburban bush, for they couldn't even safely cross the road. Around 150 of the beetles were completely new to science. This is all the more remarkable, considering that this search was carried out just 10 km from the centre of New Zealand's largest city.

Until Dr Kuschel's survey, no one had taken the trouble to look that closely at beetles in just one place. So his study has helped to show that there are far more insects in temperate countries (and hence in the world) than anyone had ever believed. And he keeps on counting: his tally in this one patch of Auckland has now reached over 1000 species. And that's just beetles.

But aren't insects a nuisance?

Many people – especially adults – often think of insects as pests. In reality though, less than 0.01 percent fall into this category. (Where they are a nuisance, the secret is to learn what conditions that insect likes and then stop giving this to them.)

Indeed, without insects, much of life on Earth would cease to exist. Without them, we would miss many of our flowers and fruits, for many need insects for pollination. Insects clean up pollutants, dung and the remains of dead plants and animals. They play a useful role in the garden and on the farm too, helping to produce and aerate the soil. Many are important tools for natural weed and pest control. Bees, wasps and cockroaches are even being trained in the same way as dogs to find unexploded landmines. We have insects to thank, too, for honey, silk, shellac and certain waxes and dyes. Insects provide important food for birds, fish, frogs, lizards and mammals. Not only that, but ...

Insects in food & medicine

Worldwide, over 1000 species of insects are used by humans as food or medicine. Indeed, it has been estimated that 80 percent of the world's population eat insects intentionally and 100 percent unintentionally (usually in processed food, like cocoa, flour, peanut butter, strawberry jam and frozen broccoli). For much of the world's population, insects provide important, cheap, low-cholesterol, high-protein food. (Per 100 g serving, the protein content of caterpillars is similar to that of beef.) On a global scale, the most popular are grasshoppers, followed by beetle grubs, caterpillars, ants and termites. Chocolate ants, fried agave worms and caterpillar crunch are all offered for sale in the United States.

However, in New Zealand few people eat insects and this is probably just as well for many are rare or threatened.

Conservation

When it comes to New Zealand's native insects and their habits, surprisingly little is known. What we do know is that most native plants are food for a specific insect. In other words, the loss of that native plant species will involve the extinction of a specific insect too. The only meaningful way to protect rare insects is by protecting their habitat; the species will then look after themselves. Indeed, because of the sensitivity of many insects to habitat modification, they are likely to become increasingly useful to us as environmental indicators for testing the overall health of ecosystems.

Just as New Zealand has many unique flightless birds vulnerable to introduced rats and mice etc, so too with its insects, e.g. wētā, giant weevils, ground beetles and flightless flies (perhaps these should be called 'walks'?).

So, rather than focus on pest insects and how to kill them, this book sets out to celebrate a largely neglected aspect of New Zealand's unique wildlife. It is intended as a tool for their protection, for this is without doubt where the bulk of New Zealand's biodiversity is found. Indeed, these humble creatures are the 'engine room' of our ecosystems.

Looking for insects

Insects are generally most active in spring and summer, so this is often the best time to look for them. Most specialise in just one kind of habitat, so learning what that habitat is for any particular insect – as indicated in this book – is often the key to finding it. With a keen eye, you could soon be making useful observations on their role in New Zealand ecology or finding species new to science.

---

* Kuschel, G. *Beetles in a suburban environment: a New Zealand case study.* DSIR Plant Protection Report No 3, DSIR, 1990.

Insect Life Cycles

A common way to group insects is according to their life cycles. Grouping insects in this way shows how primitive (or ancient) they are thought to be, as shown in the sequence below, from the 'primitive' springtails through to the 'advanced' bees, wasps and ants. This classification is useful in understanding the evolution of insects, their relationships to one another and their life cycles. However, it often does not really help the beginner when it comes to identifying an unknown insect. **For a more practical approach to insect identification, see the QuickFind Key on the facing page.**

1. PRIMITIVE SIX-LEGGED CREATURES WITH NO WINGS
[Class: Collembola & Class: Insecta; Subclass: Apterygota]

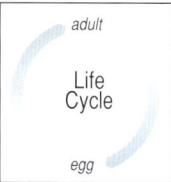

adult

Life
Cycle

egg

Over 300 million years ago, the insects (and insect-like creatures) which lived on Earth could not fly. The eggs of these creatures hatched out looking like young adults. (No metamorphosis.) Surviving examples from this group still develop in this way today and include:

springtails & silverfish

2. INSECTS WITH INCOMPLETE METAMORPHOSIS
[Subclass: Pterygota. Division: Exopterygota]

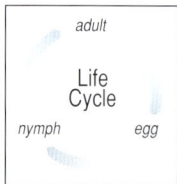

adult

Life
Cycle

nymph   egg

This group includes the first creatures on Earth ever to fly. From fossil records these can be traced back about 300 million years. All go through a series of gradual changes from young form (nymph) to adult. To change from one stage (instar) to the next, they moult their old 'skin', so these insects can all be found at various sizes. E.g. you'll find various sizes of miniature praying mantids (this group) but never miniature butterflies. Insects in this group do *not* go through a resting (pupal) stage. Examples include:

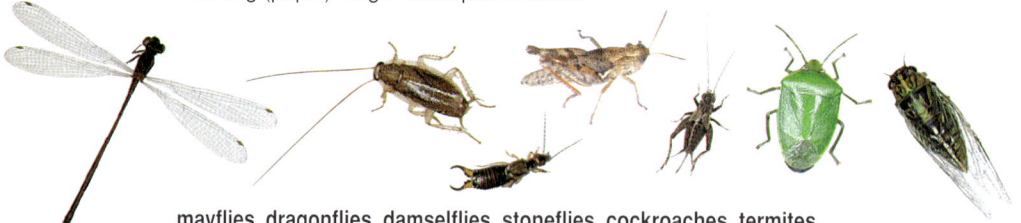

mayflies, dragonflies, damselflies, stoneflies, cockroaches, termites, praying mantids, earwigs, grasshoppers, wētā, crickets, stick insects, booklice, lice, bugs & thrips

3. INSECTS WITH COMPLETE METAMORPHOSIS
[Subclass: Pterygota. Division: Endopterygota]

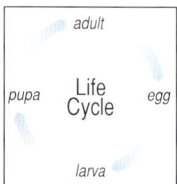

adult

pupa   Life   egg
        Cycle

larva

This group can be traced back about 290 – 245 million years. They are considered to be the most advanced insects, changing completely from the young form ('eating machines': larvae) to the adult form ('breeding machines'). For example, a caterpillar suddenly changes into a chrysalis to rest before transforming into an adult butterfly. These insects all stay the same size throughout their adult life (e.g. a small fly never grows into a big fly). The success of this arrangement is indicated by the fact that 85 percent of all living insects develop in this way. Examples include:

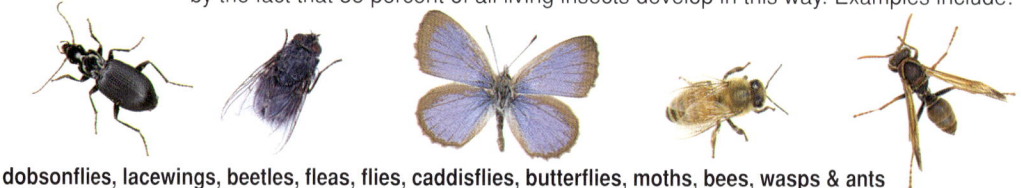

dobsonflies, lacewings, beetles, fleas, flies, caddisflies, butterflies, moths, bees, wasps & ants

QuickFind Key to Insects

Start at the top, to check the big groups first

Go to page

BUTTERFLIES & MOTHS

Scale-covered wings (not see-through).

8

BEETLES

*Hard wing-covers meeting
along a line down the back.*
[Includes: **weevils** & **ladybirds**]

42

FLIES

Have only one pair of see-through wings.
[Includes: **mosquitoes**, **sandflies** & **midges**]

56

BEES, WASPS, ANTS

*Most have a narrow waist. Those with wings
have two pairs of see-through wings.*
[Includes: **sawflies**]

67

FRESHWATER INSECTS

*The young stage of these live in water.
The adults are usually found nearby.*
[Includes: **dragonflies**, **damselflies**, **caddisflies**,
mayflies, **dobsonflies** & **stoneflies**]

74

BUGS

Have a straw-like mouth for piercing and sucking.
[Includes: **shield bugs**, **cicadas**,
aphids & **scale insects**]

82

BIG BACK LEGS

Have unusually powerful back legs.
[Includes: **wētā**, **grasshoppers**, **crickets**]

92

OTHER INSECTS

Members of smaller insect groups.
[Includes: **stick insects**, **mantids**,
cockroaches, **earwigs**, **termites**, **fleas**,
lacewings, **thrips**, **lice**, **silverfish** & **springtails**]

103

*If the creature you've found **does not have six legs**, go to **troubleshooting** (page 112).*

7

Butterflies / Pepe

[Order: Lepidoptera. Superfamily: Papilionoidea]

BUTTERFLY
(Adult)

CHRYSALIS
(Pupa)

BUTTERFLY
LIFE CYCLE
(Complete metamorphosis)

EGGS

CATERPILLAR
(Larva)

BUTTERFLIES ARE BEAUTIFUL

EVEN THOSE PEOPLE WHO INSIST that they hate insects, still love butterflies. With their large, often brightly coloured, scale-covered wings, butterflies are both beautiful and easy to recognise. Only when resting with their wings closed, do the plain undersides of their wings make them look dull and hard to find. In flight, butterflies (unlike moths) seem to have an air of contentment as they alternately flap their wings then glide.

Butterflies have a long, tubular tongue (coiled like a spring when not in use) used for sucking nectar, sweet sap or other liquids. With their stiff, thread-like antennae they smell and touch (and sometimes hear with these, too). Yet, unlike moths, most male butterflies find their female partners by sight, not by smell.

The caterpillar of each species usually eats the leaves of just one kind of plant. And as the females generally lay their eggs here, these foodplants are often the best place to look for the adult butterflies. The females test potential caterpillar foodplants by drumming their feet on the leaves, tasting the plants with the soles of their feet (particularly with their front feet).

Butterflies are less common in winter as most are either hibernating or spending the cooler months as a caterpillar or chrysalis. In the first few days of the life of a chrysalis, many of its internal organs turn to liquid as part of its miraculous transformation into an adult butterfly complete with legs and wings.

Butterflies are certainly among the world's most beautiful insects. But many are also useful as pollinators of deep, tubular flowers. However, as butterfly fanciers sometimes forget, the caterpillars of a few species can still be serious horticultural pests.

Over 20,000 species of butterflies are known worldwide, of which at least 25 are found in New Zealand (including a few which get blown here during storms). The exact total is unknown, as research at Otago Museum continues to reveal many more copper butterfly species.

Māori names for butterflies, moths and caterpillars

The name **pepe** (or **pēpepe**) means 'to flutter' and is traditionally reserved in many Polynesian languages (including some dialects of Māori) for butterflies, while others use the term more widely to include moths and even huhu beetles.

The name **pūrerehua** (also **pūrerehu**, **pūrehurehu** or **pūrēhua**) means 'flickering, dim or dark' and is more widely used for moths and similar-looking caddisflies. Yet some Māori tribes (also the natives of Hawai'i and Vanuatu) traditionally used this term to also include butterflies. Such variations reflect the close relationship of caddisflies, moths and butterflies, as recognised by modern scientists.

When it comes to caterpillars, the number of Māori names is unprecedented among Polynesian languages, where caterpillars in general (and those beetle grubs with legs) are widely known as nuhe or anuhe (Māori: **anuhe**). Including tribal variations, over 40 Māori caterpillar names have been recorded, many of them describing the ecological behaviour of a group, yet often mistakenly applied in dictionaries to a specific insect.

How to tell the difference between a butterfly and a moth:

BUTTERFLIES	MOTHS *Go to page 17*
• Antennae *always* have a clubbed tip	• Antennae feathery or pointed, *not* clubbed
• Wings *mostly* folded upright when resting	• Wings *mostly* spread flat when resting
• Fly during the day	• *Most* fly at night (though some fly by day)

Milkweed Butterflies

[Family: Nymphalidae. Subfamily: Danainae]

Also known as **wanderer butterflies**. Their front legs are short, with brush-like feet, not used for walking. Unlike many butterflies, milkweed butterflies use scent glands at the back to attract a mate. The brightly coloured caterpillars feed mostly on different kinds of milkweed [Asclepiadaceae], absorbing the toxic glycosides in these plants as protection from being eaten by predators. If the bitter-tasting butterfly is swallowed by a bird, the butterfly is often tough enough to survive being spat out again. Many of the chrysalises are decorated with silver or gold and this is the origin of the word 'chrysalis' which comes from the Greek word for 'gold'. Milkweed butterflies are sometimes regarded as a separate family: Danaidae. Over 450 species of milkweed butterflies are known worldwide; three have been seen in New Zealand, two of which have bred here.

Lesser Wanderer
Danaus chrysippus petilia
Common in Africa, the Middle East, Asia, some Pacific Islands and Australia; first spotted in New Zealand in 1904. It has been known to breed here too, but those most often seen (usually January to April) have been blown across from Australia in major storms. Like the monarch, its caterpillars feed on swan plant (*Gomphocarpus* & *Asclepias*).

Australian Blue Tiger
Tirumala hamata hamata (was *Danaus*)
Australian. Until 1995, only four sightings of this butterfly were known in New Zealand. But in April and June of that year hundreds were seen from North-West Nelson to Northland (along with large numbers of **blue moon butterflies**). From the average wind speed at the time, it was calculated that they made this passage from Australia in 54 – 60 hours. The caterpillar's main foodplants are Australian members of the milkweed family [Asclepiadaceae].

Unless otherwise indicated, all photos are life-size

Monarch / Kahuku
Danaus plexippus

The monarch arrived in New Zealand at least 120 years ago, having apparently crossed the Pacific from North America. This, New Zealand's largest resident butterfly, is common on warm sunny days in many gardens, especially near the caterpillar's food: swan plant (*Gomphocarpus*). In mid-summer, monarchs spend about two weeks as a caterpillar, two weeks as a chrysalis, then live for about two months as a butterfly.

Migration: The monarch is the only butterfly in the world known to regularly undertake a two-way migration. Indeed, one female holds the record for the longest known insect migration, having flown 3432 km from Canada to Mexico. At average speeds of up to 130 km per day, this journey would have taken almost one month, flying at altitudes of up to 1000 m. Each year, at the end of summer, at least 100 million monarch butterflies make a similar southward journey to the mountain ranges of Mexico where they hibernate in the pine forests. At the end of winter, they mate and start on their long journey back north. The most incredible thing about this northward journey is that it takes up to five generations of butterflies 'leap-frogging' each other until the great, great, great grandchildren find their Canadian summer home again! How do they know where to go? No one knows. In spite of its incredible journeys overseas, monarchs do not migrate long distances in New Zealand.

Breeding Hints: To protect the caterpillars from wasps, soldier bugs etc, throw netting over the foodplant. Also, in case the caterpillars strip the plant, keep a few spare swan plants indoors. In an emergency, mature caterpillars can also survive on milkweed or spurge (*Euphorbia*), kapok vine (*Araujia sericifera*), tweedia (*Oxypetalum caeruleum*), honey plant (*Hoya*) or slices of ripe pumpkin.

male
(with black scent pouch on back wings; the female lacks these.)

newly hatched butterfly

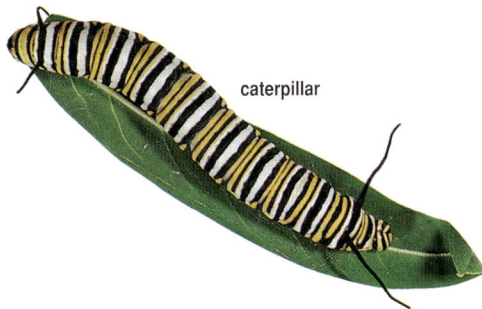

caterpillar

chrysalis

Admiral Butterflies

[Family: Nymphalidae. Subfamily: Nymphalinae]

Many admirals are very brightly coloured, but the undersides of their wings are dull, so that when the butterfly is at rest, with its wings closed, it is well camouflaged. As with the milkweed butterflies and the ringlets, the front legs of admiral butterflies are short, with brush-like feet, not used for walking. The adult males of some species are territorial, chasing other males away. About 350 species are known worldwide, of which five have so far been seen in New Zealand.

Red Admiral / Kahu Kura

Vanessa gonerilla gonerilla (was *Bassaris*)

Native Although similar butterflies are found in other countries, this red admiral is found only in New Zealand. It is usually seen from mid- to late summer and spends the winter hibernating. The butterflies are attracted to the purple flowers of the butterfly bush (*Buddleja*). The caterpillars eat nettle leaves, especially the leaves of the native ongaonga tree nettle (*Urtica ferox*). The Chatham Islands has its own subspecies (*Vanessa gonerilla ida*). The butterfly's Māori name means 'red cloak'.

Yellow Admiral / Kahu Kōwhai

Vanessa itea (was *Bassaris*)

at rest

Native Collected here on Cook's voyage in 1769, but also found in Australia. Common here in open country and gardens in late summer and autumn, mostly at low altitudes. It hibernates during winter. They are attracted to the flowers of the butterfly bush (*Buddleja*). The caterpillars feed on the leaves of common nettles (*Urtica* species). The butterfly's Māori name means 'yellow cloak'.

Australian Meadow Argus

Junonia villida calybe

Australian. These days, sightings of this butterfly in New Zealand are rare and they have never been known to breed here, but, in late 1886, literally thousands of the butterflies crossed the Tasman. The most likely place to see them is near gardens and roadsides, where they are most active in hot weather. In Australia, snapdragon (*Antirrhinum*) is one of the caterpillar's main foodplants.

Australian Painted Lady / Pepe Para Hua

Vanessa kershawi (was *Cynthia*)

at rest

Arrives in New Zealand from Australia most years, sometimes in large numbers and occasionally breeds here over summer. It flies fast and close to the ground. The undersides of the wings look like tree bark, so it is well camouflaged when resting. It will even line up its wings with the sun, so as not to leave a shadow. The caterpillars feed on various plants of the daisy family [Asteraceae], e.g. thistle, Cape weed, African daisy (*Arctotis*) and various everlasting daisies.

Unless otherwise indicated, all photos are life-size

female

male

Blue Moon
Hypolimnas bolina nerina
Seen most years on or near the west coast from late March to May, having been blown here from Australia – a journey which, with a favourable wind, might take it about three days. The female is larger, with red patches and more white on its wings. The caterpillar's known foodplants (*Portulaca, Sida* and *Alternanthera*) do grow in New Zealand, but the butterfly has never been known to breed here in the wild. Known in Australia as the **common eggfly**.

Unless otherwise indicated, all photos are life-size

Ringlet Butterflies

[Family: Nymphalidae. Subfamily: Satyrinae]

Many ringlets are found only in the mountains, others in forests, usually flying near the ground. Unlike many butterflies, ringlets will fly in the evening and on overcast days. Most are orange and black with eye-like spots ('ringlets') on the wings. These 'eyes' are believed to help scare away hungry birds. Like the milkweed butterflies and admirals, the front legs of ringlets are short with brush-like feet, not used for walking. One unusual feature is that some have ears in the bases of their wings. The caterpillars live on grasses and sedges. Sometimes regarded as a separate butterfly family: Satyridae. About 2400 species are known worldwide; eight species have been seen in New Zealand, six of them unique to this country and two introduced.

Tussock Ringlet
Argyrophenga species

Native   There are at least three very similar-looking species, all found in the native tussock of the South Island. With their wings closed, they are all very well camouflaged against the leaves as they have silver streaks on the underside of the back wings. The sleek green caterpillars feed on tall snow tussock (*Chionochloa*) and some introduced grasses. Illustrated here are an untypical *A. antipodum* without the usual ringlet wingspots (left) and *A. janitae* (right). The third named species (*A. harrisi*) is restricted to the Nelson area.

at rest

Forest Ringlet
Dodonidia helmsii

Native   Flies fast and high near the edges of forest and in forest clearings on both main islands from Lewis Pass northwards. The adult butterfly lives 3 – 4 weeks. From spring to early autumn, the green caterpillars feed at night on cutty grass (*Gahnia*) and bush snowgrass (*Chionochloa*). This butterfly has become much rarer over the past 50 years, probably as a result of the caterpillars being attacked by wasps. Also known as **Helms' butterfly**.

Butler's Mountain Ringlet
Erebiola butleri

Native   Seen in late summer, flying near the ground in the South Island mountains from North-West Nelson to Fiordland, among scrub and snow tussock at 900 – 1300 m. The male will fly long distances but the female only makes very short flights. The yellow-brown caterpillar feeds on snowgrass (*Chionochloa*).

Black Mountain Ringlet
Percnodaimon merula complex (was *Erebia pluto*)

Native   Seen high in the South Island mountains, among rock falls and scree slopes at 800 – 2000 m (though less common below 1200 m). With its velvety black wings, it is effectively solar-heated, sitting with its opened wings turned to catch the warmth of the sun, flying only when the sun shines, but hiding among rocks when a cloud passes. The dull-coloured caterpillars feed at night on blue tussock (*Poa colensoi*) & other *Poa* species. Unlike most butterflies, the female does not lay her eggs on the caterpillar's foodplant, but rather on stones where the sun's heat helps the eggs to hatch.

Blue & Copper Butterflies

[Family: Lycaenidae]

Short-lived butterflies, spending about 8 –12 days as adults. The caterpillars of some make a sweet, sticky liquid called honeydew. Some ants will even carry one of these caterpillars to their nest, then stroke (or 'milk') it to get the honeydew. In return, the caterpillar gets to eat some ant grubs. (Such behaviour has not yet been seen in New Zealand.) The adult males of some species are territorial, chasing other males away. The chrysalises of many can make squeaking or grating sounds when disturbed. About 6000 species are known worldwide, of which at least 11 are currently estimated to be found in New Zealand.

Longtailed Blue
Lampides boeticus

Almost worldwide. First seen in New Zealand about 1965 and now common from Nelson north. With its wings folded, the 'tails' on the back of the wings look like antennae, thus helping to distract insect-eating birds away from the insect's true head. The caterpillars spend their whole life feeding inside the flowers and seed pods of legumes such as gorse, broom, garden and sweet peas.

Common Blue / Pepe Ao Uri
Zizina labradus labradus

Australia's most common butterfly has probably been arriving in New Zealand on storms for centuries. But only when Europeans cleared the forest here for farms, did it find opportunities to establish itself. It is now common in gardens and farmland in the North Island and the north and west of the South Island, below 1000 m. In late summer, it flies close to the ground, often resting with its wings slightly spread. The little green slug-like caterpillars eat legumes such as white clover leaves, lucerne and birdsfoot trefoil (*Lotus*).

Southern Blue
Zizina labradus oxleyi

Native Found east of the Southern Alps. Looks very similar to the common blue, and can be best distinguished by the undersides of the wings which have dark zig-zag bands across them and a more distinctive banded border. But in Marlborough and north Canterbury, these two species hybridise, making this distinction harder to see. The caterpillars feed on various legumes including a native low-growing broom (*Carmichaelia*).

South Island male (above);
North Island male (below)

male

female

Boulder Copper
Boldenaria boldenarum (was *Lycaena*)

Native Common among tussock, especially in the South Island. The caterpillars feed on creeping pōhuehue (*Muehlenbeckia axillaris* & *M. ephedroides*) and sorrel (*Rumex*). The male's wings are iridescent purple on top. New research shows that there are many more undescribed species.

Glade Copper
Lycaena feredayi complex

Native Found along the edges of forest and lakes; hence the common name. The dark markings on the wings are heavier than on the other coppers; the underwings are yellow with a large dark triangular smudge. The caterpillars eat pōhuehue (the large-leaved muehlenbeckia, *Muehlenbeckia australis*). There are several similar undescribed species.

Common Copper / Pepe Para Riki
Lycaena salustius complex

Native Common in mid-summer in warm, open places from sand dunes to tussock hillsides. Attracted to blackberry flowers. Flies fast and jerkily, 2 – 3 m above the ground. The little green slug-like caterpillars eat pōhuehue leaves (*Muehlenbeckia* species). Note the dark wing veins of males are double; on females single and broad. Those with single thin, delicate veins belong to the similar (more strictly coastal) *Lycaena rauparaha* complex. Recent research has shown that there are several similar named and unnamed species, many of which have their own flight behaviour, flying season, foodplant and distribution.

White Butterflies

[Family: Pieridae]

Small to medium-sized butterflies, white, yellow or orange (the coloured ones being known overseas as **sulphurs**). The chemical pigments in these colours and the insects' body fluids are toxic; hence these butterflies are rarely eaten by other insects. Most are good fliers, many of them migrating long distances. About 1200 species are known worldwide; only one breeds here, but a second one has been seen (once!) in New Zealand.

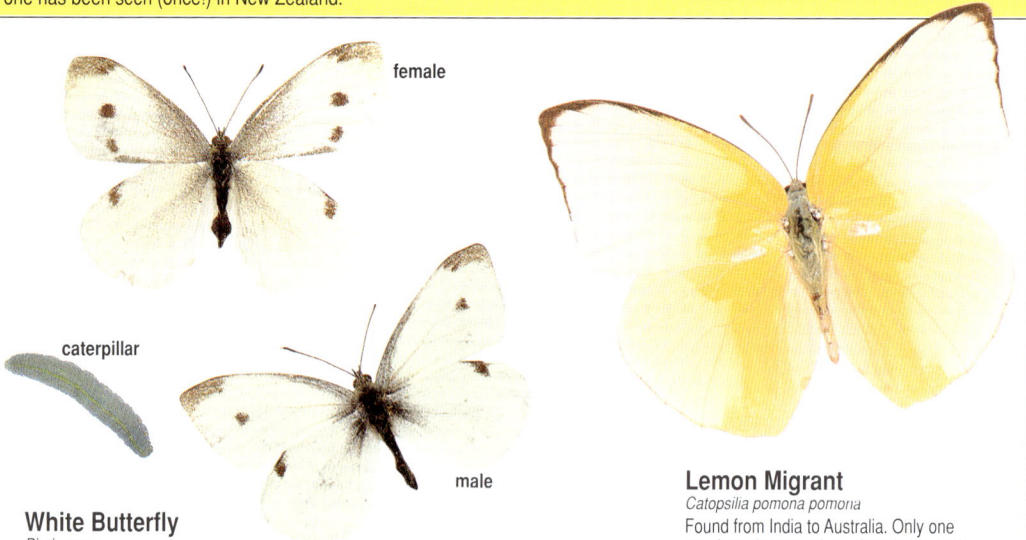

female

caterpillar

male

White Butterfly
Pieris rapae

From Europe and North America. Accidentally introduced to New Zealand about 1930 and now found throughout the country. The caterpillars (see photo) are a pest, eating the leaves of cabbage, turnip, cauliflower and nasturtium. Hence, another common name: **cabbage white**. The males have one black spot on each front wing; females two. The Māori name **pepe mā** has been translated from the English name.

Lemon Migrant
Catopsilia pomona pomona

Found from India to Australia. Only one specimen has ever been found alive in the wild in New Zealand – in Auckland – and this was some time before 1876. In India, huge and spectacular migrations of this pretty butterfly are seen. The caterpillar's foodplant is *Cassia*.

Swallowtail Butterflies

[Family: Papilionidae]

Many have 'tails' on the back wings. This family includes the world's largest butterflies, e.g. the **Queen Alexandra birdwing** (*Ornithoptera alexandrae*) of Papua New Guinea, whose wingspan can reach 28 cm. About 600 species of swallowtails are known worldwide; only one has been seen in New Zealand but it hasn't bred here.

Japanese Swallowtail
Papilio xuthus

One of the commonest butterflies in Japan during their summer. In 1996, one was seen emerging from its chrysalis in a Dunedin car yard by a woman supervising a school trip there. This yard specialises in Japanese used cars so the chrysalis is thought to have arrived with one of the cars. The caterpillars feed on plants in the citrus family [Rutaceae], so this butterfly could possibly breed here if it had emerged in the warmer north.

Unless otherwise indicated, all photos are life-size

Moths / Pūrerehua

[Order: Lepidoptera]

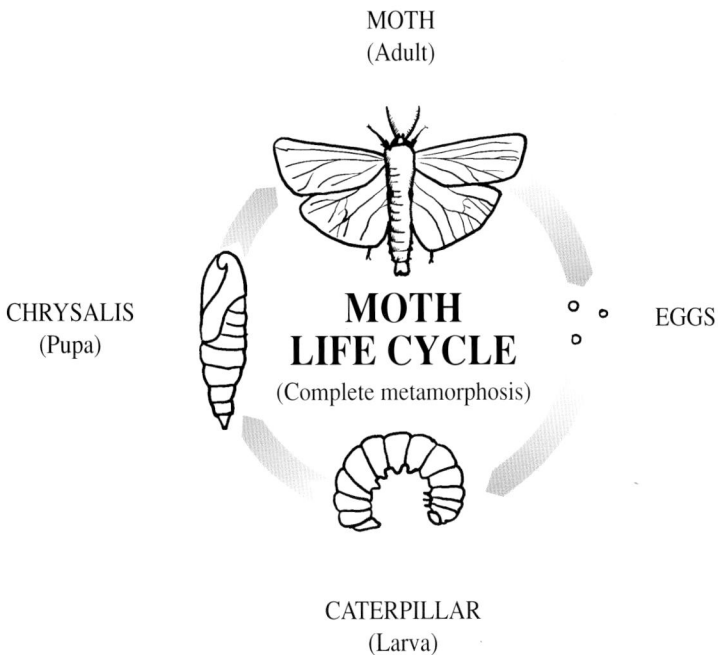

MOTH
(Adult)

CHRYSALIS
(Pupa)

**MOTH
LIFE CYCLE**

(Complete metamorphosis)

EGGS

CATERPILLAR
(Larva)

MOTHS, TOO, CAN BE BRIGHT

IT WOULD BE ALL TOO EASY to dismiss moths as dull brown things which fly into lights at night. But, in reality, many New Zealand species are brightly coloured day-flying moths every bit as beautiful as butterflies. Just take a summer trip to the South Island mountains to feast your eyes on some of the colourful loopers shown on the following pages.

Like butterflies, most moths have long, tightly curled tongues for sucking the nectar from flowers. To enable night-flying moths to find these flowers, flowers pollinated by them are usually white, often emitting a strong scent only in the evening. And since many New Zealand native plants are pollinated by such night-flying moths, this may help to explain why so few of this country's flowers are brightly coloured.

The best way to distinguish between moths and butterflies is to check out their antennae, for moth antennae have no club, or swelling, at the tip. Moths use these antennae for smelling flowers, with some species detecting flowers half a kilometre away or more. The more feathery antennae of the male moths are also used to detect special sex scents (pheromones) produced by the females. In some cases, these antennae are so sensitive that he can detect just one molecule of scent, enabling him to find a female up to 11 km away. Some moths make high-pitched calls. Many have very good hearing too, detecting sounds much higher than those which humans can hear, and are thus able to avoid the sonar squeals of hunting bats heard from up to 30 m away. Some use their antennae as ears; some have ears on their bodies; others have ears in the bases of their wings; a few hawk moths even listen with their mouths.

As with butterflies, moths are often found near the foodplant of their caterpillars, for this is where the female moth lays her eggs. She checks out the identity of each plant by tasting it, but not with her tongue. Instead, she uses her feet, her antennae or her ovipositor (egg-laying organ). In many cases, the caterpillars of related species specialise in feeding on related plants, a fact which can be helpful in finding and identifying both the caterpillars and the moths.

Most caterpillars can spin silk from their mouths, which they use to build protective cases, to climb or to 'abseil', or just to anchor themselves. By paying out such silk threads, some very young caterpillars are even picked up by the wind to 'fly' short distances. The Chinese use the threads of one species for making fishing lines. And for making cloth, caterpillar silk has been used since the time of the Aztecs, with one such moth ranking as one of the world's most useful insects: the **silkworm moth** (*Bombyx mori*) of South-East Asia, each caterpillar of which can produce a thread of silk almost one kilometre long.

Caterpillars are also an important food for many birds; others are hosts to bristle flies and parasitic wasps which lay their eggs in them as food for their young. Several caterpillars and moths were eaten by early Māori, just as many are still used, either raw or cooked, in everyday cuisine overseas today.

Moths (together with butterflies) form the world's third largest Order of insects, with about 150,000 species known worldwide, over 1700 of them in New Zealand, most of them unique to this country. Just six percent are shared with Australia. Of New Zealand's total, more than half are so-called **micro moths**: with a wingspan less than 2 cm. A selection of the larger and more distinctive species appears on the following pages.

How to tell the difference between a moth and a butterfly:

MOTHS	BUTTERFLIES	Go to page **8**
• Antennae feathery or pointed, *not* clubbed	• Antennae *always* have a clubbed tip	
• Wings *mostly* spread flat when resting	• Wings *mostly* folded upright when resting	
• *Most* fly at night (though some fly by day)	• Fly during the day	

Ghost Moths

[Family: Hepialidae]

These moths can be so slow to move that it is often possible to pick them up before they fly away. However, once they get going, many are such fast (if somewhat erratic) fliers that they are also known overseas as **swift moths**. Their front and back wings simply overlap and are not linked together in flight as with other moths. Ghost moths have no mouth, never eat and have a very short life: usually about one week. After mating, many simply scatter their eggs in the general area of the caterpillar's foodplant. Many of the caterpillars bore into turf or wood. The chrysalises are unusual in that these have rows of movable spines along their bodies, allowing them to wriggle up and down their silk-lined tunnel. This ancient insect group is named after the ghostly white look of a European member of the family. About 500 species are known worldwide; about 28 in New Zealand, all native and found only here (including one Threatened Species).

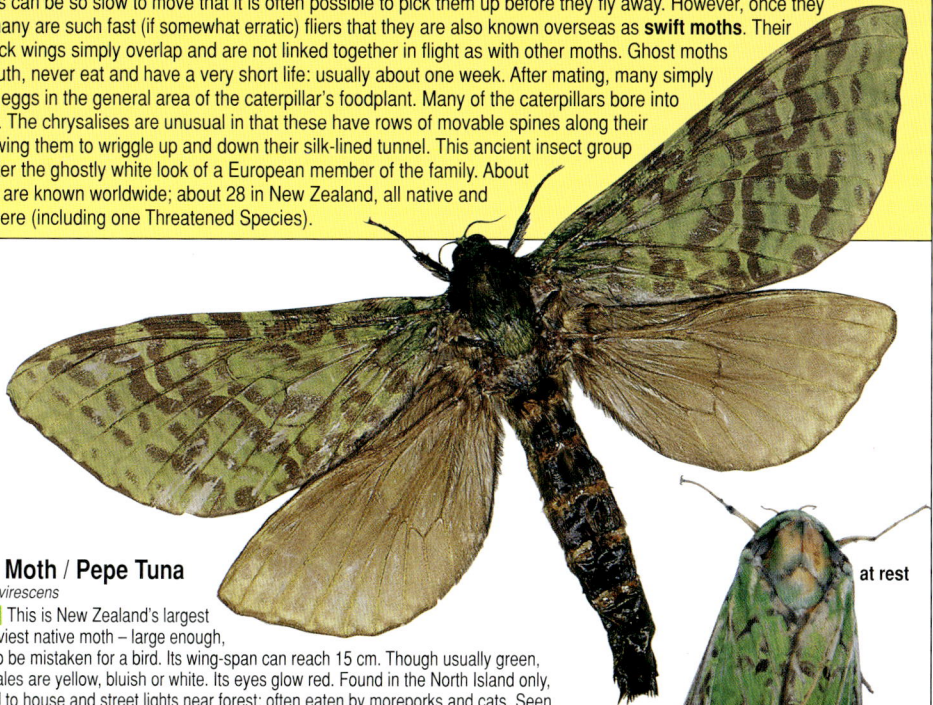

at rest

Pūriri Moth / Pepe Tuna
Aenetus virescens

`Native` This is New Zealand's largest and heaviest native moth – large enough, in fact, to be mistaken for a bird. Its wing-span can reach 15 cm. Though usually green, a few males are yellow, bluish or white. Its eyes glow red. Found in the North Island only, attracted to house and street lights near forest; often eaten by moreporks and cats. Seen all year, but mostly in spring, living only a few days, during which time they mate and the female scatters up to 2000 fertilised eggs on the forest floor. The tiny caterpillars spend their first year eating bracket fungus found on fallen logs. From there – by now much fatter – they climb a pūriri, beech, putaputawētā, makomako (wineberry), houhere (lacebark), or oak tree, to make a 7-shaped tunnel inside the trunk, where they eat the inner bark and outer sapwood for up to six more years. Meanwhile, they make a silk lid to hide the entrance hole. Māori removed these lids and poured water down to extract the mature caterpillars for food and as eel bait (pepe tuna means 'eel moth'). No wonder as, at up to 12 cm long, these are New Zealand's biggest caterpillars, hence their Māori name: **mokoroa** (long grub or caterpillar).

'vegetable caterpillar'

caterpillar

Forest Ghost Moth
Aoraia enysii

`Native` Found in forest from Mt Te Aroha to Mt Aspiring, particularly in summer. The caterpillars feed for 2 – 3 years on leaf litter, during which time they are sometimes attacked by a fungus (*Cordyceps robertsii*), which turns them into a **vegetable caterpillar** (see photo). When fresh, this strange object (**āwhato** or **āwheto**) was eaten by early Māori. When dry, it was ground up to make a blue-black dye for moko (tattoos).

Porina Moth
Wiseana species

`Native` Seen from October to January in forest and grassland. There are several similar species in different parts of the country. At rest, they hold their wings so tight against their body that the tips touch. The caterpillars (see photo) come out of the soil at night to feed on grass. These caterpillars were eaten by Māori in the same way as huhu grubs. The common name 'porina' is not Māori, but rather an old Latin name for the moth.

Unless otherwise indicated, all photos are life-size

Looper Moths / Tāwhana

[Family: Geometridae]

Closely related to butterflies and, like butterflies, many are colourful creatures which fly during the day. Many have a slender body and fine geometrical camouflage designs on their wings. Some are so patterned that they are known as **carpet moths** [Larentiinae]. At rest, most hold their wings out flat to form a broad triangle. A few rest with wings together like butterflies. Even at rest, they remain alert and are easily disturbed. Included are the **underwings** ('appear & disappear moths') which hide their brightly coloured back wings when resting, but flash these to startle predators. Looper caterpillars have the usual three pairs of true legs at the front, and two or three pairs of 'false legs' (prolegs) at the back. With no legs in the middle, their body forms a high loop with each step, as if measuring a twig. The names: **geometrids**, **loopers** or **measuring worm moths** – all refer to this. Likewise, the Māori names, **tāwhana** or **tāwhanawhana** (meaning 'bent like a bow') and **whangawhanga** ('to span with the thumb and fingers spread'). Many of the caterpillars are camouflaged with veins; some rest stretched out stiffly at an angle to look like a twig, or dangle from a branch on a thread like a spider. One of the world's largest moth families with about 20,000 species known; over 280 in New Zealand, most of them unique to this country (6 of them on the Threatened Species List). A selection of New Zealand's more common and distinctive species follows in alphabetical order of scientific name.

Swamp Looper
Adeixis griseata
Native Seen in swamps, resting with its head pointing down. Appears from January to March. The caterpillar's foodplant is unknown.

Australasian Yellow
Anachloris subochraria (was *Hydriomena*)
Native Also in Australia. Very common day-flying moth in open country throughout New Zealand at low altitudes, from November to April. The caterpillars feed on ragwort flowers and possibly also on the leaves of willowherb (*Epilobium*).

Alpine Grassland Orange
Aponotoreas insignis (was *Notoreas*)
Native A day-flying moth, common from January to March over tall tussockland on South Island mountain-sides at 900 – 1500 m. The caterpillars eat snowgrass (*Chionochloa*).

Wirerush Looper
Aponotoreas synclinalis (was *Notoreas*)
Native A day-flying moth, seen from January till March in mossy swamps near sea level in southern New Zealand. The long thin caterpillars feed on wirerush (*Empodisma*).

Riverbed Triangle
Arctesthes catapyrrha (was *Lythria*)
Native A day-flying moth seen October to March in the South Island on shingle riverbeds and stony paddocks from near sea level up to 600 m. The caterpillars eat a very wide range of low herbs.

Exquisite Carpet
Asaphodes adonis (was *Xanthorhoe*)
Native Seen resting on lichen-covered tree trunks in January and February in wet South Island forests at 300 – 1300 m. The caterpillars eat various non-woody plants on the forest floor.

Southern Green Carpet
Asaphodes beata (was *Xanthorhoe*)
Native Seen in summer in forest throughout the country, but mostly in the South Island. The caterpillars eat various non-woody plants on the forest floor.

Western Brown Carpet
Asaphodes cataphracta (was *Xanthorhoe*)
Native Seen flying during the day, December to March, on grassy slopes at 1000 – 1300 m in the South Island. The caterpillars eat mountain buttercups (*Ranunculus*).

Elegant Carpet
Asaphodes chlamydota (was *Xanthorhoe*)
Native Seen November to April in open forest and scrub on the North and South Islands, but is not common. The caterpillar feeds on various *Clematis* plants.

Orange Carpet
Asaphodes citroena (was *Xanthorhoe*)
Native Seen along the edges of forest and scrub, from December to January. The caterpillars are thought to feed on forest buttercups (*Ranunculus*).

Large Striped Carpet
Asaphodes clarata (was *Xanthorhoe*)
Native A day-flying moth seen in summer and early autumn in upland tussock country throughout. The caterpillars feed on buttercups (*Ranunculus*).

Unless otherwise indicated, all photos are life-size

Blue Carpet
Asaphodes obarata (was *Xanthorhoe*)
Native Rare. Seen December to January, along forest edges on the North and South Islands but only in a few places. It has recently disappeared from Dunedin and Invercargill. The caterpillar's foodplant is unknown.

Bright Green Carpet
Asaphodes philpotti (was *Xanthorhoe*)
Native Seen January to March in wet forests throughout New Zealand. The caterpillars eat pennywort (*Hydrocotyle*) and bitter cress (*Cardamine*).

Yellow & Brown Carpet
Asaphodes prasinias (was *Xanthorhoe*)
Native Seen in summer in forest and shrubland at about 900 m, mostly in the South Island, but also on Mt Taranaki (Egmont). The caterpillars eat buttercups (*Ranunculus*).

Green Coprosma Carpet
Austrocidaria callichlora (was *Hydriomena*)
Native Seen November to March in forest on the North and South Islands. The smooth green caterpillars feed on several species of *Coprosma*, especially karamū.

Barred Coprosma Carpet
Austrocidaria gobiata (was *Eucymatoge*)
Native Found in forest and scrub on exposed hillsides, resting with its wing patterns lined up. The caterpillars feed on several species of *Coprosma*, especially *Coprosma propinqua*.

Mountain Coprosma Carpet
Austrocidaria praerupta (was *Hydriomena*)
Native Found in mountain forest at 500 – 1000 m. One of a group of looper moths with carpet-like patterns on the wings. The smooth green caterpillars feed on *Coprosma* shrubs.

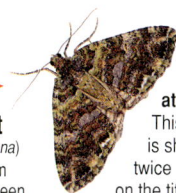

Dark Coprosma Carpet
Austrocidaria similata (was *Hydriomena*)
Native Common throughout from November to February. Has also been called the green and purple carpet moth, a name more appropriately now given to *Hydriomena purpurifera* (page 23). The twig-like caterpillars feed mostly on twiggy *Coprosma* shrubs.

at rest
This moth is shown at twice life-size on the title page.

Orange Triangle
Cephalissa siria (was *Hydriomena*)
Native Flies like a butterfly during the day in October and November in the southern South Island, at the edge of low-lying kahikatea and native beech forest. The caterpillars feed on climbing fuchsia (*Fuchsia perscandens*).

Silver Fern Looper
Chalastra aristarcha (was *Selidosema*)
Native Common in North Island forest. The caterpillars eat ponga tree fern fronds (silver fern, *Cyathea dealbata*).

Australian Pug
Chloroclystis filata

at rest

Native Self-introduced from Australia about 1970 and now very common all year throughout New Zealand from the coast to the mountains. The caterpillars feed on the flowers of shrubs, particularly gorse.

Mottled Forest Pug
Chloroclystis lichenodes
Native Found in dense forest throughout New Zealand, November to January. Pug caterpillars generally feed on flowers, but the specific foodplant of this species is unknown.

Kawakawa Looper
Cleora scriptaria (was *Selidosema panagrata*)
Native Common throughout in summer and autumn. The caterpillars (see photo) eat holes in the leaves of kawakawa, makomako (wineberry), ramarama and even introduced feijoa trees. Also known as grey evening moth.

Greater Orange Underwing
Dasyuris anceps

Native Flies strongly by day, December to February, among rocks in the mountains up to alpine altitudes. Confusingly, the back wings of specimens found in the North Island lack the orange colouring. The caterpillars eat speargrass (*Aciphylla*) and native aniseed (*Gingidia*).

Golden Spotted Looper
Dasyuris transaurea

Native Flies by day in mountain grassland in the southern South Island from November to January. The caterpillars eat the common native aniseed (*Anisotome aromatica*).

Forest Semilooper
Declana floccosa

Native Common all year, on tree trunks or posts. The twig-like caterpillars eat mānuka leaves, pine, native beech, tutu and makomako (wineberry). Called 'semilooper' as the caterpillar lifts the middle part of its body only. Also called **mānuka moth**.

at rest

Spotted Mānuka Moth
Declana leptomera

Native Seen September to March near forest and scrub on both main islands, but more common in the North Island. The twig-like caterpillars eat the leaves of various plants, including mānuka and pine.

Lawyer Pug
Elvia glaucata

Native Found in forest, mostly spring to autumn, resting with its body curled up at the back. Comes in two colour forms: one light green; the other purple.The caterpillars feed on bush lawyer (*Rubus*). (Or, in the Chatham Islands, on its introduced relative: blackberry.)

Rusty Hebe Looper
Dasyuris callicrona

Native Flies in hot sunshine over grassy slopes in the South Island at 900 – 1350 m, December to January. The caterpillars feed on one of the subalpine *Hebes*.

North Island Lichen Moth
Declana atronivea

Native North Island only. Seen November to February, resting on tree trunks, looking like lichen. Also known as **zebra moth**. The twig-like caterpillars eat five finger (*Pseudopanax*) leaves and lichen.

at rest

Blue & Orange Rock Looper
Dichromodes ida

Native Seen October to December flying during the day in rocky areas of Central Otago at 100 – 900 m. The caterpillars feed on those lichens which specialise in growing on rocks.

Orange Inanga Looper
Epiphryne charidema autocharis (was *Venusia*)

Native Seen from early December from East Cape south, to over 1500 m. The green-and-white striped caterpillars feed on inanga leaves (*Dracophyllum longifolium*).

Orange Speargrass Looper
Dasyuris partheniata

Native Flies strongly by day, October to March, from southern North Island south, in open grassy places from sea level to 1350 m. The caterpillars feed on speargrass (*Aciphylla*).

South Island Lichen Moth
Declana egregia

Native Seen in summer in the South Island only. The twig-like caterpillars feed on common and mountain five finger (*Pseudopanax*). Also called zebra lichen moth. Appears on the back of the New Zealand $100 note.

Streaked Inanga Looper
Declana glacialis

Native Flies November to January in hot sunshine in the South Island mountains at 600 – 1200 m. The twig-like caterpillars feed on inanga leaves (native grass shrubs, *Dracophyllum*). When disturbed, these caterpillars wriggle violently and fall to the ground.

Alpine Lichen Looper
Dichromodes niger (was *nigra*)

Native Flies fast in hot sunshine, December to January, near mountain rock falls and bluffs at altitudes over 1500 m in the South Island and on Mt Ruapehu. The caterpillars feed on lichens growing on stones or rocks.

Lacebark Looper
Epiphryne undosata (was *Venusia*)

Native Seen October to December throughout both main islands. The caterpillars feed on the leaves of ribbonwood (*Plagianthus*) and mountain lacebarks (*Hoheria*).

Unless otherwise indicated, all photos are life-size

cabbage tree moth caterpillars feeding

Cabbage Tree Moth
Epiphryne verriculata (was *Venusia*)
Native Seen throughout, September to March, on dead cabbage tree leaves, spreading its wings wide to neatly align its patterning with the veins of the leaves. The flat green caterpillars (see photo) hide during the day among the leaf bases, climbing out at night to eat the leaves.

at rest
The vein patterns on its wings align neatly with the veins on the dead leaves of cabbage trees, making the moth practically impossible to see until it moves.

Aristotelia Looper
Epiphryne xanthaspis (was *Venusia*)
Native Seen February to March from central North Island south. The caterpillars feed on mountain wineberry (*Aristotelia fruticosa*).

Common Carpet
Epyaxa rosearia (was *Xanthorhoe*)
Native Very common throughout. Seen all year, often around lights at night. The caterpillars feed on the leaves of various plants, including garden nasturtium and marigold (*Calendula*).

Brown Evening Moth
Gellonia dejectaria (was *Selidosema*)
Native Often drawn inside houses by lights at night, October to December. Rests with wings spread wide, aligning the patterns on its wings. The caterpillars eat the leaves of citrus and plum, also native plants such as māhoe, kareao (supplejack) and bush lawyer.

Lesser Brown Evening Moth
Gellonia pannularia (was *Selidosema*)
Native Seen in forest and shrubland throughout New Zealand, January to March. Rests with its wing patterns lined up for camouflage. The caterpillars eat the leaves of pine and many native trees.

Angle Carpet
Helastia triphragma
Native Seen August to January in dry areas of South Otago to Marlborough. Also called grey angle-wing moth. The caterpillars feed on everlasting daisy shrub, niniao (*Helichrysum lanceolatum*).

Small Hook-Tip Looper
Homodotis megaspilata (was *Asaphodes*)
Native Very common in summer in forest and shrubland throughout. Attracted to light. The caterpillars feed on fallen leaves, including those of hangehange (Māori privet, *Geniostoma*).

Gunnera Carpet
Hydriomena arida (was *Melanthia*)
Native Seen October to December in South Island forest, along damp shady banks up to 1000 m. The caterpillars feed on the mat-like solitary gunnera, *Gunnera monoica*.

Dark-Banded Carpet
Hydriomena deltoidata
Native Very common, flying both night and day in summer along forest edges throughout. This is possibly the most variably patterned moth in New Zealand. The caterpillars will eat plantain (*Plantago*).

Green & Purple Carpet
Hydriomena purpurifera
Native Seen October to November in forest throughout at 300 – 900 m, resting on tree trunks, looking like a lichen. The caterpillars feed on willowherbs (*Epilobium*).

Zigzag Fern Looper
Ischalis fortinata (was *Azelina*)
Native Common in forests, January to March, mostly in the South Island. The caterpillars eat prickly shield fern (pūniu, *Polystichum vestitum*). Also called angle-winged fern moth.

Striped Fern Looper
Ischalis gallaria (was *Azelina*)
Native Seen from December to March in forests throughout the country. The caterpillars eat the fronds of gully fern (pākau, *Pneumatopteris pennigera*).

Angled Fern Looper
Ischalis nelsonaria (was *Azelina*)
Native Found in forests throughout, February to March. The caterpillars eat hound's tongue fern (kōwaowao, *Microsorum pustulatum*) – and probably other ferns too.

Oblique-Waved Fern Looper
Ischalis variabilis (was *Azelina*)
Native Seen January to April in forest, mostly in the North Island and northern South Island. The caterpillars eat the fronds of various tree ferns.

Large Kelleria Dandy
Notoreas niphocrena
Native Active day-flying moth, seen December to February on the mountains of both islands at about 1350 m. Rests with wings held together. The caterpillars eat mat-like *Kelleria* plants. The moths pollinate the *Kelleria* flowers.

Pimelea Dandy
Notoreas perornata (was *Lythria*)
Native Active day-flying moth, common October to March in central North Island. Rests with wings held together. The caterpillars feed on the native shrub known as Strathmore weed (pinātoro, *Pimelea prostrata*). Other similar undescribed species are found south to Stewart Island.

Snowberry Yellow
Orthoclydon chloriras (was *Venusia princeps*)
Native Seen December to January in beech forests at about 750 m on both the North and the South Islands. The caterpillars feed on snowberry shrubs (*Gaultheria*)

Flax Looper
Orthoclydon praefectata
Native Found throughout in summer. The caterpillars eat slot-like 'windows' in the underside of New Zealand flax (harakeke, *Phormium*) leaves, leaving the tough top surface of the leaf intact (see photo). The 2 cm caterpillars are green when young, turning to yellow with red stripes.

flax looper damage

Orange & Purple Fern Looper
Paradetis porphyrias
Native Seen December to February, among ferns in forest clearings on both the North and South Islands. Caterpillar foodplants may include the thousand-leaved fern (huarau, *Hypolepis millefolium*).

Orange Underwing
Paranotoreas brephosata (was *Notoreas brephos*)
Native A day-flying moth, sometimes seen sitting on bare ground in hot sunshine. Common December to March from the coast to the mountains from central North Island south. The caterpillars eat willowherb (*Epilobium*).

Striped Orange Underwing
Paranotoreas ferox (was *Notoreas*)
Native Seen flying during the day, December to February, in alpine areas of eastern South Island. The caterpillars feed on various low-growing plants including the dwarf alpine daisy, *Brachyglottis bellidioides*.

Creekbed Orange Underwing
Paranotoreas zopyra (was *Notoreas*)
Native Flies by day, December to March, in mountain grasslands up to alpine altitudes on Mt Taranaki (Egmont) and in the South Island. The caterpillars eat willowherb (*Epilobium*).

Mountain Pug
Pasiphila magnimaculata (was *Chloroclystis*)
Native Found November to January, on both the main islands, mostly on the mountains, in scrubby forest at 300 – 1000 m but not common. The caterpillar's foodplant is unknown.

Green Broom Pug
Pasiphila melochlora (was *Chloroclystis*)
Native Seen in late February in forest from Taranaki south, including the South Island. The caterpillars feed on native broom (*Carmichaelia*).

Emerald Pug
Pasiphila muscosata (was *Chloroclystis*)
Native Common in summer in forest and scrub throughout. The caterpillars eat the leaves of pōhuehue (*Muehlenbeckia*) and possibly also ramarama (*Lophomyrtus*).

Horopito Flash
Pseudocoremia fascialata (was *Selidosema*)
Native In forests throughout, from January to March. On take-off, its back wings are flashed; on landing these seem to disappear along with the moth. The caterpillars feed on various native trees including horopito (*Pseudowintera axillaris* & *colorata*).

Tree Nettle Flash
Pseudocoremia insignita (was *Selidosema*)
Native Seen September to November in scrub and forest edges from Northland to Otago. The name 'flash' refers to the back wings being flashed on take-off; these seem to disappear along with the moth on landing. The caterpillars eat tree nettle (ongaonga, *Urtica ferox*).

Conifer Flash
Pseudocoremia leucelaea (was *Selidosema*)
Native Seen September to November in forest throughout. Its back wings are flashed on take-off but, on landing, the disappearance of these creates the illusion of the moth also disappearing. The caterpillars feed at night on miro, tōtara and pine leaves.

at rest

Celery Pine Looper
Pseudocoremia monacha (was *Selidosema*)
Native Very common in summer at alpine altitudes (up to 1500 m) in the ranges of North and South Islands. The caterpillars feed on various kinds of celery pine (*Phyllocladus*).

Brown Forest Flash
Pseudocoremia productata (was *Selidosema*)
Native Common in forest throughout. Attracted in late summer to the flowers of the small white rātā vine. On landing, the brighter back wings seem to disappear along with the moth. The caterpillars feed on the leaves of a wide range of trees and shrubs.

Yellow Broom Looper
Samana falcatella
Native Seen near the edges of scrub and forest in February. North and South Islands. The caterpillars feed on New Zealand broom (*Carmichaelia*).

Hook-Tip Fern Looper
Sarisa muriferata (was *Gargaphia*)
Native Found all year in forests throughout. The caterpillars feed on hound's tongue fern (kōwaowao, *Microsorum pustulatum*) and leather-leaf fern (ngārara wehi, *Pyrrosia eleagnifolia*). When disturbed, these caterpillars wriggle violently.

Tutu Green Spindle
Tatosoma lestevata
Native Seen January to February in scrub and forest on both North and South Islands. The front wings have four vertical wavy lines on them. The body is spindly. The caterpillars feed on the native tutu shrub (*Coriaria*).

Kāmahi Green Spindle
Tatosoma tipulata
Native In forest, summer and autumn, from southern North Island south. Spindly body; long 'beak'. The caterpillars feed on kāmahi (*Weinmannia*) and native beech (*Nothofagus*).

Five Finger Looper
Xyridacma alectoraria (was *Epirhanthis*)
Native Common from November to February in forest and scrub throughout New Zealand. The caterpillars feed on the leaves of the native five finger (*Pseudopanax arboreus*).

Tarata Looper
Xyridacma ustaria (was *Epirhanthis*)
Native Seen from October to December in forest throughout New Zealand. The caterpillars eat the leaves of tarata (*Pittosporum eugenioides*) and kōhūhū (*Pittosporum tenuifolium*).

Broom Flash
Pseudocoremia melinata (was *Selidosema*)
Native Found along the edges of scrub and forest in December. In flight, the eye latches onto the bright colour of the back wings. When, on landing, these suddenly disappear, the moth itself seem to vanish. The caterpillars feed on New Zealand broom (*Carmichaelia*).

Common Forest Looper
Pseudocoremia suavis (was *Selidosema*)
Native Very common in farmland and forest throughout, in spring, summer and autumn. Attracted to light. The caterpillars eat the leaves of rātā, tawa, tōtara, *Macrocarpa* and pine.

Common Fern Looper
Sestra flexata
Native Common September to March in scrub and forest throughout. The caterpillars feed on bracken (*Pteridium*), sweet fern (*Pteris*) and water fern (*Histiopteris*). To escape predators, these wriggle violently, fall to the ground and dig themselves into the leaf litter.

Barred Pink Carpet
Xanthorhoe semifissata
Native Common from August to February throughout. The name 'carpet' refers to a group of loopers with carpet-like wing patterns. The caterpillars feed on various low-growing plants including watercress.

Large Hebe Looper
Xyridacma veronicae (was *Epirhanthis*)
Native Seen from August to November in scrub throughout New Zealand, often entering houses. The caterpillars feed at night on koromiko (*Hebe*).

Owlet Moths

[Family: Noctuidae]

Fat-bodied, dull-coloured moths, many of which have owl-like 'eyes' on their wings. They fly mostly at night (hence: **noctuid**) and rest with their wings folded roof-like over their body. In bright light, their eyes glow red, due to a network of tiny air tubes at the back which act like mirrors. Some can make sounds by rubbing their legs on the edge of their wings. Most have ears – not on their head, but further back: on their bodies. With these, they can hear – and avoid – hunting bats. A few have brightly coloured back wings, hidden beneath the front wings during the day when the moth is resting. When disturbed, the moth flashes this brighter colour to startle predators. Some overseas owlet moths have the oddest diets: one species sucks blood, and others are known to suck the tears of cattle and yak. At night, the caterpillars of many species (**cutworms** or **armyworms**) damage cultivated plants. When food is scarce, some overseas species migrate in such huge numbers that trains have been brought to a standstill by their wheels slipping on crushed caterpillars. All have three pairs of true legs plus five pairs of 'false legs' (prolegs). One of the world's largest moth families with about 22,000 known species; over 170 in New Zealand, most of them unique to this country (of which three are Threatened Species, one presumed extinct). A selection of the more common and distinctive species follows in alphabetical order of scientific name.

caterpillar

at rest

chrysalis

Bogong Moth
Agrotis infusa
Australian. A nuisance at the 2000 Sydney Olympics, when large numbers were drawn to the floodlights. Often blown across the Tasman Sea in spring, but it doesn't breed here. After proper preparation, these were traditionally eaten by the Australian aborigine.

Spring Dune Cutworm
Agrotis innominata
Native Found on the coast throughout from September to December. The caterpillars scurry over the sand – sometimes even in daytime – feeding on dune plants such as shore bindweed (nihinihi) and marram grass.

Greasy Cutworm
Agrotis ipsilon aneituma
Native Found throughout much of the world, with large numbers arriving some years from Australia. Seen most of the year flying around lights at night. The greasy-looking caterpillars (see photo) come out of the soil at night, cutting through the stems of garden plants near ground level. These were a serious pest on kūmara crops and are known in Māori as **ngūharu**, **mūharu** or **mūwharu** ('mud insect').

Greater Alpine Grey
Aletia virescens
Native Common in shrub-grassland up to 1000 m, throughout the South Island north to Central North Island. Seen late summer, resting on rock outcrops and attracted to light. The green-headed, green-and-white striped caterpillars feed on grasses.

Small-Eyed Owlet
Austramathes purpurea
Native Common in autumn, in forest and scrub throughout. The common name does not refer to the moth's true eyes, but to the 'eye patterns' in the centre of its front wings. The caterpillars feed on māhoe (whiteywood, *Melicytus*) leaves.

side view
Showing the moth's distinctive, humped-looking back, with prominent tufts of hairs.

Silver Y Moth
Chrysodeixis eriosoma
Native Found from India to New Zealand. The moth has a silver marking on each front wing like the letter 'Y'. Seen side on, the moth has a distinctive shape (see photo). Often seen in summer, around sunset, feeding on the nectar of flowers such as marigolds. The **green semilooper** caterpillars eat the leaves and fruits of many garden plants, including tomato, bean and potato, but also the native poroporo shrub and rengarenga lily.

Spangled Green Owlet
Cosmodes elegans
From Australia. Seen on both main islands, mostly in autumn on the coast. The caterpillars feed on native shore lobelia (punakuru, *Lobelia anceps*) and verbena. Known in Australia as the green blotched moth.

Unless otherwise indicated, all photos are life-size

caterpillar

chrysalis

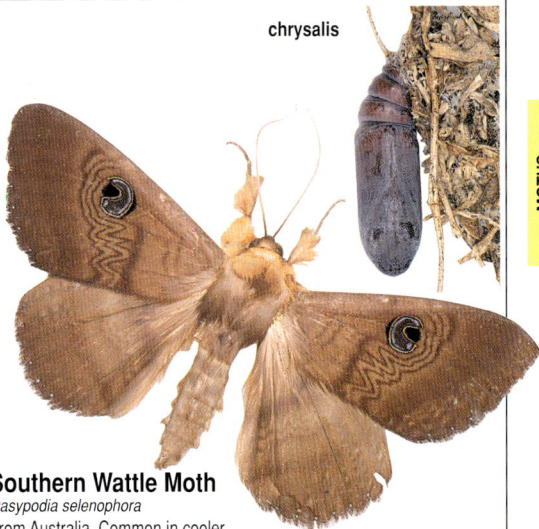

Northern Wattle Moth / Pepe Atua

Dasypodia cymatodes

From Australia. Common as far south as Nelson, February to April. Attracted to lights. The caterpillars (see photo) eat the leaves of wattle trees. Known to early Māori who found the odd moth blown in from Australia before the first wattle trees were planted here, hence the Māori names: **pepe kēhue**, **pepe atua** and **para kori tāua**, all of which refer to the belief that these mysterious moths were the returning spirits of ancestors. (A similar belief about noctuid moths is found in Madagascar.) Also known as **owl**, **moon** or **peacock moth** from the 'eye' pattern on the wings, shining like a new moon or like the tail feathers of a peacock.

Southern Wattle Moth

Dasypodia selenophora

From Australia. Common in cooler climates, particularly in the South Island, February to April. Unlike the northern species, its wings are golden underneath. Also known as **peacock moth** or **moon moth**, from the eye-patterns on the front wings. Australians know it as granny moth or old lady moth, distinguishing it from *Dasypodia cymatodes* which they call northern brown house moth. The caterpillars feed on wattle leaves.

at rest

Orange Peel Moth

Diarsia intermixta (was Graphiphora compta)

Probably flew here from Australia. Also found elsewhere in the South Pacific. Seen throughout New Zealand in summer and autumn. Also called dotted border moth. The caterpillar's foodplants include nettles, white mustard and Cape weed.

Māhoe Stripper

Feredayia graminosa (was Erana)

Native Seen from October to January in or near forest on both main islands, but more common in the North Island. The caterpillars strip māhoe (whiteywood, *Melicytus*) leaves. Also called green māhoe moth.

Fox's Owlet

Graphania brunneosa (was Melanchra)

Native Seen from November to December in forests from Waikato southwards. The caterpillar's foodplant is unknown.

Green-Toothed Owlet

Graphania chlorodonta (was Melanchra)

Native Seen from November to December in wet forest throughout New Zealand. The caterpillars feed on various plants found growing on the forest floor.

Red Owlet

Graphania chryserytha (was Melanchra)

Native Seen in shrubland and grassland in the southern South Island in December. The caterpillar's foodplant is unknown.

Desert Owlet

Graphania disjungens (was Persectania)

Native Seen November to January from the Central Plateau south, up to 1650 m. The moth has net-veined wings. The caterpillars feed on grasses.

Dunedin Owlet

Graphania fenwicki (was Melanchra)

Native Found in forest and shrubland in southern South Island in September. The caterpillars feed on plants of the forest floor.

Green-Marked Owlet

Graphania insignis (was Melanchra)

Native Very common throughout New Zealand all year, especially in autumn and early winter. The caterpillars feed on various low-growing plants.

Alpine Treasure Owlet

Graphania maya (was Melanchra)

Native Seen September to March in grassland and shrubland on both main islands from 600 m to over 1500 m. The caterpillars feed on non-woody plants.

Unless otherwise indicated, all photos are life-size

Common Garden Owlet
Graphania mutans (was *Melanchra*)
Native Very common October to April in grassland, shrubland and forest throughout (at all altitudes). The caterpillars feed on many low-growing plants, including ragwort, groundsel and plantain (*Plantago*).

Giant Speargrass Owlet
Graphania nullifera (was *Aletia*)
Native Seen December to May in the South Island and central North Island. Attracted to lights. The orange caterpillars burrow into the soft stems of speargrass (*Aciphylla*).

Black & White Owlet
Graphania paracausta (was *Melanchra*)
Native Seen October to February, mostly in the mountains of the South Island and central North Island. Also known as the orange-marked moth. The caterpillars feed on grasses.

Green Carpet Owlet
Graphania plena (was *Melanchra*)
Native Found near forest throughout New Zealand, October to May. Also known as the common green cutworm. The caterpillars feed on a wide range of plants including *Fuchsia*.

Large Grey Owlet
Graphania ustistriga (was *Melanchra*)
Native Common throughout New Zealand from August to March. Attracted to light. The caterpillars feed on the leaves of various plants including native pōhuehue (*Muehlenbeckia*) and pine (*Pinus*), often high up in the trees.

Tomato Fruitworm
Helicoverpa armigera conferta (was *Heliothis*)
Almost worldwide. Common in summer on farms and gardens throughout. Flies day and night. The caterpillars eat the buds, flowers and fruits of many plants including tomato, beans, pumpkins, maize and thistle, then burrow underground to hibernate as a chrysalis.

Common Snowgrass Owlet
Ichneutica ceraunias
Native Common in summer in the mountains of the South Island and central North Island; also down to sea level in Southland. Sometimes flies during the day. The caterpillars feed on snowgrass (*Chionochloa*) and fescue (*Festuca*).

Lindsay's Alpine Owlet
Ichneutica lindsayi
Native Seen December to January in the mountains of Otago and Stewart Island. The caterpillars are thought to feed on snowgrass (*Chionochloa*).

Streaked Alpine Owlet
Ichneutica nervosa
Native Found in the South Island mountains in December. The caterpillars are thought to feed on snowgrass (*Chionochloa*).

Pōhuehue Owlet
Meterana coeleno (was *Melanchra*)
Native Found on the North and South Islands, September to January. The caterpillars feed on pōhuehue (*Muehlenbeckia*).

Kōwhai Owlet
Meterana decorata (was *Melanchra*)
Native Found on the North and South Islands, August to March. The caterpillars feed on kōwhai (*Sophora*).

Lawyer Owlet
Meterana diatmeta (was *Melanchra*)
Native Found on the North and South Islands, September to March. The caterpillars feed on the prickly vine known as bush lawyer (*Rubus*) and on kaikōmako (*Pennantia*).

Exquisite Olearia Owlet
Meterana exquisita (was *Melanchra*)
Native Found in forest and shrubland on both main islands, October to February, but not common. The caterpillars feed on a small-leaved tree daisy (*Olearia*). It is disappearing from some areas due to loss of suitable habitat.

Grand Olearia Owlet
Meterana grandiosa (was *Melanchra*)
Native Seen in forest and shrubland in May, mostly in the southern South Island but also in the southern North Island. Becoming less common due to loss of habitat. The caterpillars feed on a small-leaved tree daisy (*Olearia*).

Patē Owlet
Meterana merope (was *Melanchra*)
Native Found on both main islands, October to April. Groups of caterpillars gather under leaves by day, feeding at night on patē (seven finger, *Schefflera*) and on mountain lacebark (*Hoheria glabrata*).

Southern Pimelea Owlet
Meterana meyricci (was *Melanchra pictula*)
Native Common in summer, mostly high in the South Island mountains. Also called scarce green cutworm moth. The caterpillars feed on the native daphne (*Pimelea*).

Patchwork Owlet
Meterana pauca (was *Melanchra*)
Native Found at 500 – 1000 m in the wet western forests on both islands, December to March. The caterpillar's foodplant is unknown.

Northern Pimelea Owlet
Meterana pictula (was *Melanchra rhodopleura*)
Native Found from the coast to the mountains in central and eastern North Island and western South Island. The colourful caterpillars feed on various native daphnes (*Pimelea*). Protected as a Category I Threatened Species.

Mottled Brown Owlet
Meterana stipata (was *Melanchra*)
Native Found in forest and shrubland in the South Island and southern North Island. The caterpillars eat pōhuehue (*Muehlenbeckia australis*).

Yellow-Bordered Owlet
Meterana tartarea (was *Melanchra*)
Native Found in forest and shrubland in the South Island and along the west coast from Taranaki to Wellington, December to May (but mostly in autumn). The caterpillars feed on a small-leaved *Coprosma* shrub.

Transwinter Owlet
Meterana vitiosa (was *Melanchra*)
Native Seen all year in forest and shrubland on both main islands. The caterpillar feeds on a small-leaved *Coprosma* shrub.

caterpillars

at rest

Northern Armyworm
Mythimna separata (was *Aletia unipuncta*)
Exotic. Found in the warmer parts of the North Island and northern South Island. The caterpillars feed on grass and cereal crops. Also known as the **cosmopolitan armyworm**.

Southern Armyworm
Persectania aversa
Native Very common throughout New Zealand. The velvety caterpillars feed on grasses, sedges and cereal crops. Also known as **streaked armyworm**.

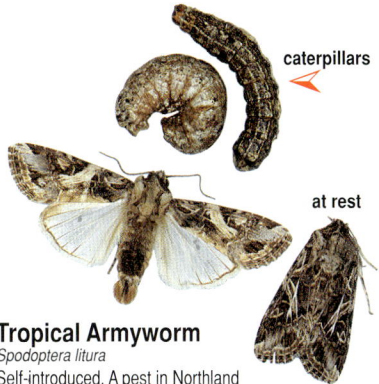

Tropical Armyworm
Spodoptera litura
Self-introduced. A pest in Northland and Auckland, where it has now become established. It lays its eggs in fluffy masses on the sides of buildings. The caterpillars eat clover, beans, celery, silver beet, kūmara and cabbage. Also known as **cluster grub**.

Unless otherwise indicated, all photos are life-size

Fruit-Piercing Moth
Othreis materna (was *Elygea*)
Regularly arrives in New Zealand from the tropics but has never established itself here. The moth damages citrus and other fruit by piercing the skin to suck the juice. The caterpillars feed on plants in the moonseed family [Menispermaceae].

caterpillar

Grapevine Moth
Phalaenoides glycinae (misspelt *Phalaenodes*)
Accidentally introduced from Australia about 1940. A day-flying moth with furry orange legs, seen in spring in northern North Island only. The caterpillars eat the leaves and young fruit of grapevines (also *Fuchsia*).

Comma-Mark Cutworm
Proteuxoa comma (was *Rictonis*)
Native Seen from November to February along forest edges, in shrubland and grassland throughout. The front wings bear a small comma-shaped mark. The caterpillars feed on various plants including pine trees.

at rest

Slender Owlet
Rhapsa scotosialis
Native One of New Zealand's commonest forest moths, recognised by its triangular shape. Seen all year. The caterpillars feed at night on recently fallen leaves and hanging moss.

at rest

caterpillar

Slender Burnished Brass
Thysanoplusia orichalcea
From West Africa to Australia. Arrived here in 1984. Now common in northern New Zealand. The wings appear to be gold-plated. The caterpillars eat soybean plants, potatoes, parsley, carrots and cabbage. Also called **soybean looper** (but is not a true looper).

Orange Astelia Wainscot
Tmetolophota purdii (was *Leucania*)
Native Common from December to January in forest and scrub throughout. 'Wainscot' refers to the wood grain pattern on the wings. The caterpillars eat holes in the leaves of the native bush lilies (*Astelia* & *Collospermum*).

Common Dotted Wainscot
Tmetolophota semivittata (was *Leucania*)
Native Seen October to January in grassland throughout, especially in areas of high rainfall. 'Wainscot' describes the grain-like pattern on the wings. The patterned caterpillars feed on grasses.

at rest

Chocolate Swamp Wainscot
Tmetolophota similis (was *Persectania*)
Native Seen from December to January in peat lands throughout, but with a rather patchy distribution. Note the grain-like design on the wings. The caterpillars feed on red tussock (*Chionochloa rubra*).

Flax Notcher
Tmetolophota steropastis (was *Persectania*)
Native A common wainscot moth seen from November to January near swamps throughout. At night, the caterpillars eat New Zealand flax (harakeke, *Phormium tenax*) and toetoe (*Cortaderia*), leaving characteristic notches along the edges of the leaves.

Dark Underwing Wainscot
Tmetolophota sulcana (was *Leucania*)
Native Found in late summer and autumn in forests in the North and South Island. The moth has a grain-like wing pattern. The caterpillars feed on the pūkio sedge, *Carex secta*.

Hawk Moths

[Family: Sphingidae]

Large moths with bullet-shaped bodies, thick antennae and very long tongues. Their front wings are long and narrow, usually about twice as long as the back wings. Like hawks, they are very strong fliers, reaching speeds of 50 km/h or more, many migrating huge distances (e.g. from Africa to northern Europe), some occasionally landing on ships at sea. They can even fly backwards. For just 15 – 30 minutes at dawn and dusk, they rush from flower to flower, hovering like humming birds, collecting nectar with their very long, coiled 'tongues'. Indeed, some overseas orchids and morning glory plants are totally dependent on the exceptionally long tongues of hawk moths for their pollination. One South American species has a tongue over 30 cm long (the full width of this opened book), holding the record for the longest tongue of all insects. In human terms, this is equivalent to being able to lick an ice cream on the other side of the road. Another extremely unusual feature is that some hawk moths are known to be able to listen with their mouths. Most of the caterpillars are large, with a small spine sticking up at the back (see photo below). The sphinx-like way these rear up to defend themselves gives this group the alternative name of **sphinx moths**. When disturbed, these caterpillars are able to make squeaking or grating sounds. Over 1000 species are known worldwide, three of which have so far been seen in New Zealand. Of these, only one regularly breeds here.

Convolvulus Hawk Moth / Hīhue
Agrius convolvuli

Native Arrived here in pre-European times. With wings closed, the moth is remarkably well camouflaged against the grey-brown bark of a tree trunk. From this hidden pose, it can then startle its enemies simply by flicking its wings open to reveal its strikingly striped body. It is sometimes seen in the evening, hovering over flowers or attracted to lights. The moth's Māori names (**hīhue, wenewene** or **kōwenewene**) all refer to the gourd plant (hue or wenewene, *Lagenaria siceraria*) which Māori once cultivated, as the adult moth was often seen sucking nectar from its flowers. The large caterpillar (**hōtete, kauā** or **kauwaha**) – see photo – was commonly roasted and eaten. This caterpillar was also a major pest in their plantations as it eats the leaves of kūmara, before burrowing into the ground in February to become a chrysalis (**pūngoungou, tīngoungou, tūngoungou** or **tīngoingoi**). Māori children have long played the traditional game of holding this chrysalis upside down between their fingers and asking it questions; a nod (tūngou) means 'yes' – hence the name; a wriggle: 'no'. The moth hatches the following summer. The moth's native foodplants are thought to be the native bindweeds (*Calystegia* species).

spine

caterpillar
Formerly roasted and eaten by Māori.

Silverstriped Hawk Moth
Hippotion celerio (was *Deilephila*)
Found worldwide, this moth has been arriving occasionally in New Zealand over the past one hundred years but it has not yet been known to breed here. The caterpillar's foodplants include taro, fuchsia and grape vine. Also known as vine hawk moth.

Unless otherwise indicated, all photos are life-size

Emperor Moths

[Family: Saturniidae]

Large, fat, hairy moths. Their large wings have staring, goggle eye-patterns to scare off birds. The further apart these 'eyes' are, the bigger the strange animal seems to be. The outer tip of the front wing is also often stretched out in a curve, rather like the head of a snake, a feature thought to help scare off birds in countries where snakes are found. Note the short, wide, feather-like antennae on the males. The adult moths have no mouth, never eat and are usually found resting among fallen leaves at the base of trees. The largest tropical species (**Atlas moth**, *Attacus atlas*) is king among moths, having the largest wing area of any insect. In general, emperor caterpillars are large too, covered in bumps with tufts of spines and long hairs (like rows of old-fashioned shaving brushes). When fully grown, these caterpillars make dense cocoons which they attach to their foodplant. About 1200 species are known worldwide, of which two breed in New Zealand.

female

male

cocoon
The caterpillar takes about 10 hours to spin sufficient silk to make this.

caterpillar

Gum Emperor

Opodiphthera eucalypti (was *Antheraea*)
Introduced from Australia about 1939. Common from Nelson north. The moths are seen near gum trees in mid-summer. These live for no more than a couple of days and never eat. They fly both day and night and are attracted to light. The caterpillars are large with bright knobs and spines (see photo) and eat the leaves of gum trees (*Eucalyptus*), Californian pepper trees (*Schinus molle*), silver birch, apricot and even grapevines. To spin a cocoon (see photo) takes them about 10 hours.

Unless otherwise indicated, all photos are life-size

Tree Of Heaven Silk Moth
Samia cynthia

Found naturally from North India to South China, but also lives in the US and Europe. Discovered in Auckland in 1982 and now established in and around Albert Park from specimens which escaped from Auckland University. The caterpillars feed on tree of heaven (*Ailanthus potentia*), where the cocoons can be seen as clusters of dead leaves in the tree tops over winter. Potentially, a commercially viable producer of silk. Also called cynthia moth or **Ailanthus silk moth**.

Bag Moths
[Family: Psychidae]

The caterpillars of bag moths spend their whole lives inside little home-made cases, rather like sleeping bags – feeding through a hole in the top of the bag, while using an opening in the bottom for their droppings. Many of the female moths are maggot-like with no wings, eyes, legs or antennae, and stay in (or near) these bags their whole lives. The males have thin, often translucent, wings and have a telescopic body to reach into these bags. Neither male nor female moth ever eats, both generally living for just a few hours. So how do such stay-at-home moths colonise the world? The answer lies in the caterpillars, for they can not only walk long distances, but – attached to branches – are known to float across rivers and oceans and even be carried overland by tornado. About 600 species are known worldwide; over 50 in New Zealand, most of them unique to this country.

male

the bag in which the caterpillar lives

Common Bag Moth / Pū A Raukatauri
Liothula species

Native Common, although the flying (male) moth is rarely seen. At night, the caterpillar (still inside its bag) eats the leaves of native plants such as mānuka, kānuka, tauhinu (*Ozothamnus*) and neinei (*Dracophyllum*), also the introduced willow, wattle, pine, broom, feijoa and macrocarpa. The Māori name translates as the flute of Raukatauri, goddess of music, who lives inside the bag. Also called **whare atua**, **kopa** or **kopi**. There are now known to be at least two species.

Lichen Bag Moth
Cebysa leucotelus

Arrived from Australia about 1981. It often comes into houses. The female is brightly coloured and is sometimes mistaken for a beetle or wasp. She hops about a bit but can't fly. But the brown-and-cream male can fly and is active during the day. The caterpillar (inside its bag) eats algae and lichen.

female

male

Little Log Cabin Bag Moth
[Undescribed species]

First noticed in the Auckland area about 1980, having most likely arrived from the Indo-Malay region. The caterpillar lives in an odd-looking spiral of vegetation, like a miniature log cabin. This is often noticed slowly moving over the outside walls of houses and on fence posts, but no one has ever studied it, so the moth still has no scientific name.

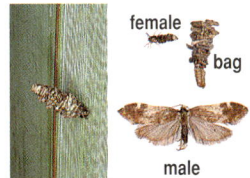

female

bag

male

Unless otherwise indicated, all photos are life-size

Snout Moths

[Superfamily: Pyraloidea: Families: Crambidae & Pyralidae.]

These moths generally have a short 'snout', formed by two finger-like sensory organs (palps) held out in front of the head. Most are small and dull-coloured, with long legs. At rest, many look very slender. Some wrap their wings around their body like a rolled up newspaper or look like a sleek paper dart. Others are a wider triangle shape (like a V-bomber). Many are important pests. The caterpillars typically roll, or tie up, leaves as a safe, tasty home, or dig tunnels into roots and soft stems. Overseas, some even live in sloth droppings or animal horn. The Pyralidae are also known as **pearl moths**, while the Crambidae are often called **grass moths**. Together, these form one of the world's largest moth groups with about 24,000 known species; over 255 in New Zealand, most of them unique to this country (including three Threatened Species of 'grass moths'). A selection of the more common and distinctive species follows in alphabetical order of scientific name. (Those featured are all 'grass moths' except for the introduced **wattle gall moth** and the two **meal moths**.)

Clematis Triangle
Deana hybreasalis (was *Nesarcha*)

Native Seen November to March (sometimes also in winter) in forest and towns throughout, but not common. Seems to wear bobbysocks. The caterpillars feed on buttercups and clematis (both Ranunculaceae).

Arrowhead
Diasemia grammalis

Native Flies fast during the day, April to October, in dry scrub and grassy areas throughout, from the coast to about 1000 m. Has arrow-like markings on its front wings. The caterpillars feed in the leaf litter.

Bold Scoparia
Eudonia aspidota (was *Scoparia*)

Native Very common from November to January at the edge of forest from southern North Island south. Rests with wings swept back. Also called black & white-barred scoparia. The caterpillars are thought to feed on moss.

Little Orange-Spot Scoparia
Eudonia minualis (was *Scoparia chimeria*)

Native Common from December to January in forest throughout New Zealand. At rest, its wings are swept back close to the body. The caterpillars tunnel inside the stems of mosses.

Greater Orange-Spot Scoparia
Eudonia submarginalis (was *Scoparia*)

Native Seen November to March in forest throughout, resting on trees and rocks, with its wings swept back. The caterpillars feed in moist turf.

Mountain Scoparia
Eudonia trivirgata (was *Scoparia*)

Native Seen October to March in open grassy areas throughout, but commonest in the mountains at 1000 – 1300 m. Rests with wings swept back. The caterpillars are thought to feed on moss.

Wattle Gall Moth
Gauna aegusalis (was *aegalis*)

at rest

From eastern Australia. The tiny caterpillars of this (and two other smaller moths) tunnel into the large brown lumps (rust fungus galls, *Uromycladium*) found on green wattle branches (*Racosperma decurrens*) – see photo on right. The moth rests in a most unusual pose, with its back end curled straight up (see photo above).

wattle gall (caused by a rust fungus)

Yellow Silverling
Glaucocharis auriscriptella (was *Diptychophora*)

Native Found flying during the day, November to January, in damp forest throughout New Zealand. Also called silver-marked yellow moth. The caterpillars feed on moss.

Swan Plant Moth
Glyphodes onychinalis

From Australia. First found in New Zealand in 1986; seen mainly in Auckland, often coming into houses, presumably attracted to light. The caterpillars feed on swan plant flowers (*Gomphocarpus*).

Tropical Grass Webworm
Herpetogramma licarsisalis

Almost worldwide, particularly in the tropics. Established itself in northern Northland in 1999. At night, the caterpillar eats grasses – especially kikuyu – causing serious damage to pasture. The 2 cm long, dark brown to pale green caterpillars live in a silk-lined tube of grass leaves near the surface of the soil.

Unless otherwise indicated, all photos are life-size

Pond Moth
Hygraula nitens (was *Nymphula*)
Native Also in southern Australia. The underwater caterpillars are common in ponds and lakes throughout, where they use hair-like gills to breathe and live inside a case attached to a foodplant such as Canadian pondweed (*Elodea*). The moth is seen in summer.

Golden Brown Fern Moth
Musotima nitidalis
Native Also found in Australia. Common throughout New Zealand in early summer; again in early autumn. A delicate, ethereal-looking moth. The bright green caterpillars feed on ferns.

Mire Grass Moth
Orocrambus aethonellus (was *Crambus*)
Native Flies during the day in the South Island, December to January on damp ground and in wetlands. Rests with wings curled lengthwise like a rolled up newspaper. The caterpillars feed in the new shoots of sedges etc in moist turf.

a grass moth
at rest

Common Grass Moth
Orocrambus flexuosellus (was *Crambus*)
Native Very common in grassland throughout, from spring to autumn, flying during the day. Rests with its wings snug against its body. The caterpillars (known as **sod webworms**) feed on seedlings and young shoots in turf.

Wetland Orange
Orocrambus heliotes (was *Crambus*)
Native Flies fast in hot sunshine, January to February, in damp, mossy places on both main islands. Rests with wings curled like a rolled up newspaper. The caterpillars feed in moist turf.

Scabweed Snout
Orocrambus xanthogrammus (was *Crambus*)
Native Seen from December to February from central North Island to Southland. Rests on riverbed shingle, with wings curled like a rolled up newspaper, but is easily disturbed during the day. The caterpillars feed on mat daisy (scabweed, *Raoulia*).

Indian Meal Moth
Plodia interpunctella (was *Tinea*)
Worldwide. Accidentally introduced. The maggot-like caterpillars are common in food cupboards, where they spin silk tubes and eat nuts, raisins, chocolate and various kinds of flour, including 'Indian corn' (maize) – hence the common name.

Meal Moth
Pyralis farinalis
Accidentally introduced. Common on food stored in damp places, especially on flour. The caterpillars spin tubes of silk which provide them with a safe place from which to feed.

Shining Scoparia
Scoparia diphtheralis
Native Common throughout, especially near forest, around lights on summer nights. The sparkle ('shining') on the front wings is more evident on North Island individuals. The caterpillars (known as **sod webworms**) feed on grass and seedlings in turf.

Boot Scoparia
Scoparia ustimacula
Native Seen throughout, usually in forest, from October to January. The front wings are marked with a dark boot-shape. The caterpillars are thought to feed on mosses. (One of about 40 forest *Scoparias*.)

Chequered Alpine Snout
Tauroscopa trapezitis
Native Seen flying during the day in the South Island mountains from November to February. The caterpillar's foodplant is unknown.

Blue-Grey Rock Snout
Tawhitia glaucophanes (was *Tauroscopa*)
Native The moth appears in January and is seen flying in hot sunshine in the mountains of the South Island at 1200 – 1800 m. The caterpillar's foodplant is unknown.

Rusty Dotted Triangle
Udea flavidalis (was *Mnesictena*)
Native Seen throughout most of New Zealand, particularly in late summer, flying both day and night. The caterpillars feed on soft-leaved plants, including borage and pōhuehue (*Muehlenbeckia*).

Dusky Nettle Triangle
Udea marmarina (was *Mnesictena*)
Native Common throughout New Zealand, December to March. The caterpillars eat stinging nettle leaves (*Urtica*) and parataniwha (*Elatostema*).

Kōwhai Moth
Uresiphita polygonalis maorialis
(was *Mecyna maorialis*)
Native Often seen in late spring, flying in strong sunlight, throughout New Zealand. The spotted caterpillars feed on kōwhai (*Sophora*), introduced brooms, lupin, gorse and clover.

Leafrollers / Tīkopa

[Family: Tortricidae]

Small, often dull-coloured moths. At rest, the wings of many species form a neat bell shape, giving them the name **bell moths**. When spread, their front wings look almost rectangular. The caterpillars are fast movers and can go in reverse. Most make themselves a safe home by rolling or folding up leaves and tying them with silken webbing which they produce from their mouths; others tunnel into fruit, seeds or soft stems. Some of the caterpillars are pests, damaging orchard fruit and plantation forests. Formerly, Māori looked out for these folded leaves, to collect and eat the caterpillars, naming them **moka** or **tīkopa** (from kopa, meaning 'bent' or 'folded'). About 5000 species are known worldwide; about 185 in New Zealand, most of them unique to this country.

Umbrella Fern Bell Moth
Apoctena clarkei (was *Planotortrix*)
`Native` Seen in North Island forests in summer. The caterpillars feed on the fronds of the umbrella fern (waekura, *Sticherus cunninghamii*).

Greater Beech Leafroller
Apoctena pictoriana (was *Planotortrix*)
`Native` Seen mostly in native beech forest, often at high altitudes, January to April, from Wellington south. The caterpillars feed on various New Zealand beech trees (*Nothofagus*).

Tiger Bell Moth
Apoctena tigris (was *Planotortrix*)
`Native` Seen in forest throughout New Zealand in January, among the dead fronds of *Dicksonia* tree ferns. The caterpillars are thought to feed on these tree ferns.

Cabbage Tree Bell Moth
Catamacta lotinana
`Native` Seen December to January in the North and South Islands. The young caterpillars tunnel inside the bases of cabbage tree (*Cordyline*) leaves, later moving to the tip of the youngest leaf, rolling it into a tube, in which to safely develop into a moth.

at rest

Black-Lyre Leafroller
'Cnephasia' jactatana (was *Batodes*)
`Native` Common throughout in forest, scrub and orchards, except in winter. The caterpillars feed on a wide range of plants including kiwifruit, plum, gum and pine. With its wings closed, the dark hook shape on each front wing together look like a lyre.

Blackheaded Leafroller
Ctenopseustis obliquana
`Native` Particularly common in the northern North Island. The black-headed caterpillar feeds on pōhutukawa, plum, peach and pine trees and is a pest in kiwifruit orchards. There is also a **brown-headed leafroller** (*C. herana*).

Codling Moth
Cydia pomonella (was *Laspeyresia*)
Accidentally introduced from Europe and now common throughout New Zealand. Flies December to January but not attracted to light. Named after a kind of apple. The grub-like caterpillars tunnel inside apples and pears. Also spelled: codlin moth.

Ponga Ugly Nestmaker
Ecclitica torogramma
`Native` The moth is well camouflaged when resting on the silver undersides of ponga (*Cyathea dealbata*) fronds. The untidy nests of the caterpillars distort the young fronds.

Sharp-Tipped Bell Moth
Epalxiphora axenana
`Native` Found mostly in summer, near forest in the North Island. The female has more pointed wings. The stripe-headed caterpillars feed on a very wide range of trees, shrubs and low-growing plants. Also called brindled bell moth.

Lesser Beech Leafroller
Epichorista emphanes
`Native` Seen flying during the day around the tops of the trees from December to January in beech forest. The caterpillars eat the flowers and new leaves of native beech trees (*Nothofagus*).

Lightbrown Apple Moth
Epiphyas postvittana (was *Tortrix*)
Australian. Accidentally introduced about 1891, and now common throughout New Zealand. The caterpillars feed on many plants including apple leaves and the surface of the fruit. Also called **apple leafroller**.

Alpine Daisy Rosette-Borer
Gelophaula aenea (was *siraea*)
`Native` Flies by day in January at altitudes over 1500 m in the South Island mountains. The male (pictured) is orange and purple-brown; the female cream. The caterpillars feed in the heart of large, mountain daisy plants (*Celmisia*).

Oriental Fruit Moth
Grapholita molesta (was *Cydia*)
Accidentally introduced in 1973. Now found in commercial orchards north of about Palmerston North, where the caterpillars feed on the stems and fruit of peaches, nectarines and other fruit. The moth flies both day and night.

Yellow Field Bell Moth
Merophyas leucaniana (was *Tortrix*)
`Native` Common throughout, seen in the evening, flying close to the ground in grassy places, September to April. The caterpillars eat native daphne (*Pimelea*), native sea spurge (waiūatua, *Euphorbia glauca*) and various clover-like plants.

Greenheaded Leafroller
Planotortrix excessana group
`Native` One of a group of native leafrollers, various members of which are common in summer throughout. The green-headed caterpillars feed on native broad-leaved trees and shrubs but have since adapted to apple, pear, plum, *Camellia* and some exotic conifers.

Painted Wedge
Pyrgotis plagiatana (was *Capua*)
`Native` Common in forest clearings throughout, September to June. At rest, its wings are held roof-wise like a wedge (not a bell). Note the half-moon on the front wings. The caterpillars feed on various plants, including wineberry (makomako), cherry and English oak.

Unless otherwise indicated, all photos are life-size

Tiger Moths
[Family: Arctiidae]

Many are brightly coloured, day-flying moths. They rest with their wings held roof-like over their fat, hairy bodies. Some can protect themselves with a horrible smelling, yellow liquid which they squirt from two openings behind their 'collar'. Several are poisonous to birds. With special drums on the sides of their bodies, many can make very high-pitched clicking, twittering, rustling, crackling, chirping or grating sounds, too high for us to hear but which may confuse hunting bats. They are mostly slow, clumsy fliers. Indeed, the females can be so full of eggs that they hardly fly at all and remain hidden under rocks. The caterpillars make a cocoon with a mixture of silk and hairs from their own body. Inside this, they are safe to turn into a chrysalis. About 2500 species are known worldwide; about eight in New Zealand.

at rest

at rest

caterpillar
A favourite of shining cuckoos (pīpīwharauroa).

Magpie Moth / Mōkarakara
Nyctemera amica

There are two very similar species: this one from Australia and a native species (*N. annulata*), which has much smaller patches of white on its wings. In Auckland and Nelson, at least, these two species are known to interbreed to produce hybrids. Very common day-flying magpie-coloured moths, often mistaken for a butterfly. The furry caterpillars (English: **woolly bear**; Māori: **tuahuru** or **tūpeke** – see photo – eat the leaves of daisy-like plants such as ragwort and cineraria. This makes both the caterpillars and the moths poisonous to lizards and most birds (although the shining cuckoo is obviously unaffected).

Cinnabar Moth
Tyria jacobaeae

Bred in huge quantities on butterfly farms in England for introduction to New Zealand in 1929 to help control ragwort. (But it has proven to be ineffective.) Day-flying and very distinctive, often being mistaken for a butterfly. Common after November, mostly in the lower North Island and upper South Island. The caterpillars eat the leaves and flowers of ragwort, making both the caterpillar and the adult moth poisonous to birds.

Crimson Speckled Footman
Utetheisa pulchelloides vaga

From the Indo-Australian region, this day-flying moth is found throughout most of New Zealand (common in places) in summer, but rarely survives the winter here. The caterpillars eat plants in the borage family [Boraginaceae]. Although suitable foodplants are found in New Zealand, this moth is not so far known to breed here.

Western Tiger Moth
Metacrias erichrysa

Native Found along the western side of the South Island and southern North Island. The males fly during summer days, while the flightless female is hidden away under rocks. The caterpillars feed on grasses and other low-growing herbs, but first they eat their own mother.

Eastern Tiger Moth
Metacrias huttoni

Native Found in the alpine regions of eastern South Island from Marlborough to Otago. The male flies during summer days. The flightless female hides under rocks. The caterpillars feed on grasses and other low-growing herbs.

Southern Tiger Moth
Metacrias strategica

Native Found in grassy areas, from South Canterbury to Southland. The male flies during summer days. The female is almost wingless and never flies. The caterpillars feed on grasses and other low-growing herbs.

Clothes Moths
[Family: Tineidae]

Small, narrow-winged moths which rest with their wings folded roof-like over their body. They are often seen running around on walls etc, rather than flying. The caterpillars of many species make cases to live in. Over 2000 species are known worldwide; over 100 in New Zealand, most of them unique to this country.

at rest

at rest

Dead Sheep Moth
Monopis ethelella

Australian. Now common year round in farmland throughout New Zealand. Also known as the spot and cream-stripe moth. The caterpillars are common on dead sheep, where they feed on decaying wool.

Dusky Scuttler
Opogona omoscopa (was *Hieroxestis*)

Introduced. Found almost worldwide. Now one of the commonest moths in New Zealand. Seen November to February, from about Nelson north, often inside homes. The caterpillars feed in leaf litter, on dead and dying plants. Known in Australia as the **detritus moth**.

Large Pale Clothes Moth
Tinea pallescentella

Introduced. Widespread around homes. The whitish caterpillar feeds on wool, hair and feathers in open or unheated buildings.

Casemaking Clothes Moth
Tinea pellionella

Accidentally introduced. Found in dark places in homes throughout New Zealand. The creamy-white, eyeless caterpillars hide in strong cases of silk and wool, and eat clothing.

Unless otherwise indicated, all photos are life-size

Litter Moths

Small moths, resting with their wings held flat or roof-wise. The small caterpillars feed on leaf litter or on dead wood. New Zealand and Australia are unusual in having so many moth species which specialise in this habitat. In native forest, a hundred of these caterpillars can sometimes be found in just one square metre of the forest floor, where they build fine silk runways between the fallen leaves. (This family previously included **flat moths** – below – as a subfamily.) More than 6000 species are known worldwide (most of them from Australia); about 260 in New Zealand, most of these unique to this country.

Whiteshouldered House Moth
Endrosis sarcitrella (was *lacteela*)
Found worldwide. Seen November to March, resting on walls in homes, garages and sheds. Also in birds' nests. The caterpillars eat stored seeds, carpets and even wine corks.

Pink-Tipped Yellow Moth
Gymnobathra flavidella (was *Gelechia*)
Native   Common from November to January in forest from the North Island to central South Island. The caterpillars tunnel inside rangiora branches (*Brachyglottis repanda*).

Small Angle-Wing Moth
Gymnobathra hyetodes
Native   Common in forest in summer on the North Island and northern South Island. The caterpillars feed on dead wood and branches.

Gregarious Tineid
Hierodoris atychioides (was *Heliostibes*)
Native   Very common throughout, December to January. Flies fast by day. The caterpillars often live in large groups, webbing together leaves of small-leaved trees and shrubs, such as mānuka, rimu, tauhinu, kahikatea and macrocarpa.

Orange Flash
Hierodoris illita (was *Heliostibes*)
Native   Flies like a rocket in hot sunshine, November to February. Seen in scrub and forest margins on both main islands. The caterpillars feed in the live stems of tutu (*Coriaria*).

Brown House Moth
Hofmannophila pseudospretella (was *Borkhausenia*)
Introduced. Seen November to February throughout New Zealand. Usually seen resting on damp house walls, but also found in birds' nests. The caterpillars feed on clothes, carpets, furniture and wine corks.

Green Lichen Tuft
Izatha peroneanella
Native   Common near native forest throughout, December to January. Some are almost blue. Looks like lichen. Its front wings each have a tuft of raised scales. The caterpillars tunnel inside the dead branches of trees such as wineberry (makomako) and apple.

White Lichen Tuft
Izatha picarella (was *acmonias*)
Native   Looks like lichen and has a tuft of raised scales on each front wing. Rests on trees and fences in the South Island, December to January. (A similar moth, *Izatha churtoni*, is found in the North Island.) The caterpillars feed on dead wood.

Yellow Litter Moth
Tingena armigerella (was *Borkhausenia*)
Native   Common in the North Island, on tree trunks and fences, from November to January. Falls to the ground when disturbed. The chocolate-coloured caterpillars feed on fallen leaves.

Flat Moths

Small, flat-bodied moths with broad, arched front wings which they hold out flat. The small caterpillars feed on living plants. Previously included as a subfamily of the **litter moths** [Oecophoridae] – above. More than 600 species are known worldwide; about 15 species in New Zealand, most of them unique to this country.

Tarata Flat Moth
Nymphostola galactina
Native   Found mid-summer in forest in the North Island and north-eastern South Island. The caterpillars feed on various shiny-leaved native plants including broadleaf (*Griselinia*), tarata and ramarama.

Mountain Beech Moth
Proteodes carnifex
Native   Very common in some years in mountain beech forest in the North and South Islands. Can also be yellow or pink. The caterpillars feed on mountain beech leaves (*Nothofagus solandri* var. *cliffortioides*).

Fiordland Flirt
Proteodes clarkei
Native   Seen in Fiordland only, in January, at about 1200 m. The caterpillars feed on the native grass tree known as pineapple scrub (*Dracophyllum menziesii*).

Unless otherwise indicated, all photos are life-size

Tussock Moths
[Family: Lymantriidae]

Dull-looking moths, similar to owlet moths (page 26), except that they are hairier. The irritant hairs act as a defence and are often placed among their eggs as protection. The females are sometimes wingless. The adult moths never eat. The caterpillars are far more spectacular: even hairier than the moths, often with brush-like (or 'tussock'-like) tufts along the back and sides. About 2600 species are known worldwide. New Zealand has no native species and only one introduced species is so far established here.

male

female (at rest)

Gypsy Moth
Lymantria dispar (was *Porthetria*)

One of the world's worst forest pests. Already, several clusters of egg cases have been found (and successfully intercepted) on container ships and log ships arriving from northern Asia and on imported used Japanese cars. Once established, the caterpillars, swinging from a silk thread, can be lifted several hundred metres off the ground and be carried by the wind. In North America, where the moth was deliberately introduced to produce cheap silk, the gypsy moth has escaped to become a serious nuisance.

Painted Apple Moth
Teia anartoides

From southern Australia, this moth was first found in New Zealand in 1983 in Dunedin and again in Glendene (Auckland) in May, 1999. At the time of writing, it is established here also in Avondale, Kelston, Titirangi and Mt Wellington. The caterpillars (see photo) feed on a very wide range of plants including wattle, pine and apple trees, roses and geraniums. To date, caterpillars have also been found on kōwhai and ribbonwood (*Plagianthus regius*). The female moth cannot fly, but the caterpillars – swinging on a silken thread – can be carried short distances by the wind.

male

female

caterpillar

Whitespotted Tussock Moth
Orgyia thyellina

First spotted in New Zealand in an east Auckland garden in 1996. The caterpillars are such a serious forest and horticultural pest overseas that several million dollars were spent on spraying the area with organic pesticides from DC6 planes and helicopters to eradicate the moth. The moth is believed to have arrived in New Zealand originally on an imported used vehicle. Some of the female moths have no wings.

Burnet Moths
[Family: Zygaenidae]

Mostly brightly coloured daytime visitors of flowers. Many look like wasps and contain high concentrations of hydrogen cyanide in their blood, making them poisonous to birds and other predators. Also called **forester moths**, or **leaf skeletonisers**, after the habits of the caterpillars. The slow-moving caterpillars are covered in small warts with tufts of hairs. About 800 species are known worldwide; one in New Zealand.

Bamboo Moth
Artona martini

From China, Taiwan, Japan and Vietnam. First discovered near Whangarei in about 1997, having probably arrived on board a yacht or cargo ship. The caterpillars feed on bamboo leaves. The moth is likely to spread throughout New Zealand. It may prove helpful in the control of wild bamboo but is also likely to become a pest on ornamental bamboos. The caterpillars are 25 mm long, yellow with tufts of irritating black hairs.

Unless otherwise indicated, all photos are life-size

Cabbage Moths
[Family: Plutellidae]

Small moths. Most of the caterpillars live in shoots, buds or fruits, or web leaves together. (Previously included in the Yponomeutidae family.) Over 400 species are known worldwide; about 40 in New Zealand, most of them unique to this country.

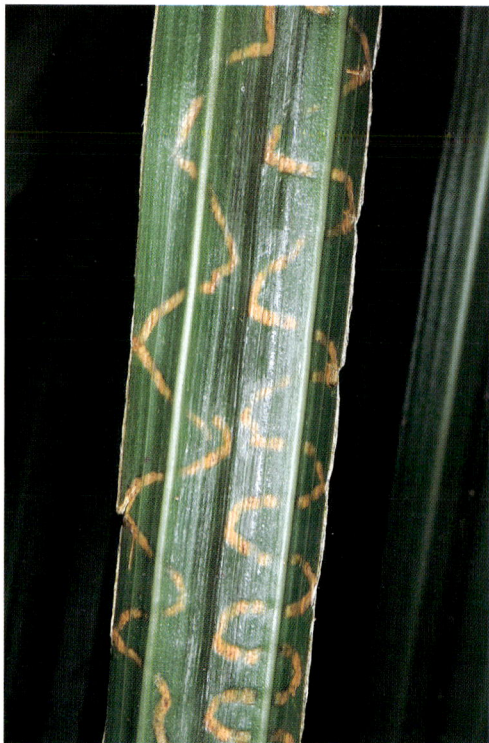

zig-zag leaf mine in *Astelia* leaf

Astelia Zig-Zag Moth
Charixena iridoxa
Native Seen December to January, flying by day on both the main islands. The caterpillars live in the heart of mountain astelia plants (kakaha, *Astelia nervosa*), tunnelling down in a zig-zag path as the leaf grows (see photo).

Diamondback Moth
Plutella xylostella (was *maculipennis*)
Almost worldwide. Accidentally introduced and now found throughout New Zealand, flying October to March. Also called **cabbage moth**, as the caterpillars often eat small holes in cabbages. In Europe, it regularly migrates across both the North Sea and the Mediterranean. A cream diamond pattern appears on its back, once the moth closes its wings.

Nīkau Moth
Doxophyrtis hydrocosma
Native Common in January in the north of the North Island, usually resting on nīkau palm trunks with its head pointing down. These and the cocoons are usually found on the leaf-scar rings on the trunk. The caterpillars tunnel inside the fruit and occasionally the bases of the leaves.

Snoutlet Fruit Moths
[Family: Carposinidae]
Small moths with a long 'snout'. Most have raised tufts of scales on their front wings and most of the caterpillars feed on fruits, including berries. About 275 species are known worldwide; 25 in New Zealand, all unique to this country.

Lichen Snoutlet
Heterocrossa eriphylla
Native Seen September to April in forest, but not common. Well camouflaged against lichen. The caterpillars live under injured bark (e.g. of pūriri) feeding on the soft tissue which grows over the wound. Compare with the **green lichen tuft** (*Izatha peroneanella*), page 38.

Plume Moths
[Family: Pterophoridae]
Small, delicate moths with very long, thin legs and body, and odd-looking, narrow, feather-like wings, spread wide like the wings of an aeroplane (or like the letter 'T'). Weak fliers, never found far from their caterpillars' foodplants. The moths feed at night, but are easily disturbed in daylight. About 500 species are known worldwide; over 20 in New Zealand, most of them unique to this country.

Common Hebe Plume Moth
Platyptilia falcatalis
Native Common throughout from December to January. Also known as the common brown plume moth. The caterpillars feed inside the unopened new buds of koromiko (*Hebe salicifolia* & *stricta*).

Leaf Moths
[Family: Thyrididae]

Many of these moths are patterned to look like leaves. The caterpillars of many species tunnel into the stems of plants, making the stem swell to form a gall, which the caterpillars then use as food. Most are found in the tropics. Over 250 species are known worldwide; only one in New Zealand.

pōhuehue stem gall

Pōhuehue Gall Moth
Morova subfasciata
Native Found below 500 m throughout. The males are seen flying fast in hot sunshine, November to February. But, surprisingly, the females shun the day and fly only at night. She lays her eggs in the stem of the large-leaved and small-leaved pōhuehue (*Muehlenbeckia axillaris* & *complexa*). This stem then swells to make a gall, providing food for the caterpillars (see photo).

Clearwing Moths
[Family: Sesiidae (was Aegeriidae)]

Most of these moths have long, narrow, transparent wings and fly during the day, defending themselves by looking and flying like bees or wasps. In flight, they even buzz like bees. Some take this disguise a step further and pretend to sting. About 1000 species are known worldwide; only one in New Zealand.

Currant Clearwing
Synanthedon tipuliformis (was *Trochilium*)
Accidentally introduced to New Zealand from Europe. Seen flying on summer days in the South Island and southern North Island, or resting on black currant and gooseberry bushes. The caterpillars tunnel inside the branches of these plants.

Leafminer Moths
[Families: Gracillariidae, Lyonetiidae, Nepticulidae]

These are so-called **micro moths**, whose tiny, pale caterpillars tunnel inside leaves, leaving pale, squiggly, see-through lines. With the clear outer surface of the leaf left intact and the consequent inner humidity, these tunnels act like miniature hothouses for the rapid development of the caterpillars. Each species specialises in the leaves of a different plant, with specific species known for example on wattle, kauri, lancewood, karamū, azalea, silver beech, hazel, oak and convolvulus. Broom has a twigminer. About 3000 species are known worldwide; about 60 in New Zealand. (Note that similar squiggly lines are also left by the tiny burrowing maggots of **leafminer flies** – see page 66.)

Wattle Miner
Acrocercops alysidota
[Family: Gracillariidae]
From Australia. The moth is seen from September to November. As the common name suggests, the tiny caterpillars tunnel inside the leaves of wattle trees.

pattern in kauri leaf left by the caterpillar

Kauri Leafminer
Acrocercops leucocyma
[Family: Gracillariidae]
Native The tiny caterpillars tunnel inside the leaves of the kauri tree, leaving meandering silver-coloured lines like the scribbles of a silver pen.

Unless otherwise indicated, all photos are life-size

Beetles / Pāpapa

[Order: Coleoptera]

BEETLE
(Adult)

PUPA

BEETLE
LIFE CYCLE
(Complete metamorphosis)

EGGS

GRUB (LARVA)
with or without legs

AN INORDINATE FONDNESS FOR BEETLES

WHEN ASKED WHAT HIS STUDY of biology had taught him, J. B. S. Haldane replied that he'd learnt of God's 'inordinate fondness for beetles'. Indeed, there are more beetle species on Earth than all the world's plants put together.

Instead of front flying wings, beetles have hard, movable wing-covers (elytra). At rest, these fold down to protect the beetle's back wings, meeting in a straight line along the centre of the beetle's back. (On flightless beetles, these covers are sometimes fused together.) It takes so much energy for a beetle to take off, that most first need to 'shiver' for a while to warm up. Once airborne, the beetle's wing-covers are held up where they can be used for gliding and steering.

A beetle's antennae are used partly as 'feelers' but mostly to smell. On the males, these antennae are often larger to help them find the females. All beetles have chewing mouths. Many are useful flower pollinators.

Beetles range in size from a fraction of a millimetre to more than 20 cm long (almost the height of this page). The world's heaviest insect, the male African **goliath beetle** (*Goliathus* species), can weigh up to 100 g – so heavy in fact that, when flying into houses, it can crash right through glass windows. The bodies of most beetles are very strong and well armoured, with some being able to carry 800 – 1700 times their own weight (equivalent in human terms to three people carrying a 747 jumbo jet).

The grubs of most species eat a completely different diet from the adults. Both the beetles and their grubs are an important food for many birds and the larger grubs are eaten by many people too (e.g. **huhu** and **sago grubs**).

The places in which beetles are found range from coastal beaches, underground caves and hot springs to mountain altitudes over 3700 m.

About 40 percent of all insect species are beetles, making this the largest Order of insects in the world. About 370,000 species are known worldwide; over 5500 in New Zealand, 90 percent of these unique to this country. Most are found only in native forest so their survival depends on the protection of this unique habitat. Many are flightless, some being found only on off-shore islands. Like canaries in a coal mine, beetles provide us with sensitive indicators of habitat damage.

Māori beetle names

Traditionally, beetles were grouped by Māori into broad behavioural categories, a few tribal names for which are still in use. For example, **mumu** (or **mumutawa**, or **tanguru**) includes the rounded beetles, like scarabs, ladybirds and leaf beetles, many of which fly in swarms, often with a humming sound.

Traditionally, **pāpapa** (or **pāpaka**) are the broad, flat, scuttling beetles (like tiger beetles) and other scuttling, beetle-like creatures such as slaters and cockroaches. The name means 'flat' or 'lying close to the ground'.

Tātaka traditionally refers to beetles (and some moths) which fly around clumsily at night (e.g. longhorn beetles, like the well-known 'huhu'). It means 'to turn or roll from side to side' or 'to take a circuitous route'.

In modern Māori, however, the names pāpapa, pāpaka or **pītara** (from the English word 'beetle') are widely used to include all beetles.

Throughout much of Polynesia, the name **huhu** (in its various forms) refers to all legless wood-boring beetle grubs. Those with legs are grouped with caterpillars.

Longhorn Beetles

[Family: Cerambycidae]

Long, narrow, flat beetles with very long, swept-back antennae, often two-thirds as long as the beetle's body (even longer on males). Many can make sounds, either by rubbing their back legs against the edge of their wing-covers or by nodding their neck to grind a joint in the middle section of the body. These noises are thought to scare off enemies. They can defend themselves by **biting**. Many are good fliers. The adult beetles generally feed on flowers, leaves or bark, but the grubs tunnel into dead wood or live trees, carrying yeast in their guts to help digest the wood. These grubs are so plump and rich in fat that they are among the most popular edible insects worldwide. In captivity, longhorn grubs have lived for up to 45 years. Sometimes known overseas as **timber beetles**. About 30,000 species are known worldwide; over 180 in New Zealand, most of them unique to this country (including three Threatened Species). The most common and distinctive New Zealand longhorns are here shown in order of size.

huhu grub
Eaten raw or cooked, or used as fishing bait.

Huhu Beetle / Tunga Rere
Prionoplus reticularis
Native   New Zealand's largest and heaviest beetle, seen in and around native and exotic forests throughout. Also known in Māori as **pepe te muimui**. In spring and summer, it often flies into lights or crashes against windows. The large white grubs tunnel into old damp logs, eating rotten wood, especially dead pine and rimu. But the adult beetle (tunga rere) never eats and lives for about two weeks only. It can squeak. To Māori, only the grub is known as **huhu** (also **tunga**); this is sometimes eaten raw, roasted or fried, and is also used as fishing bait.

Spiny Longhorn
Blosyropus spinosus
Native   Rare, but occasionally found in forest throughout. This large flightless beetle has four large spines in front of the wing-covers and another two on the head. The grubs tunnel into the rotting wood of dead trees such as manoao (silver pine), native beech, tawa and grass tree (*Dracophyllum*). Also known as spiny silver-pine borer. A Category I Threatened Species.

Kānuka Longhorn
Ochrocydus huttoni
Native   Looks like a small huhu. Can fly. The grubs tunnel into the live wood of various trees including native beech, mānuka and kānuka. These grubs are extracted from their tunnels and eaten by kākā. Also known as pale brown longhorn.

Burnt Pine Longhorn
Arhopalus tristis (was *ferus*)
Accidentally introduced from Europe in the mid-1950s and now found throughout the North Island and northern half of the South Island. It flies soon after dark and often lays its eggs in recently burnt pine trees – hence the name.

Variegated Longhorn
Coptomma variegatum
Native   Found in forest on both the main islands from September to March, on and in various dead trees including kōwhai, tawa and wattle. Can fly. Also called **tawa longhorn**.

Borneo Longhorn
Euryclelia cardinalis
The grubs of this beetle were intercepted in timber and posts arriving from Borneo in 1958 and 1960. In order to identify the beetle, this specimen was reared by the Forest Research Institute from one of these grubs. (This species is just one example of such interceptions.)

Large Green Longhorn
Calliprason marginatum (was *Pseudocalliprason*)
Native   Found only in North Island forests. The grubs tunnel under the bark, and later into the wood, of tāwari (*Ixerba brexioides*). The adult beetles are seen October to May and can fly.

Unless otherwise indicated, all photos are life-size

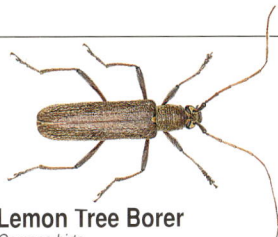

Lemon Tree Borer
Oemona hirta

Native Found in the North Island and around Nelson. The grubs tunnel into the live branches of citrus trees, grape and many native plants, particularly māhoe and rangiora trees. The adult beetle is common in summer, flying at night; it eats pollen and often squeaks when handled. The grubs are attacked by the **lemon tree borer parasite** (page 72).

Two-Toothed Longhorn
Ambeodontus tristis

Native 'Two-toothed' refers to the points on each side of the beetle's body, just in front of its front legs. The white grub (3 cm long) tunnels into dead trees and damp, sawn timber, leaving tunnels much larger than that of 'borer' (page 53). These tunnels are etched with crescent-shaped lines where the grub has been gnawing from side to side. Favourite timbers are rimu, kahikatea and macrocarpa. The flying beetle is usually seen in autumn and avoids light. Found throughout.

Pallid Longhorn
Calliprason pallidum (was *Stenopotes*)

Native Found throughout. The grubs tunnel into the dead wood of conifer trees, including kahikatea, rimu, miro, tōtara, tānekaha, larch, pine, Douglas fir and dawn redwood. The adult beetle can fly and is seen on white rātā flowers at night. Smells of lysol.

Orange & Black Longhorn
Gastrosarus nigricollis

Native Flies fast in hot sunshine imitating a spider-hunting wasp. Common on and around mānuka flowers on both the main islands. The grubs bore into – and kill – thin branches of many kinds of trees and shrubs, including mānuka and mingimingi.

Wattle Longhorn
Bethelium signiferum

Australian. Accidentally imported to New Zealand with hardwood piles in the 1840s. It breeds under the bark of dead and dying wattle and gum trees, where the grubs feed on the surface of the sapwood, leaving meandering grooves. The beetle can fly.

Squeaking Longhorn
Hexatricha pulverulenta

Native The grubs tunnel just under the bark of various dead and dying trees, especially native beech, and pine. The flying beetles are found throughout from August to April and live for up to three months. When held, they squeak. The grubs are attacked by the **lemon tree borer parasite** (page 72).

Tiger Longhorn
Aridaeus thoracicus

Australian. First seen in New Zealand in 1954, having probably arrived on gum (*Eucalyptus*) logs. It has so far been seen in Taranaki, Bay of Plenty and the Coromandel. This beetle runs over flowers and can also fly. The grubs live in dead wood such as mangrove (mānawa) and gum trees.

Striped Longhorn
Navomorpha lineata

Native Also known as **candy-striped longhorn**. The grubs tunnel into the live twigs of various trees and shrubs, including pine. The adult beetles appear in late spring and summer, flying during the day and eating pollen. North Island only. The grubs are attacked by the **lemon tree borer parasite** (page 72).

Speckled Longhorn
Xuthodes punctipennis

Native The beetle is found in the North Island at night on white rātā flowers and can fly. The grub feeds on the dead wood of various trees including karaka, silver birch and Lombardy poplar.

Elegant Striped Longhorn
Calliprason elegans (was *Drotus*)

Native Found in a few areas of scrubland and forest in the North Island only, flying in spring and summer. The grubs are known to feed in mānuka and in turpentine scrub (*Dracophyllum uniflorum*). (This specimen was photographed near Whitianga on the Coromandel.)

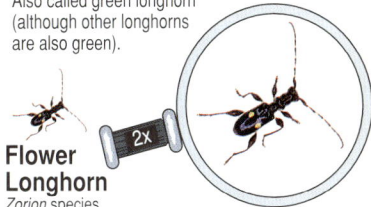

Common Eucalypt Longhorn
Phoracantha semipunctata

Australian. Accidentally imported about 1874 in hardwood piles. The grubs are found under the bark of dead and dying gum trees, feeding on the sapwood and leaving wide, meandering grooves. The adult beetles are most often seen in summer. Can fly.

Velvet Eucalypt Longhorn
Tessaromma undatum

Australian. First noticed here in 1904. The beetles and their grubs are found under the bark of dead or dying gum trees (*Eucalyptus*), often finding their way into houses with firewood. The flying beetle emerges in spring and autumn, and is attracted to lights at night.

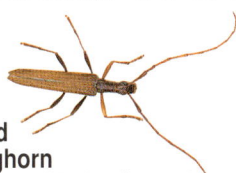

Hissing Longhorn
Tetrorea cilipes

Native The adult beetle is found in forest and scrub on both the main islands, November to March. It can fly and makes hissing sounds when disturbed. The grubs feed in the wood of five finger trees (*Pseudopanax*).

Sinclair's Longhorn
Calliprason sinclairi

Native Found in forest December to February, from Northland to mid-Canterbury. Can fly. The grubs tunnel into dead wood, including branches of trees such as pigeonwood (porokaiwhiri) and miro. Also called green longhorn (although other longhorns are also green).

Flower Longhorn
Zorion species

Native Small, brightly coloured flying beetles, common throughout, feeding on nectar and pollen in the flowers of native and introduced plants (including citrus). The grubs live under the bark or in dead branches and are found in large numbers on shelter belt prunings. About 10 species are now known.

Scarab Beetles

[Family: Scarabaeidae]

Includes **chafers** [Melolonthinae] and **dung beetles** [Scarabaeinae]. Common beetles with roundish, often shiny, bodies and strong digging legs. They have moveable, leaf-like clubs on the end of their antennae with which to smell. Most species eat leaves, roots, dung, or the rotting remains of plants. One kind even lives in the rectum of a kangaroo. The grubs are curled like the letter 'C'. To the ancient Egyptians, the pupal stage of the scarab or dung beetle symbolised the mummification of their dead for, in their religion, the appearance of these beetles signalled the return of the sun and the eternal nature of the human soul. Thus, images of the scarab were hewn from rock or formed in clay to make amulets and seals, and their round form remains popular in African jewellery today. (See also grass grub, below, for a parallel in Māori culture.) Scarabs include not only many of the world's heaviest insects (*Goliathus* species), but also the most beautiful: the iridescent, **leaf chafers** [Rutelinae] of the tropics. Worldwide, the grubs are popular as human food. About 16,500 species are known worldwide; over 140 in New Zealand, most of them unique to this country (including 12 Threatened Species). A selection of the more common and distinctive species follows in alphabetical order of scientific name. (Note that these could be confused with **leaf beetles**, page 54.)

Tasmanian Grass Grub

Acrossidius tasmaniae (was *Aphodius*)
Accidentally introduced from south-eastern Australia. The grubs live in tunnels in the soil, coming out at night to eat grass leaves, which they often drag into the tunnel. Common in gardens and farmland on both the North and South Islands. The beetle can fly.

Black Beetle

Heteronychus arator
Accidentally introduced in the 1930s from South Africa. Flies mostly on warm autumn evenings and sometimes attracted to lights at night. Both the beetles and the grubs feed on the roots of grass and other crops. Common in warmer parts of the North Island.

Large Sand Scarab / Mumutawa

Pericoptus truncatus
Native By day, this large beetle lies buried deep beneath the sand above high water mark. At night, it leaves clear tracks in the sand with its broad digging legs or flies about noisily (in spring). The grubs live under logs and eat rotten driftwood and dead marram grass roots. Found from Christchurch north. Smaller species, **small sand scarab** (*Pericoptus* species), are more common in some places.

Mumu Chafer

Stethaspis longicornis
Native Found in forest in the northern half of the North Island. Looks like the tanguru chafer but without the faint yellow stripe down its back. Its buzzing flight can be heard in the early evening in summer. The grubs feed on tree roots. Traditionally, the names mumu, tanguru and mumutawa are used interchangeably for a whole group of round beetles.

Mexican Dung Beetle

Copris incertus
American. Introduced to the Whangarei and Nelson regions in the 1950s to help dispose of farm dung. The male has a horn at the front, used for digging and fighting. On farms, the beetles fly around looking for dung to feed to their underground grubs. They can bury a sheep pat in less than a week. Often flies into house lights.

female

male
(with horn at front)

Yellowspotted Chafer

Odontria xanthosticta
Native Often seen flying in autumn and winter in native forest, farmland and gardens where the grubs eat grass roots or attack young trees.

Cromwell Chafer

Prodontria lewisii
Native The only beetle in New Zealand to have a protective reserve devoted to it. Discovered about 1900 and so far found only in rough pasture around Cromwell in Central Otago. The grubs feed on the roots of silver tussock (*Poa cita*). In summer, the adult beetle is found in soft sand, emerging at night to eat golden scabweed (*Raoulia australis*), field speedwell (*Veronica*) and sorrel (*Rumex*). Eaten by little owls, hedgehogs and wild cats. Protected as a Category A Threatened Species. Flightless.

Jewel Chafer

Stethaspis pulchra (was *Chlorochiton pulcher*)
Native The adult beetles are seen November to December at Titan Rock (1250 m) and Gow Burn in the Garvie Mountains of South Otago. Because of their short flying season, they are rarely seen. Similarly colourful alpine and subalpine species are found in North-West Nelson, Paparoa Range and Tararua Range.

Grass Grub / Tūtaeruru

Costelytra zealandica
Native These chafers fly in buzzing swarms at dusk in summer, eating huge quantities of the leaves of trees, shrubs and vegetables. In winter, the grub lives in the soil, eating the roots of grass and other plants, often killing them. Found throughout, but causing the most damage in Otago and Southland. Formerly eaten by Tūhoe Māori, they were known also as **manu a Rehua** (bird of the summer star, Antares) in reference to the season in which the flying beetle appears.

grub

Australian Dung Scarab

Onthophagus species
One of two similar species of Australian beetle, the first of which appears to have arrived here in the 1870s in stable manure imported with farm animals. The beetles feed on wet cow, horse or sheep dung and bury this as food for their grubs. Useful cleaners of farms. Found on both the main islands. Can fly.

Mānuka Chafer / Kēkerewai

Pyronota festiva
Native Swarms on warm days in spring and summer. It feeds on mānuka leaves, but often falls into streams and gets eaten by trout, as described by another Māori name, **kerewai**, meaning 'to drift on water'. Usually green, but can be blue, orange, red or purple. The grubs eat roots. Tūhoe Māori collected the adult beetles for food, pounding them with raupō pollen for steam-cooking. Also known as **manu a Rehua** (bird of the summer star, Antares, from the season in which the beetle flies) or as **reporepowai**.

orange form

Tanguru Chafer

Stethaspis suturalis
Native Distinguished from the mumu chafer by the yellow stripe on its back. Common in summer in native forest and pine plantations over most of New Zealand, flying with a buzzing sound soon after dark. The large white grubs (**papahu**) feed on tree roots.

grub

46

Unless otherwise indicated, all photos are life-size

Ladybirds / Mumutawa

[Family: Coccinellidae]

These little, round, short-legged beetles are often brightly coloured, many of them spotted (hence a modern Māori name: **pāpapa kōpure**). Many are useful in the garden, eating aphids, mealybugs, scale insects and mites. The adult beetles can eat about 100 aphids a day, their little caterpillar-like grubs: about 50. Both grubs and adults can ooze drops of bitter, orange-yellow blood from their knee joints, making them poisonous to birds. The beetles were used medicinally to treat colic, measles and toothache, and were dedicated in the Middle Ages to the Virgin Mary with the name 'Beetle of Our Lady', a name later shortened to 'ladybird'. Most can fly. In Europe, huge swarms are common. The children's rhyme: 'Ladybug, ladybug fly away home, Your house is on fire, your children do roam' referred to the plight of ladybirds when the hop vines were burned after the harvest in England. About 5000 species are known worldwide; about 40 in New Zealand, more than half of them native. Pictured are the conspicuous ones.

Twospotted Ladybird
Adalia bipunctata
Introduced from Europe. Common in southern New Zealand, where they are found mostly on trees (but also on lucerne), eating aphids. Can fly.

Flax Ladybird
Cassiculus venustus
Native Found in the North Island on New Zealand flax (*Phormium*) and cutty grass, where they apparently eat mealybugs. Can fly.

Orangespotted Ladybird
Coccinella leonina
Native Has 16 orange spots on its black back. Both adults and grubs eat mostly aphids found on grasses, speargrass and tussock. Seen throughout, from sea level to subalpine altitudes. Can fly.

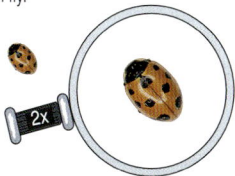

Elevenspotted Ladybird
Coccinella undecimpunctata
Introduced from England in 1874 to help control aphids. Now common in gardens and orchards here, where they lay their eggs in the soil. In its lifetime, each ladybird can eat 1000 aphids. Can fly.

Double-Cross Ladybird
Coelophora inaequalis
Arrived here from Australia or the Pacific Islands about 1960. On each wing-cover is a black Maltese-style cross. It eats aphids and can fly. Also called **variable ladybird**.

Mealybug Ladybird
Cryptolaemus montrouzieri
Introduced from Australia to help control mealybugs. It can fly. The grubs of this ladybird are cleverly disguised to look just like the mealybugs they eat.

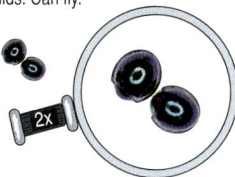

adult

grub

Steelblue Ladybird
Halmus chalybeus
Introduced from Australia to control scale insects on citrus. Also eats aphids. Common in warm native forest and gardens, especially on lemon trees from Nelson north. Can also appear green. Can fly.

Antipodean Ladybird
Harmonia antipoda
Native Found in North Island forest where they have been seen on leaves and under the bark of dead rimu trees (although this one landed on a café table in Titirangi). Can fly.

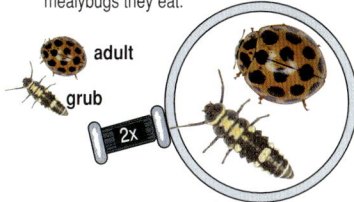

Large Spotted Ladybird
Harmonia conformis
Introduced from Australia. This has 20 large black spots, 18 of them on the wing-covers. Common in the north. The adults and grubs (see photo) feed on aphids. The adult can fly.

grub

adult

Fungus-Eating Ladybird
Illeis galbula
From Australia. Has a black 'batman' design on its bright yellow back. It is seen in the vegetable garden where it eats powdery mildew, a kind of fungus common on the leaves of pumpkins, courgettes, etc. Can fly.

Cardinal Ladybird
Rodolia cardinalis
Accidentally introduced from Australia. Some were taken from New Zealand to California in 1888, helping to save their citrus trees from a plague of **cottony cushion scale insects** (page 91). Uncommon here now. Can fly.

Yellow-Shouldered Ladybird
Scymnodes lividigaster
Introduced. Found in North Island gardens, where it feeds on aphids. Can fly.

Unless otherwise indicated, all photos are life-size

Weevils

[Superfamily: Curculionoidea. Family: Curculionidae]

These beetles have a long 'snout' (with their mouth at the tip), so are also known as **snout beetles** (later translated into Māori as **pāpaka nguturoa**). Many of the females use these 'snouts' to bore holes in plants to lay their eggs. They have elbowed antennae. Most are small. All feed on plants and many are crop pests. Rather than use pesticides to control them, the Yukpa people of Venezuela and Colombia eat them; likewise the Pedi people of South Africa. The grubs are C-shaped and legless. Weevils comprise the largest animal family in the world, with over 48,000 known species; over 1540 in New Zealand, most of them unique to this country (including almost 20 large, flightless Threatened Species).

Flax Weevil
Anagotus fairburni
Native Flightless. Discovered in 1931. Once widespread, now found mainly on rat-free islands such as the Poor Knights, down to the off-shore islands of Fiordland; also in the Tararua Ranges, hiding during the day deep inside the bases of flax bushes. At night, the grubs and adult weevils feed on both species of native flax (*Phormium*). A Category C Threatened Species.

Helms' Beech Weevil
Anagotus helmsi
Native Found from Mt Te Aroha to Stewart Island. The adult weevil is active at night but cannot fly. The grub tunnels into all five species of native beech (*Nothofagus*), also blue Douglas fir and pine.

Tussock Weevil
Anagotus lewisi
Native Flightless. Found in the South Island, where the grubs feed on tussock plants. The adult weevil feeds on various plants, including snowberry (*Gaultheria*). Eaten by rats.

Astelia Weevil
Anagotus oconnori
Native Flightless. Lives in the mountains, especially in the Tararua Ranges and North-West Nelson, where they feed on *Astelia* plants. Eaten by rats.

Stephens Island Weevil
Anagotus stephenensis
Native Flightless. Now restricted only to Stephens Island (near the Marlborough Sounds). The grubs tunnel into wood, especially of ngaio and karaka trees. The adult weevils eat ngaio leaves. Protected as a Category B Threatened Species.

Fivefinger Weevil
Ectopsis ferrugalis
Native The adult is thought to feed on the nectar of five finger flowers (*Pseudopanax arboreus*). When disturbed, it imitates a chip of wood by drawing its legs up underneath, folding up its long 'nose' into a little groove underneath. Note the flat slope at the back end. Flightless.

Vegetable Weevil
Listroderes species (incl *costirostris*)
Introduced from South America. Found from about Oamaru north. The adult weevil and its grubs are a nuisance in vegetable gardens, feeding on leaves. All the adults are females for they don't need a male to reproduce. They have wings but seldom fly.

Speargrass Weevil
Lyperobius coxalis
Native Flightless. Found in South Island tussock grassland at 1200 – 1600 m, where it feeds on speargrass and native aniseed plants. Two very similar large, flightless weevils (*Lyperobius*) are on the Threatened Species List.

Longnosed Kauri Weevil
Mitrastethus baridioides
Native Found throughout the North Island. In summer, the little white grubs tunnel into the wet dead wood of kauri and pine trees. The adult beetles are common under bark from January to April and can fly.

Whitefringed Weevil
Naupactus leucoloma (was *Graphognathus*)
Accidentally introduced from South America via the USA in 1945 and now found from Ashburton north. The grubs are a pest, eating plant roots. At night, the adult weevils eat leaves, though these are less of a nuisance than the grubs. Flightless.

Twospined Weevil
Nyxetes bidens
Native The adult weevil is common in flowers, where it feeds on pollen. Can fly. The grubs live in trees and vines, making the plant produce lumps (galls) which provide the grubs with an on-going supply of food.

Black Vine Weevil
Otiorhynchus sulcatus
Introduced from the northern hemisphere. It feeds at night on various plants including grape vines, strawberry and black currant. All the adults are females, for these weevils don't need males to reproduce. Flightless.

Garden Weevil
Phlyctinus callosus
Introduced from Ethiopia. Now found from Nelson north. The tiny orange-headed grubs feed on the roots of various garden plants including carrots and parsnips. The flightless adults are active at night.

Elephant Weevil
Rhyncodes ursus
Native On summer nights, these crawl slowly over the trunks of native trees including beech, kauri, taraire, rimu and mountain neinei, feeding on sap. Can fly. The grubs tunnel into the dead branches and trunks of these trees and are attacked by the **giant ichneumonid wasp** (page 72).

Fourspined Weevil
Scolopterus species
Native Often knocked out of native flowering plants in summer, where they eat pollen during the day. Can fly. The grubs feed in dead wood. One species feeds on the dead stems of the mamaku tree fern.

Rice Weevil
Sitophilus oryzae
Introduced from the Indo-Malayan region. This and the similar **granary weevil** (*Sitophilus granarius*) are common in stored seeds. The female lays one egg in each seed. Here, the white legless grub feeds before climbing out as an adult to fly and mate. The cycle takes about one month at 26°C.

Unless otherwise indicated, all photos are life-size

Giraffe & Seed Weevils

[Superfamily: Curculionoidea. Family: Brentidae]

Also called **primitive weevils**. Like true weevils, these have a long snout for boring into plants. The longer snout of the female allows her to drill more deeply to create safe egg-laying sites. Their antennae can be either straight or slightly elbowed. The family includes two very different groups: (1) tiny, pear-shaped insects [Apioninae] and (2) very long, narrow creatures [Brentinae]. Not surprisingly, some regard these subfamilies as separate families. About 2500 species are known worldwide; about six in New Zealand.

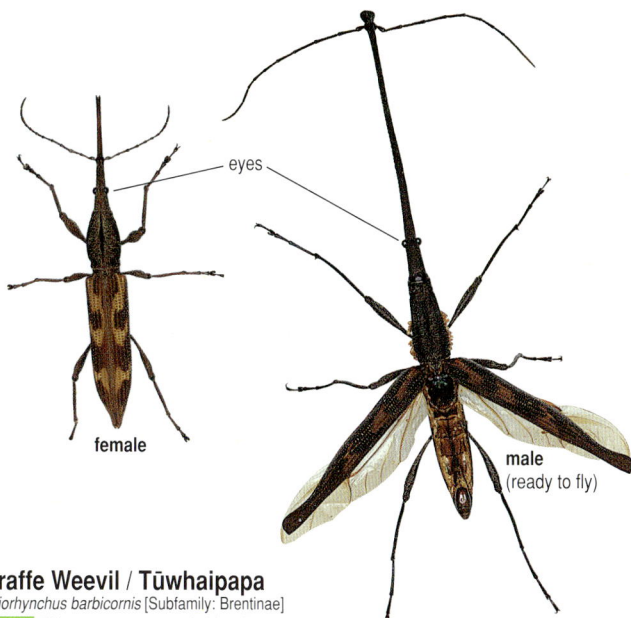

eyes

female

male
(ready to fly)

adult weevils climbing out
of cracked gorse seed pods

4x

BEETLES

Giraffe Weevil / Tūwhaipapa

Lasiorhynchus barbicornis [Subfamily: Brentinae]

Native This strange creature is New Zealand's longest beetle. The larger male has its antennae at the tip of its 'nose'. The female has them further back near its eyes, leaving its mouth free to bore into the bark of dying trees or logs to lay its eggs (October to March). Males fight with their 'noses'. Common in spring and summer on trunks and logs in native forest in the North Island and northern South Island, mostly at lower altitudes. The grub tunnels for two years into rotten or dying trees and is thought to feed on the fungi and yeast growing inside. The hole the adult makes as it leaves the wood is not round but square. This adult lives for just two weeks and – most remarkable of all – it can fly! Similar-looking insects elsewhere are found mostly in the tropics. The insect's canoe-like shape is recorded in the same Māori name being given to the god of a newly-made canoe: tūwhaipapa. Also known as **tūwhaitara**. Sometimes mistaken for a stick insect (page 104).

Gorse Seed Weevil

Exapion ulicis [Subfamily: Apioninae]

Introduced from Britain in 1931 to help control gorse. By 1947, 235,000 of them had been released here. Now very common. The female chews a hole in the young seed pods and lays her eggs inside. The grubs and adults feed on the seeds, but the adult weevils feed on the needles too. Unfortunately, gorse in New Zealand produces seeds twice a year but there is only one generation per year of the weevils. They can fly.

Fungus Weevils

[Superfamily: Curculionoidea. Family: Anthribidae]

Adult fungus weevils are often found on dead wood, under loose bark and inside seed pods, where they eat mostly fungi. Unlike ordinary weevils, their *antennae are not elbowed*. On some males, these can be much longer than their body, making them easy to confuse with small longhorn beetles (page 44). The grubs live mostly inside the dead and dying branches of trees and shrubs. About 3000 species are known worldwide; over 60 in New Zealand, most of them unique to this country, several found only on offshore islands.

Wattle Gall Weevil

Araecerus palmaris

Australian. First found in New Zealand in 1894. They can jump or fly and are found all year, usually on rust fungus galls (*Uromycladium*) on wattle trees (see photo on page 34). The grubs tunnel into these large brown lumps to feed. The grubs are also found in dried up lemons, figs, loquats and apples.

Nikau Anthribid

Arecopais spectabilis

Native Very common running around inside the sheaths of fallen nikau fronds, but also found on cabbage trees, flax, perching lilies and kiekie, where they feed on the tiny fungi found growing on these plants. Seen all year, but especially in spring and summer. It can fly.

Lacebark Fungus Weevil

Hoherius meinertzhageni

Native This greenish fungus weevil is found September to April, from Christchurch north and can fly. The grubs feed in mountain lacebark, ribbonwood and saltmarsh ribbonwood.

Unless otherwise indicated, all photos are life-size

Ground Beetles

[Family: Carabidae]

Most are fairly flat, shiny, brown or black beetles with fine grooves along the wing-covers, long legs for running and strong jaws for hunting. Larger ones **can bite**. Those with an unpleasant smell are known in Māori as **kurikuri**, referring to this smell as being dog-like. Overseas species, known as **bombardier beetles**, can even fire clouds of hot irritating gases at their enemies. Most of the grubs are active hunters too, so these likewise have strong jaws and legs. Ground beetles are common under stones, logs and leaf litter or on rotting tree trunks. A few can be found high up in forest trees. Others are found along the banks of streams, rivers or lakes or in coastal sand dunes. Most are active only at night. To find them, just look under stones, loose bark and logs. About 29,000 species are known worldwide; about 430 in New Zealand (excluding **tiger beetles** – below), most of them unique to this country. One of New Zealand's largest beetle families. Most native species are flightless (so their wing-covers are joined together) and around 50 of these are Threatened Species.

Cosmopolitan Ground Beetle
Laemostenus complanatus
A frequent flier, helping it spread throughout much of the world. It can also climb. Accidentally introduced to New Zealand by boat and now common throughout the country in old wood piles, under stones in gardens and on farmland. It is active at night and is found throughout the year, but not seen in dense forest. Eaten by hedgehogs.

Snail-Eating Ground Beetle
Maoripamborus fairburni
Native Found mainly in Northland (although subfossil remains have also been found in central North Island caves). At night, it uses its unusually long, narrow head to get into the shells of native snails, first biting the snail's foot and then following the snail into its shell as it withdraws. The snail tries to defend itself with thick slime, but the beetle dissolves both the slime and the snail with special chemicals. Flightless. A Category I Threatened Species.

Stephens Island Ground Beetle
Mecodema costellum costellum
Native A flightless beetle which hides during the day under logs and stones in open forest on Stephens Island (near the Marlborough Sounds). It hunts at night. Note the narrow 'waist' in front of the wing-covers; New Zealand has about 60 species of such **waisted ground beetles** (all *Mecodema* species), of which this is the largest. A Category A Threatened Species.

Metallic Green Ground Beetle
Megadromus antarcticus
Native Very common in the Canterbury Plains of the South Island, where it is sometimes known as the **Alexander beetle**. Seen throughout the year, mostly in dry forest but also in farmland and town gardens. Active mostly at night. Flightless. It can defend itself with a strong smell and powerful bite. Eaten by hedgehogs.

Bubbled Ground Beetle
Megadromus bullatus
Native Seen September to April in Fiordland, from near sea level right up to alpine altitudes, mostly in wet forest. Active at night, hiding under logs during the day. Flightless. Its back is patterned like a row of chains. It can defend itself with a strong smell and a powerful bite.

Stinking Ground Beetle
Plocamostethus planiusculus
Native Common all year from Te Aroha to northern South Island, usually found under damp, rotting logs in native forest, coming out at night to feed on insects. Flightless. It has a powerful bite and a horrible smell which can cling to one's fingers for hours. One of about 150 similar-looking common native ground beetles.

Tiger Beetles

[Family: Carabidae. Subfamily: Cicindelinae]

Included in the **ground beetle** family (above). Most have bone-coloured, spotted designs on their backs. They are active during the day, hunting non-stop, hence the common name. They have particularly long legs for fast running. Indeed, overseas species can reach speeds of up to 2.6 km/h, making them among the fastest runners in the insect world (but not as fast as some cockroaches). About 2000 species are known worldwide; about 12 in New Zealand, all unique to this country.

common tiger beetle nesting holes

Common Tiger Beetle
Cicindela tuberculata (was *Neocicindela*)
Native Active on warm days, running over dry clay banks, taking quick, short flights, hunting other insects. They live in colonies. At night, they burrow just beneath the surface of the soil. The grub (**penny doctor**, **hāpuku**, **kūi** or **muremure**) lives in a deep, narrow tunnel (15 cm deep) in bare ground for more than a year, eating insects which walk by. In the South Island, the similar-looking *Cicindela latecincta* is more commonly seen.

Sand Dune Tiger Beetles
Cicindela perhispida (was *Neocicindela*)
Native There are several colour forms, depending on the sand in which they live – pale if found on silica sand, dark on iron sand, or brown if living on sand from sedimentary rock. They are fast runners, often flying over one metre when disturbed, making them very hard to catch.

Unless otherwise indicated, all photos are life-size

Click Beetles / Tūpanapana

[Family: Elateridae]

Also known as **skipjacks**. These beetles can be recognised by the pointed back corners of the front, bell-like section of the body (thorax), and by their clicking behaviour. (Tūpanapana means 'to keep twitching'.) This click sends the beetle leaping to heights of up to 30 cm (equivalent in terms of human body length to being able to leap onto the roof of a three storey building), with an acceleration up to 400 G (or over 30 times that of a space rocket). They do this by popping a peg-and-socket joint under their belly. The beetle may land back in the same spot, or up to 30 cm away. This feat allows the beetle to make a quick getaway or to right itself if it lands upside down. The loud click that it makes is also effective in startling predators. At night, most adult click beetles eat leaves, pollen and nectar. Many of the slender grubs live underground for many years, feeding on plant roots (**wireworms**); others are found in rotting logs. Such grubs from rotting logs are used in parts of Japan as food. About 9000 species are known worldwide; over 135 in New Zealand, most of them unique to this country. New Zealand currently has four Threatened Species.

grub (pasture wireworm)

Cook Strait Click Beetle
Amychus granulatus

Native This beetle has long lost its ability to click or fly. The adults feed at night on the sap oozing from tree trunks and the grubs are thought to feed on the roots of forest trees and shrubs. It is now restricted to islands in the Marlborough Sounds. Protected as a Category B Threatened Species.

Three Kings Click Beetle
Amychus species [Undescribed species]

Native Like the Cook Strait click beetle (left) and the **Chatham Island click beetle** (*Amychus candezei*), this large, well-camouflaged, bark-like beetle has long lost its ability to click or fly. It is known only from Great & South West Islands in the Three Kings Islands group (off the northern tip of the North Island). Protected as a Category I Threatened Species.

Common Click Beetle
Conoderus exsul

From Australia. This beetle flies into houses in summer. The tough wire-like grub (**pasture wireworm**) is common in garden soil, eating potatoes, plant roots, maggots and other grubs.

Acutewinged Click Beetle
Metablax acutipennis

Native This beetle is seen in forest from November to January and can fly. The grub tunnels under bark and into recently dead wood (especially of hīnau), eating both the wood and other grubs.

Striped Click Beetle
Metablax cinctiger

Native Found on trees and shrubs in North Island forest from January to March. It can fly. The grubs feed in dead branches and tree trunks. A similar-looking, but larger, undescribed species (*Metablax* species) from Spirits Bay is on the Threatened Species List.

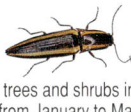

Wakefield's Click Beetle
Thoramus wakefieldi

Native The beetle is found on the forest floor, but the large grub lives in rotting logs, where it eats the wood-boring grubs of longhorn beetles. This is the largest of New Zealand's flying click beetles, so has also been called the **giant click beetle**.

Darkling Beetles

[Family: Tenebrionidae]

Hard-bodied beetles, with long cylindrical grubs, found mostly under bark, logs and stones, eating rotten wood, lichens, fungi and other decaying plants. Most are black or brown. Many overseas species live in deserts where some have been seen doing 'headstands' to tip droplets of dew from their back into their mouths. Named for their love of the dark (active at night). Many produce smelly, bad-tasting chemicals to put off would-be predators. When picking them up, these chemicals can leave a smelly yellow stain on your fingers. During the day you will find them under stones and logs; go out with a torch at night to find them on tree trunks. About 17,000 species are known worldwide; about 150 in New Zealand, most of them unique to this country (including two Threatened Species).

Australian Darkling Beetle
Amarygmus species

Accidentally introduced from Australia. Common in northern New Zealand. The grubs and beetles are found in forest, farmland and gardens, in holes or under the loose bark of standing dead trees such as wattle, pine and gum. Can fly.

Lichen Darkling Beetle
Artystona species

Native Common in forest, where the grubs burrow into the dead branches of many trees. The adults are seen at night on tree trunks and fence posts, feeding on lichens. Flightless.

Seaweed Darkling Beetle
Chaerodes trachyscelides

Native Common on beaches, where they are found under seaweed or driftwood. They have a bubble-like shape, similar to a scarab beetle (page 46). Flightless.

False Wireworm
Mimopeus opaculus

Native The beetle and its grubs are common south of Auckland in dry, rotten wood in the forest, and under stones. The worm-like grub looks similar to a wireworm (top right). The beetle produces a bad smell to put off predators, but is nevertheless a favourite food of tuatara. Flightless.

Yellow Mealworm
Tenebrio molitor

Introduced. These live in dark corners of warehouses where flour is stored. Can fly.
The grubs are used as food for pets, such as parrots and fish, and are used as bait for catching fish. In the USA, some specialty restaurants serve them too, stir-fried or as a dessert in the form of 'mealworm chocolate chip cookies'.

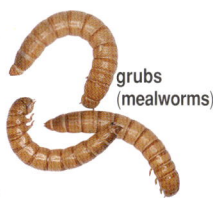

grubs (mealworms)

Dented Beetle
Uloma tenebrionoides

Native The beetles and grubs are common in and under rotten logs from both native and introduced trees. The beetle has a tarry smell and can fly. Its common name refers to the male which has a dent just behind its head.

Unless otherwise indicated, all photos are life-size

Stag Beetles

[Family: Lucanidae]

Most male stag beetles have large jaws which, on some tropical species, can be enormous – like stag antlers. Such large-jawed males sometimes tackle each other head on, using these 'antlers' as weapons, each trying to flip its rival over onto its back. Most stag beetles are brown or black, and many have elbowed antennae with fixed 'leaves' at the ends used for smelling. At night, the adult beetles feed on fruit juices or the sap of trees. The C-shaped grubs eat rotten wood, living for up to six years, but the adults generally live for a few weeks only. About 1300 species are known worldwide; about 30 in New Zealand, most of them unique to this country, including four flightless Threatened Species and several other large, flightless species found only on offshore islands.

female

male

Earl's Stag Beetle
Dendroblax earlii

`Native` The flying beetles are sometimes seen on spring and summer evenings. The grubs live in the soil and are thought to eat grass roots. Found throughout most of the country.

Helms' Stag Beetle
Geodorcus helmsi

`Native` New Zealand's largest stag beetle. Flightless. On rat-free islands, it can (with its jaws) reach 42 mm long and 2 cm wide. It is most often found in the wettest rainforests of South Westland and Fiordland, where it is sometimes seen during the day at the base of kahikatea trees or feeding on sap bleeding from tree trunks. The grub lives in rotten wood.

Golden Stag Beetle
Lamprima aurata

Known in Australia as the golden stag beetle, it has found its way across the Tasman (probably on imported timber) and has been found at Puha near Gisborne. It breeds in rotten logs and stumps; the beetle is usually found nearby and can fly.

Parry's Stag Beetle
Mitophyllus parrianus (was *Ceratognathus*)

`Native` The beetles are found all year in forests throughout the country, on trunks and branches, or flying into lights. The grubs live in sound or rotting wood.

Reticulate Stag Beetle
Paralissotes reticulatus

`Native` The beetles are found under the loose bark of living trees, particularly native beech (*Nothofagus*). Both the beetles and the grubs can also be found under old logs on the forest floor. Flightless.

Brown Stag Beetle
Ryssonotus nebulosus

An Australian beetle first noticed in New Zealand in Gisborne in 1950. It has since been found in Auckland, preferring to breed in the dead wood of privet, oak, gum and wattle trees, where the grubs can be found tunnelling. The adult beetle appears at dusk in summer and can fly.

Rove Beetles

[Family: Staphylinidae]

These can curl or wag their long, flexible bodies like a tail (giving many smaller ones the general appearance of earwigs – but without the nippers). Most are brown or black. They have strong jaws and very short wing-covers. Many can defend themselves with an unpleasant smell from a pair of stink glands on their tail end. Both the beetles and the grubs are found on the ground under rotting wood, dead animals or seaweed, where they eat other insects. Some are useful for controlling insect pests. Named from the Dutch 'roof kever' (robbery beetle) from their habit of stealing meat. For a sweet substance they produce, some species are 'farmed' by **ants** just as we keep cattle. Some have been observed communicating with ants using the ant's antennal language: their so-called 'antennal fingering'. Over 29,000 species are known worldwide; over 1020 in New Zealand, most of them unique to this country. Many are tiny (including two Threatened Species, both about 3 mm long).

Large Coastal Rove Beetle
Cafius litoreus

`Native` Common on the beach, just above high water mark, feeding on kelp fly maggots found in decaying seaweed. Can fly.

Devil's Coachhorse
Creophilus oculatus

Possibly native. Smells like rotten fish. Common near rotting plants and dead animals. Its common name comes from an old belief that a related European beetle carried away the corpses of sinners. Note the orange-red spot behind each eye. A strong flier, attracted to lights.

Metallic Green Rove Beetle
Thyreocephalus orthodoxus

Introduced from Australia. Very common in gardens and paddocks, sometimes in forest. Strong-smelling. Can fly. Both the adult beetles and the grubs help control insect pests in soil and grass.

52

Unless otherwise indicated, all photos are life-size

Borer Beetles
[Family: Anobiidae]

Small beetles with a hood-shaped head. Both the beetles and the grubs are found in dead trees, logs and timber. The grubs of several species bore into the wooden structure of houses and furniture. Others are found in dried food, woollen clothes, bookbindings, leaf litter and fungi. To help the grubs digest wood, many have fungal yeast cells in their gut or cultivate these in the tunnels in which they feed. These yeast cells are found on the beetle egg, conveniently entering the grub's gut when it eats its own shell. About 1500 species are known worldwide; over 40 in New Zealand, 30 of them native.

borer damage

Large Borer / Uhu
Hadrobregmus magnus
Native At 6 – 8 mm long, this beetle is larger than the common European house borer. The grub prefers damp and rotting rimu and tōtara. It will not attack dry wood. When the adult beetle moves out, it leaves an exit hole twice as wide as those from the European house borer. Found throughout. Can fly. The Māori name (a variation of 'huhu') refers to the grubs of a whole range of wood-boring beetles.

House Borer
Anobium punctatum
From Europe, but now found throughout New Zealand. This beetle is just 2 – 6 mm long, yet the grub can destroy untreated timber (especially sapwood) used in buildings and furniture. The grubs live for up to five years, but the adult beetle lives for no more than a month and never eats. In summer, this flying adult beetle emerges from the wood, chewing its way out (without swallowing) – gnawing through sheet lead if necessary.

Lax Beetles
[Family: Oedemeridae]

Soft-bodied, small-headed beetles with a narrow 'neck'. From their knee joints, they can bleed a fluid, called *cantharidin*, a chemical which **makes blisters on the skin when touched**. This is collected from one overseas species for medicinal use. A dose of 70 grams is enough to kill a person. The beetles are found on flowers and leaves and are common near driftwood along the coast, but a few can also be found inland – even as far from the sea as the South Island mountains. The grubs feed on dead and rotting wood. Also called false tiger beetles or **blister beetles** (but the name 'blister beetle' is often used overseas to refer to a closely related family not found in New Zealand: Meloidae). About 600 species are known worldwide (mostly from the tropics); about 20 in New Zealand, most of them unique to this country.

Spotted Lax Beetle
Parisopalpus nigronotatus
From Australia. Easily recognised by the dark spots on its wing-covers. The beetles eat nectar and pollen. Found from Nelson north, on the beach or on the ground. At night, they often fly into lights. The grubs live in dead and rotting wood. Particularly common near mangroves.

Dark Patch Lax Beetle
Thelyphassa diaphana
Native Very common under driftwood along the shoreline throughout New Zealand. Cream with a long chocolate-coloured patch on its back. Note the short wing-covers.

Striped Lax Beetle
Thelyphassa lineata
Native Note the long dark stripes. In late spring and summer, these beetles often fly into houses, attracted by the lights. Otherwise, they are usually found on the flowers of native shrubs, where they are thought to feed on pollen and nectar. Along with their yellowish grubs, they are common in rotten wood on the forest floor throughout.

Jewel Beetles

[Family: Buprestidae]

Beetles with a bullet-shaped body and large eyes; most feed in flowers. The grubs tunnel into wood, so they are sometimes known as **metallic wood borers**. The grubs of many species are known to carry yeast in their gut to help digest the wood. Most are from tropical forests, where they can be the most stunning metallic colours: brilliant greens, reds or blues, often with stripes, bands or spots. Such gorgeous beetles have long been used for decorative purposes and jewellery, both by local people and for trade to western tourists. Some tropical species have heat sensors in their legs for finding freshly burned trees, which make good egg-laying sites. About 15,000 species are known worldwide; three in New Zealand, two of them native.

Golden Buprestid
Buprestis aurulenta

From the north-west coast of the United States. The beetle is occasionally found alive in New Zealand, but is not so far known to breed here. The grubs bore into the old wood of pine trees and Douglas fir (which used to be imported for house framing). The grubs can live for up to 47 years, which may qualify this beetle as being the world's longest-living insect. The beetle can fly.

Beech Buprestid
Nascioides enysi

Native Both the beetles and their grubs are found only in native beech forest where they feed on unhealthy trees. The grub tunnels under the bark, feeding on the outer sapwood. The adult beetle is seen in spring and summer, eating the leaves. On hot sunny days, it flies. There is a pair of gold markings on each wing-cover.

Leaf Beetles

[Family: Chrysomelidae]

Smooth, hairless beetles, many of them rounded like a large ladybird (page 47). Several have strong back legs for jumping, hence overseas common names such as **kangaroo beetles** or **flea beetles**. The beetles and their grubs eat the stems, leaves or roots of plants. Many are pests. The maternal females of several species have been seen guarding their eggs and grubs from predators. Among the insects of the tropics, this family contains some of the most spectacularly beautiful metallic species. About 35,000 species are known worldwide; over 150 in New Zealand, most of them unique to this country.

Bronze Beetle
Eucolaspis brunnea

Native Very common in late spring and early summer in the northern North Island. At night, the beetle flies about, eating the leaves of trees and shrubs, leaving 'shot-holes'. It is a pest in orchards, where it also damages fruit. The grubs live in the soil.

Eucalyptus Tortoise Beetle
Paropsis charybdis

Arrived from Australia about 1916. A pest in gum forests (*Eucalyptus*) as the beetles and grubs eat the leaves. In winter, the beetle hibernates under loose gum bark. It can fly.

West Coast Leaf Beetle
Chalcolampra speculifera (was *Eualema*)

Native Found in South Island forest, mostly along the West Coast. One of New Zealand's largest and most handsome native leaf beetles, but little is known about it.

Three Kings Leaf Beetle
[Undescribed species]

Native Found only on the Three Kings Islands.

Diving Beetles / Tātaka Ruku

[Family: Dytiscidae]

Smooth, dark, shiny, flattened, boat-shaped beetles with large back legs and paddle-like feet, hunting in still or flowing water. While underwater, they carry a spare supply of air under their wing-covers, both to breathe and to help them float back quickly to the surface. Both the adults and their larvae (**water tigers**) hunt small insects, including mosquito larvae, but also fish and frogs. In the Philippines, the larvae are eaten fried, grilled or sautéed with vegetables. Similarly in the Kwangtung Province of China these are farmed and served in restaurants. About 3500 species are known worldwide; about 16 in New Zealand, all native. Some of these survive in cold alpine lakes at 1700 m; others live in warm thermal pools near Rotorua; several small species have even been found in underground waters.

Large Diving Beetle
Homeodytes hookeri

Native New Zealand's largest water beetle. Sometimes found in ponds and deeper lakes, mostly in the North Island but also in the Nelson area. Can fly.

immature form
The underwater larva of this diving beetle

Cosmopolitan Diving Beetle
Rhantus suturalis (was *pulverosus*)

Native Also found overseas. Common throughout New Zealand in ponds, water troughs and the edges of lakes. Flies on summer nights, making a humming sound.

Unless otherwise indicated, all photos are life-size

Hide Beetles

[Family: Dermestidae]

Most adult hide beetles feed in flowers, eating nectar and pollen. It is the grubs which give the beetles their name, for these feed frantically on bones and dried meat as well as on the skins, fur, leather and wool of dead animals. In times of food shortage, these grubs can reduce their body size, cast off their old skin and eat it. Also known as **carpet beetles** or **larder beetles**. About 950 species are known worldwide; about 17 in New Zealand, most of them native.

Varied Carpet Beetle
Anthrenus verbasci
Introduced. The harmless adult beetles are found in spring on various flowers and can fly. It is the grubs which are a nuisance, as they eat untreated woollen carpets and clothes. These grubs are 6 mm long, brown with cream stripes.

Netwinged Beetles

[Family: Lycidae]

Brightly-coloured, soft-bodied beetles. Their flattened wing-covers have a delicate network of veins, making these beetles look like moths. These covers are widest at the back, giving the beetle a pear-like shape. Many have corrosive blood, distasteful to predators. So effective is this deterrent, that their unusually bright colouring is often very convincingly mimicked by completely unrelated beetles and even moths. About 3500 species are known worldwide (most of them tropical); only one in New Zealand.

Redwinged Lycid Beetle
Porrostoma rufipenne (was *Metriorrhynchus*)
From Australia. These beetles are often seen flying on warm days, feeding in flowers on nectar and pollen. Easily mistaken for a moth. The grubs live under the bark of fallen logs. Found from Nelson north.

Pill Beetles

[Family: Histeridae]

Small, dark, glossy beetles, round or oval, flat and solidly-built, with elbowed antennae. The wing-covers stop short at the back end. Many of the grubs and adult beetles are found on rotting animals and plants or dung, where they eat maggots and grubs. Others are found under bark, inside the tunnels of wood-boring insects, or in the nests of birds, ants or termites. Also called **hister beetles**. About 3000 species are known worldwide; about 30 in New Zealand, most of them unique to this country.

Large Pill Beetle
Aulacosternus zelandicus (was *Sternaulax*)
Native The beetles and grubs have been found under the bark of dead karaka trees. The beetles are also attracted to the gum bleeding from nīkau palms. Can fly.

Pintail Beetles

[Family: Mordellidae]

Wedge-shaped beetles with a humped back and a spine at the tail end. This spine provides support during a spring-loaded take-off. They are common on flowers and can jump to escape, so are also known as **tumbling flower beetles**. The grubs live in dead wood. About 1500 species are known worldwide; about six in New Zealand.

Large Pintail Beetle
'Mordella' antarctica
Native Common throughout in summer, feeding in flowers, particularly on sun-drenched mānuka and rātā. When disturbed, they can jump or fly away. The grubs live in dead wood.

Flies / Ngaro

[Order: Diptera]

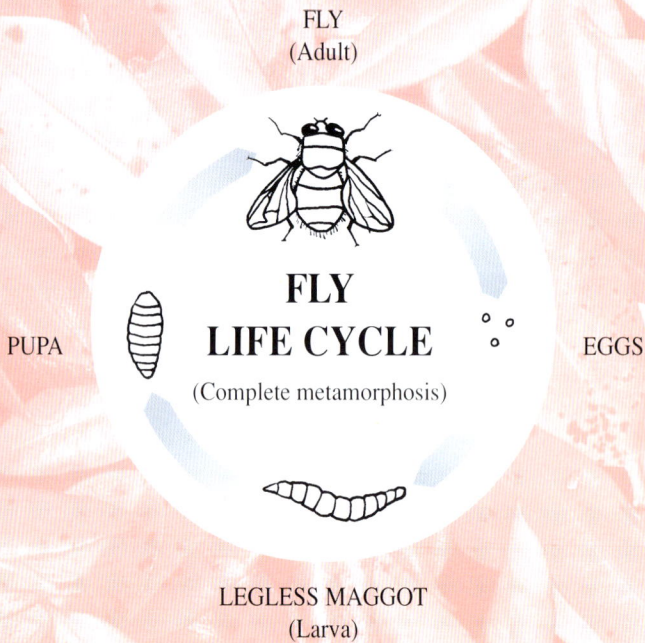

FLY
(Adult)

**FLY
LIFE CYCLE**

(Complete metamorphosis)

PUPA

EGGS

LEGLESS MAGGOT
(Larva)

JUST ONE PAIR OF WINGS

EVEN THE MENTION OF flies is enough to make most people wince. True, house flies and blowflies do spread diseases, and many other flies have sufficiently gruesome habits to inspire horror movies, but many more are useful. Most adult flies visit flowers for nectar, thus playing a key role in pollinating plants. Several are proven tools in natural pest and weed control. On the farm, they clean up dung and the remains of dead animals. And overseas, the maggots, pupae and adults of many larger species are widely appreciated as food or used medicinally.

Note that not all flying insects are flies. True flies [Diptera] have only two flying wings – never four. The other two are just tiny waggling 'drum sticks' (called halteres) which the fly uses to keep its balance while flying. These are easily seen on the giant crane fly photo (page 58).

Flies have no jaws, eating instead by sucking and sponging, tasting food either with their feet or with their tube-like mouth (proboscis). Their eyes can be so large that they almost cover the whole head, especially on male flies where the eyes may even meet in the middle. A female's eyes rarely meet. Flies range from tiny midges, the size of a metal pinhead, to an overseas robber fly up to 8 cm long (half the width of this page).

Most Diptera are not only fast fliers, but also incredibly acrobatic and precise in the way they steer, allowing them, for example, to somersault and land on ceilings. Unlike beetles, they need no warm-up exercises before take-off, frequently reaching impressive speeds (almost instantly) of 300 wingbeats per second. The record is held by a biting midge which can reach about 2000 wingbeats in one second, i.e. in the time it takes to say the word 'wingbeat'. It is no surprise then that up to one-third of a fly's body weight may be in its wing muscles.

The maggots of flies are found in the most surprising places, including hot springs. One Californian species even lives in swamps of crude oil.

Flies are the world's fourth largest Order of insects, with about 122,000 species known worldwide; over 2000 in New Zealand.

FLIES

Māori fly names

As in other Polynesian languages, the Māori word '**ngaro**' (or **rango**) traditionally refers to stout, fat-bodied flies [Brachycera] such as houseflies and blowflies, but also to similar-looking flying insects such as bees and wasps.

The more delicate (and often long-legged) flies [Nematocera] are known both by Māori and throughout Polynesia as **waeroa** (long leg), **namu** or **naonao**.

Nowadays, however, the Māori name **ngaro** is often used for all flies, distinguishing these from **pī** for bee (sometimes also for wasp) and **wāpi** for wasp.

Flies can be divided into two main groups:

THIN-BODIED FLIES	Go to page 58
[Suborder: Nematocera]	

Includes the delicate, lightly-built flies. Their maggots all have an obvious head. Also called Ancestral Flies since these are closely related to the earliest fossil flies (which looked like modern crane flies).
Examples: **crane flies**, **mosquitoes**, **midges**

FAT-BODIED FLIES	Go to page 62
[Suborder: Brachycera. Divisions: Orthorrhapha & Cyclorrhapha]	

Includes the fat-bodied flies, which have short, stout antennae. Unlike the thin-bodied flies (above), the maggots of these have no obvious head.
Examples: **blowflies**, **house flies**, **hover flies**

Crane Flies / Matua Waeroa [Family: Tipulidae]

The world's biggest fly family. These flies generally have long wings, long thin bodies and very long fragile legs (and are therefore named after the long-legged wading bird: a crane). Also called **daddy longlegs** (not to be confused with daddy longlegs spiders). The Māori name 'king mosquito' also describes how they look, although crane flies eat nectar and never bite. They fly slowly, using their long legs to help them glide. Common in native forest, pākihi bogs, scrubland, alpine tussock, tarns and in farmland. Some live only in the spray of waterfalls or on the coast between the tides. The soft, rubbery maggots live in rotting plants, wet soil or near water. Some of these are called **leatherjackets** because of their tough coat. Large numbers of such leatherjackets were collected and eaten by the Californian Indians. About 15,000 species are known worldwide; about 600 in New Zealand (including two Threatened Species). Strangely, many of New Zealand's crane flies – particularly the females and the more southern species – have no wings. (Perhaps these should be called 'crane walks'?)

Giant Crane Fly
Austrotipula hudsoni (was *Tipula dux*)
Native In terms of wingspan, this is certainly New Zealand's largest fly. It is found in wet forest from Rotorua south. The maggots are thought to live in freshwater seepage.

halteres
(see page 57)

House Crane Fly
Leptotarsus species
Native Common in gardens and often seen hanging on walls indoors, with its wings spread. (Note that *Zelandotipula novarae* is also common in these places.)

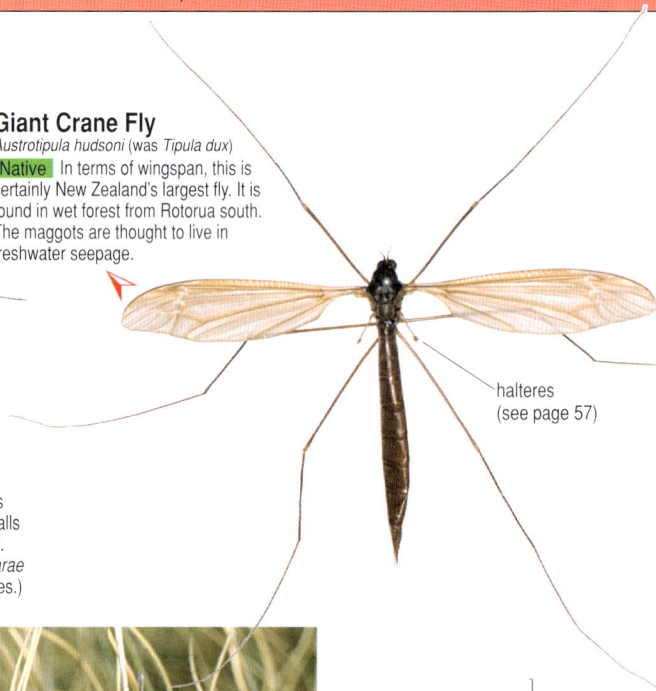

Mountain Crane Fly
Leptotarsus (Macromastix) montanus
Native Found from Arthur's Pass south in subalpine tussock. The maggots ('leatherjackets') live in the soil at the base of tussock plants.

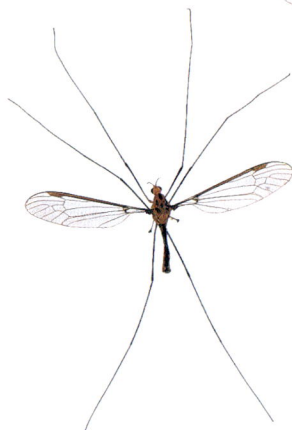

Orange Crane Fly
Leptotarsus ferruginosus (was *ferruginea*)
Native Found in damp forest in the North Island. The maggots ('leatherjackets') are thought to live and feed in the soil.

Unless otherwise indicated, all photos are life-size

Fungus Gnats

Fragile, slender flies found in damp, shady places, often in large numbers. The common name refers to the fact that most species in this group are attracted to fungus. However, the larvae of New Zealand's most famous species (and many other Keroplatidae) spin sticky webs instead, to trap small insects. The main families of fungus gnats in New Zealand are Mycetophilidae, Keroplatidae and Ditomyiidae. About 4000 species of these are known worldwide; over 280 in New Zealand, all but one of them unique to this country. Also in this superfamily are **black fungus gnats** [Sciaridae], of which New Zealand has a further 50 species or more.

FLIES

glowworm larva shown at twice life size

New Zealand Glowworm / Titiwai, Pūrātoke

Arachnocampa luminosa [Family: Keroplatidae]

Native New Zealand's Waitomo caves are famous worldwide for the twinkling lights created by these insects, where a good display looks like thousands of stars in the Milky Way. But glowworms are also common throughout New Zealand on the walls and ceilings of many caves and on damp road banks and river banks. Here, the larvae (i.e. the 'worms'; pūrātoke) live in a slimy tube-like nest. From this, each one sends down up to 70 sticky 'fishing lines'. A blue-green light in the creature's tail attracts flying insects, which get stuck in these lines. The larva then grabs the line with its mouth and pulls up its meal. The adult fly (titiwai), on the other hand, never eats, lives for just two or three days and flies at night with a buzzing sound. The female fly uses its tail-light to attract a mate. Similar species are also found in eastern Australia and Tasmania, but the New Zealand species is unique to this country. (Not to be confused with a group of unrelated luminous beetles found overseas: the **firefly beetles** [Family: Lampyridae], whose light-producing larvae are also known as glowworms.)

adult fly

glowworm shown actual size

Unless otherwise indicated, all photos are life-size

Mosquitoes / Waeroa

[Family: Culicidae]

Waeroa means 'long-legged'; also known in Māori as **namu** (in line with other Polynesian languages) or as **namu katipō**. Also called **mozzies**. The females of most species need to suck blood for their eggs to ripen. The males do not suck blood. Both feed on sap and nectar. They can beat their wings at more than 500 times per second. The larvae (**wrigglers, ngarangara**) live in any still water (where they are eaten by ducks, frogs, water beetles and some fish). Each wriggler filters over two litres of water a day, sieving out tiny food particles. Overseas, *Anopheles* mosquitoes carry malaria, killing over 1,200,000 people ever year – more than any other insect. (These malarial mosquitoes can be recognised by the way they hold their back end up at a steep angle when resting.) Most species do not bite people, but specialise either in sucking the blood of other mammals, or frogs, lizards, birds, even other insects. About 3100 species are known worldwide; 16 in New Zealand (although few normally bite people). An unusual native one – the **saltpool mosquito** (*Opifex fuscus*) – breeds in salt water pools close to the high-tide mark.

adult drinking the author's blood

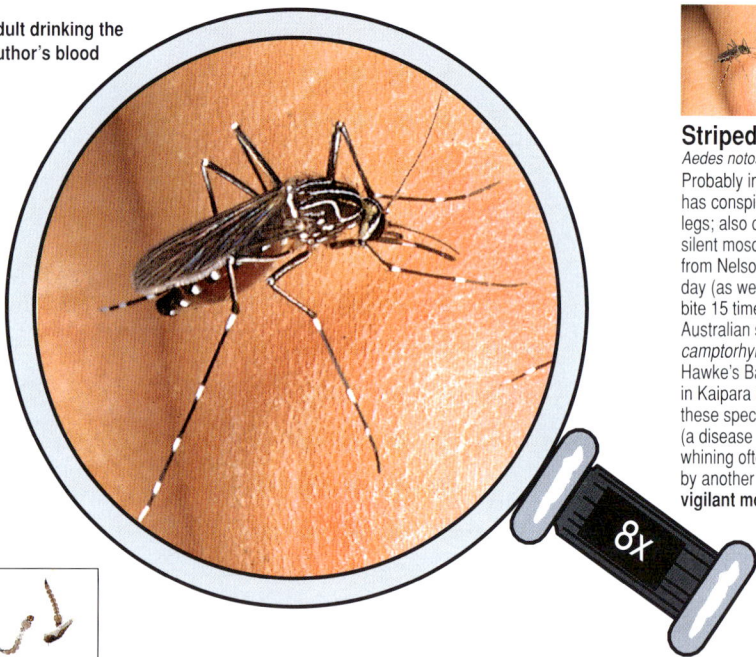

mosquito wrigglers (these larvae live in water)

Striped Mosquito
Aedes notoscriptus

Probably introduced from Australia. It has conspicuous white bands on its black legs; also called **tiger mosquito**. This silent mosquito is the one most often seen from Nelson north, as it **bites** during the day (as well as at night). Each one can bite 15 times a day. The almost identical Australian **saltmarsh mosquito** (*Aedes camptorhynchus*) recently arrived in Hawke's Bay and is now established in Kaipara Harbour. In Australia, both these species carry Ross River Fever (a disease so far not found here). The whining often heard at night is made by another species (rarely seen): the **vigilant mosquito** (*Culex pervigilans*).

Window Flies

[Family: Anisopodidae]

Slender-bodied flies with relatively short legs, and patterned wings which are folded at rest on top of one another. Named from the fact that they often come indoors and are seen on windows, trying to get out. They breed in rotting compost and manure. About 100 species are known worldwide; five in New Zealand.

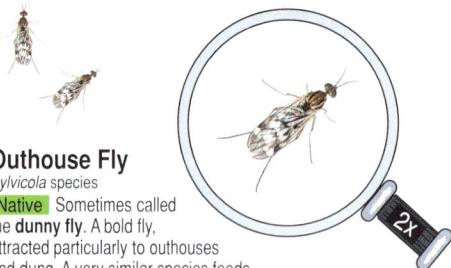

Outhouse Fly
Sylvicola species

`Native` Sometimes called the **dunny fly**. A bold fly, attracted particularly to outhouses and dung. A very similar species feeds on rotting plants or fruit and is very common around houses. Although often mistaken for a mosquito, these flies do not bite.

March Flies

[Family: Bibionidae]

Dark, hairy flies, the males of which have large heads with eyes touching; the females have smaller heads with eyes separated. They are slow fliers, often visiting flowers. Named from the month in which northern hemisphere members of this family begin to fly. The maggots are found in soil, leaf litter, dung and compost. About 780 species are known worldwide; eight in New Zealand, all unique to this country.

Blossom Fly
Dilophus nigrostigma

`Native` Found throughout New Zealand, feeding in flowers where, like bees, they help pollination. The male fly is entirely black; the female is red at the front, grey at the back. Both have a long head, like a horse. Also known as **swamp fly**. The maggots are found on the ground, eating rotting plants.

male

Unless otherwise indicated, all photos are life-size

Black Flies / Namu
[Family: Simuliidae]

Tiny, blackish, hump-backed, biting insects. The females need to suck blood for their eggs to mature. The eggs, larvae and pupae are attached to rocks or plants in clean *running* water. The larvae feed by sieving tiny food particles from swift-flowing water. In the USA, they are known as buffalo gnats, in Canada as black flies and in Europe as Columbian gnats. Most New Zealanders know them as sand flies (a name used overseas for a group of **moth midges** [Psychodidae]). Also known in Māori as **namu poto** (the short namu). About 1500 species of black flies are known worldwide; about 13 in New Zealand, only four of which usually bite people.

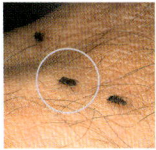

Sand Fly / Namu
Austrosimulium species

Native Found throughout New Zealand, but in greatest numbers on warm, sunny, humid days in Westland and Fiordland, where up to 70 can be squashed with one clap of the hands. Only the females **bite**, appearing to prefer penguins to people. They also feed on nectar. The two main people-biting species here – you need a microscope to tell the difference – are: the **New Zealand black fly** (*Austrosimulium australense*) and the **West Coast black fly** (*Austrosimulium ungulatum*). Most people just call them sand flies.

Biting Midges / Naonao
[Family: Ceratopogonidae]

Tiny flies found near water, known in North America as '**no-see-ums**' or '**punkies**'. An alternative form of the Māori name is **ngaungau**. The adult females of many species suck blood from a wide range of animals including people; one kind even feeds on mosquitoes, sucking the blood the mosquito has already collected. Other species visit flowers and are important crop pollinators. They mate while flying. The worm-like maggots of most species develop in water. About 4000 species are known worldwide; 33 in New Zealand.

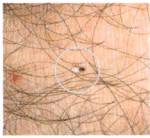

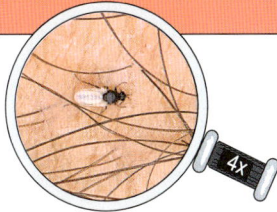

Coastal Biting Midge
Styloconops myersi

Native Smaller than a sandfly (only 1.5 mm long), but its **bite** can be more painful and irritating. Found on beaches around Nelson, Bay of Plenty, North Cape and the Coromandel.

Non-Biting Midges
[Family: Chironomidae]

These hump-backed flies look like mosquitoes but have no sucking tube (proboscis); they do not bite. Common in damp places, they fly in large swarms. They mate while flying. Some have such hairy feet that they can walk on water. The males have very feathery antennae. The maggots live for two or three years, eating rotting plants and small animals, but the adult flies never eat and live for no more than a few weeks. Also called **gnats**. A few live in salt water. One kind is so common over Lake Nyasa in the African Rift Valley that these are caught, pressed together, then eaten in the form of a sticky loaf-sized mass called 'kungu cake'. Kungu cake looks like a large muffin and is said to taste like caviar. About 5000 species are known worldwide; over 100 in New Zealand.

Common Midge
Chironomus zealandicus

Native Although this fly does not bite, it often flies in large, dense swarms, getting into people's eyes, mouth, nose or ears. The long, red maggots (**bloodworms**) contain myoglobin, helping them to live in stagnant water. These can survive hot springs at 34°C.

a swarm of **common midges** (not life-size)

Unless otherwise indicated, all photos are life-size

Blowflies / Ngaro Iro [Family: Calliphoridae]

Fat, bristly, buzzing flies, often with a metallic colour. Many are attracted to sweet substances, vomiting their last meal onto their food to help turn it to liquid, then drinking this mixture through a straw-like feeding tube. The maggots (**iro**) feed on dead (and sometimes on live) animals, dung and rotting plants. One kind (**cluster fly**) feeds on earthworms. Overseas, some seek out frogs and toads to fasten eggs to their eyes. Many are a serious nuisance on farms (see below). Yet blowfly maggots have also been widely used medicinally to clean up slow-healing wounds and after surgery to remove dead tissue. While doing this, the maggots excrete a healing compound called *allantoin*, which is now synthesised for the same purpose. Many of the maggots are useful too for cleaning up the smelly remains of dead animals. Blowfly maggots were eaten by early Māori and, in many countries, these remain a culinary delicacy, for example in China where blowfly maggots are farmed, then dried in the sun. About 1200 species are known worldwide; over 50 in New Zealand. (See also the **New Zealand bat fly** – page 66.)

NZ Blue Blowfly / Rango Pango
Calliphora quadrimaculata
Native Common in native forest, but also comes into houses in summer and autumn, often surviving cold weather. Its eggs are laid on dead animals, rotting plants or woollen clothes, where the maggots then develop. With its shiny, dark purplish-blue body, this fly is also known as a **bluebottle**.

Brown Blowfly / Rango Tuamaro
Calliphora stygia
Introduced from Australia by early settlers and now common throughout New Zealand from late spring to autumn. Found also in New Guinea and the Solomon Islands. Covered in golden brown hairs. It is a nuisance to farmers since it lays eggs on sheep, the developing maggots burrowing into the live animals to feed. This is called fly-strike.

maggots

European Blowfly
Calliphora vicina
Introduced. A common shiny blue fly. It often survives cold weather and is one of the first blowflies to appear in spring, attracted into houses by the smell of cooking. Its eggs are laid on dead animals and meat scraps.

Hairy Maggot Blowfly
Chrysomya rufifacies
From Asia, the Pacific and Australasia. It has narrow black lines across its iridescent green back. Unlike the green and brown blowflies, the maggots of this fly only infest those sheep which already have an existing wound. As the name suggests, the maggots are hairy.

Australian Sheep Blowfly
Lucilia cuprina
A recent arrival from Australia, now found throughout New Zealand. A serious nuisance to farmers. The flies are attracted to moist wool, where they lay their eggs; the maggots then burrow into the flesh of the living sheep. Known in Australia as the 'king of terror'. Hard to distinguish from the green blowfly.

Green Blowfly
Lucilia sericata
Introduced from Europe in about 1870. Can be bright shiny green, or copper coloured. It feeds on flowers but lays its eggs on sheep (and other animals). The developing maggots burrow into the live sheep to feed. Also common in summer on dog droppings and dead animals. In captivity, a single fly has been known to lay up to 2000 eggs. Also called **greenbottle**.

House Flies [Families: Muscidae & Fanniidae]

Like blowflies, many of these spread diseases by vomiting their last meal onto human food when they land on it. Many are skilled at somersaulting in midair to land upside down on ceilings. The maggots feed on dead animals, dung, silage or compost. Over 3500 species are known worldwide; over 200 in New Zealand, most of them unique to this country.

Bat-Winged Fly
Exsul singularis
[Family: Muscidae]
Native Common in the western Southern Alps, particularly around streams at 760 – 1830 m (although once thought to be rare). The flies are hunters, chasing and attacking other soft-bodied flying insects such as caddisflies. The male, in particular, uses its large black wings like solar panels to absorb warmth from the sun, helping it acquire the energy to fly in its cold mountain home. (The female has smaller, paler wings.)

Lesser House Fly / Ngaro Huka
Fannia canicularis [Family: Fanniidae]
Introduced. Small groups are often seen in summer, flying in circles indoors or under trees. Particularly common near chicken farms. They frequently land on people's faces. When shaken off, they often land back in the same place. They cannot bite. Some people mistakenly believe these grow into the larger common house flies (but little flies never grow into big flies). The Māori name (translation: sugar fly) refers to the way this fly often lands in sugar bowls.

Common House Fly
Musca domestica [Family: Muscidae]
Very common worldwide. Often breeds in moist animal manure, but their ideal breeding ground is household food waste or heaps of lawn clippings. Here, the maggots feed, hatch, turn into pupae and then to adult flies – the whole cycle sometimes taking less than two weeks. Besides being annoying in the house, they spread diseases and often leave fly spots on the ceiling and on light cords. They cannot bite. Can fly at 6-8 km/h.

Biting Stable Fly
Stomoxys calcitrans [Family: Muscidae]
Introduced by early settlers. Both the male and female flies **bite** people, cows and dogs to suck their blood. The maggots feed in unturned compost and in farm or stable dung, so this fly is especially common near dairy farms and riding stables.

False Stable Fly
Muscina stabulans [Family: Muscidae]
Found worldwide. Often confused with the biting stable fly, the difference being that this fly sucks its food and doesn't bite. The maggots feed in rotting vegetable and animal matter. The fly can be completely covered in mites, which are not parasites but use the fly only for transport.

Flesh Flies

[Family: Sarcophagidae]

The front section of the body (thorax) is striped from front to back. These large, grey and black, bristly flies are common in summer around rubbish dumps and on the flower-heads of long grasses. Many give birth to live maggots, which they drop onto compost, manure or onto dead or living animals. Some overseas species even lay their maggots on the wounds of people. Many are useful for cleaning up dung and the remains of dead animals (hence the name). About 2500 species are known worldwide; four in New Zealand.

European Flesh Fly
Jantia crassipalpis (was *Sarcophaga*)
Introduced. Common in the North Island in farmland and gardens. These drop large live maggots – much larger than those of the common house fly.

Striped Dung Fly
Oxysarcodexia varia (was *Hybopygia*)
Accidentally introduced from South America. These breed in compost and cow dung. Groups are often seen on grasses. They are attracted to human sweat and look like a small European flesh fly.

Hover Flies / Ngaro Paira

[Family: Syrphidae]

FLIES

Very fast fliers with big eyes. Some look like bees or wasps (page 69). On warm, sunny days, they are often seen hovering, as if glued in one spot, suddenly darting off or doing an instant 180° turn. They can make complete somersaults in one hundredth of a second. Often seen resting on leaves, but they feed on the nectar and pollen in flowers. Females often need to eat pollen before their eggs will develop. Most are important pollinators of plants. Also called **flower flies**. Larger ones make a harmonious buzz (hence the Māori names: **ngaro tamumu** and **ngaro tara**). Many of the maggots live in mud and liquid manure and breathe using a snorkel-like tail. Others eat small insects such as aphids. About 6000 species are known worldwide; over 40 in New Zealand.

rat-tailed maggot

Drone Fly
Eristalis tenax
From Europe. This looks and buzzes just like a honey bee, visiting flowers for nectar and pollen. The drone fly can be distinguished by its much larger eyes, no pollen bags on its legs and no sting. It also has a more darting flight. Maggots eat dung and mud at the bottom of stagnant, polluted water, their telescopic breathing tubes giving them the name: **rat-tailed maggots**.

Threelined Hover Fly / Ngaro Tara
Helophilus trilineatus (was *seelandica*)
Native Often seen on windows. The name refers to the three broad black stripes behind the head. Like the drone fly, its maggots are also 'rat-tailed' (with a long breathing tube) and live in water containing rotting plants, animals or dung.

2x

Metallic Blue Hover Fly / Ngaro Tamumu
Helophilus hochstetteri
Native Often seen on flowers, collecting nectar and pollen. The maggots live in water containing rotting plants, animals or dung.

Unless otherwise indicated, all photos are life-size

Bristle Flies

[Family: Tachinidae]

Fat, bristly flies which visit flowers. The maggots live and feed inside live spiders, caterpillars, beetles, bugs, grasshoppers and other insects, and have proven to be one of the most useful tools for the chemical-free control of many insect pests. The adult fly may lay its eggs *on* the host; inject these eggs *into* its host; lay them *nearby*; or *attach* them to the host's foodplant. Some even thrust the eggs directly into their host's mouth. The maggot begins by eating the non-vital parts of the host's body such as fat and blood, getting air either by making a hole in the host's body or by tapping the host's air, or blood, supply. Also known as **parasitic flies** or **tachinids**. One of the world's largest fly families with about 8000 species known; over 100 in New Zealand.

Large Bristle Fly
Bothrophora lupina (was *zelobori*)
Native Found in forest, where the maggot is thought to feed inside the soft grubs of the large green **mumu** and **tanguru chafer beetles** (page 46).

Ginger Bristle Fly
Protohystricia species
Native Seen in late spring, resting in the sun or flying over grassland in search of **porina moth caterpillars** (page 19). The fly drops live maggots nearby. These seek out the caterpillars, then bore their way inside to devour their host.

Australian Leafroller Tachinid
Trigonospila brevifacies
Introduced to help control **leafroller caterpillars** (page 36). Often seen in northern and central New Zealand, resting on leaves. The female looks for a leafroller caterpillar to attach its chalk-white eggs to. When the egg hatches, the maggot eats the caterpillar. Unfortunately, its impact on harmless native leafroller moths is largely unknown.

Soldier Flies

[Family: Stratiomyidae]

Soldier flies have broad, flat bodies and rest with their wings folded on top of one another. Although named after the bright soldier-like colours of many overseas species, many look like black hunting wasps (page 71). They are often seen on windows or resting on leaves and flowers. Most are thought to feed in flowers. The flat, leathery maggots tend to look as if they've been run over by a bulldozer (with the track-marks still there). Some of the maggots feed on plant sap; others live among rotting plants; a few live in water, shaving the algae off leaves; still others are carnivorous. Those which live in water are (or were) collected and eaten by the Yukpa Indians of South America. About 2000 species are known worldwide; over 30 in New Zealand, most of them unique to this country.

American Soldier Fly
larva
Hermetia illucens
Found over much of the world, arriving in New Zealand about 1956. Common in northern North Island, in summer and often noticed on windows. They can be recognised by two clear 'windows' in the abdomen. The maggot (photo) and pupa are found among rotting plants, particularly in very wet, sour compost heaps.

3x

Green Soldier Fly
Beris species
Native Flat, shiny green flies, found throughout. The flat maggots are found in rotting vegetation.

Garden Soldier Fly
Exaireta spinigera (was *Neoexaireta*)
Introduced from Australia in about 1900. Found all year, often coming into houses where they are noticed running across windows. The adult flies feed in flowers, on nectar and pollen. The maggots and pupae live in compost heaps.

Australian Soldier Fly
Inopus rubriceps
From Australia. The maggots have been a pest here since the 1940s, sucking sap from the roots of grass and other crops. The flies themselves are often seen in summer and autumn on windows in northern New Zealand; these do not eat and live for only a few days.

Unless otherwise indicated, all photos are life-size

Bot Flies [Family: Oestridae]

As adult flies, these mottled, silver-grey insects never eat, but produce live maggots which they squirt – while flying – into the nose or eyes of large animals, including people. The maggots then wander about in the animal's throat, nasal passages or head, feeding on blood. Swellings caused by these feeding maggots are sometimes known as **warbles**. Most large animals are somehow instinctively afraid of the flies, even though the adult bot fly doesn't actually bite. In spite of such parasitic habits, the Dog Rib Indians of Canada had no hesitation in eating bot fly maggots raw. About 80 species are known worldwide; four in New Zealand.

Sheep Nasal Bot Fly
Oestrus ovis
Introduced. The female flies past a sheep (or goat) and fires a maggot into its nose. When mature, the maggot is sneezed onto the ground to develop into a fly. The maggots bother the sheep, but rarely kill them. In rare instances, they can also fire these maggots into a person's eyes but, in this case, the maggots thankfully survive for no more than a few days.

Robber Flies [Family: Asilidae]

Bristly-legged flies with widely-spaced eyes. Like hawks, they dive onto the back of other insects in flight (even bees and wasps), using their large claws to get a grip as they bite the soft neck of their prey. After paralysing them, the fly sucks out the insides of its captive. Also called **assassin flies**. The largest ones overseas are among the largest of all flies – up to a scary 8 cm long. Their eggs are laid in soil or on, or inside, plants. The maggots live in soil or rotten wood and eat most things. About 5000 species are known worldwide; about 20 in New Zealand (including six Threatened Species).

note the large claws

Common Robber Fly
Neoitamus melanopogon
Native Common in sunny forest clearings, where the adult fly can catch insects as large as a cicada or bumble bee. Also seen on house windows near forest.

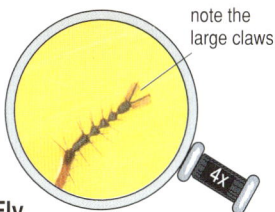

Bladder Flies [Family: Acroceridae]

These hump-backed flies appear swollen – like a bladder. The head is so small that it seems to be all eyes, these eyes almost joining as one. Their eggs are laid on grass or twigs, or are dropped in flight. Once hatched, the maggots find young spiders, crawl inside their body and eat their internal organs. Also known as **small-headed flies**. About 520 species are known worldwide; about 10 in New Zealand.

Bladder Fly
Ogcodes brunneus (was *Oncodes*)
Native Often seen laying patches of black eggs on fence wire, twigs and grass stems.

Gad Flies [Family: Tabanidae]

Fat flies with a big head. Gad is an old name for a metal spike used for goading animals, referring to the fact that the females of many overseas species give painful bites to people and farm animals, sucking their blood (often spreading diseases); the males cannot bite and feed mainly on nectar. Fortunately, few species found in New Zealand bite animals. Also called **tabanids**, **clegs**, **deer flies** or **horse flies**. The maggots live in water, mud, moss or other damp places. About 4000 species are known worldwide; about 20 in New Zealand.

Bush Gad Fly
Scaptia adrel
Native Often seen in native forest, resting on tree trunks. Also hovers about two metres above the ground in clearings or flies back and forth between flowering shrubs. Looks like a very large blow fly with a tuft of white hairs on each side. It breeds in damp mud or moss. The maggot is carnivorous.

Seaweed Flies [Family: Coelopidae]

The maggots of these flies feed only in decaying seaweed which has been washed onto the shore. When a wave submerges the hairy adult fly in the sea, it just bobs back up to the surface and is still dry enough to take off from the water. Also known as **kelp flies**. Less than 25 species are known worldwide, eight of them in New Zealand, all native.

note the hairy legs

Hairy Kelp Fly
Chaetocoelopa littoralis
Native Swarms are sometimes found around rotting seaweed, which their maggots feed on. The flies have long, hairy legs, which enable them to walk on water.

Stiletto Flies [Family: Therevidae]

These flies often have a pointed back (like a stiletto), making them look rather like robber flies (above, left). Most live near sand on beaches or riverbeds. The worm-like maggots live in sand or loose soil, where they are fast-moving hunters of grubs and earthworms. About 800 species are known worldwide; 70 in New Zealand (including about a dozen Threatened Species).

Beach Stiletto Fly
Megathereva bilineata
(was *Anabarrhynchus*)
Native Seen on the beach in summer. The long, cream or pink maggots burrow in the sand, hunting a variety of other small creatures.

Leafminer Flies [Family: Agromyzidae]

A group of flies known from the leafmining habits of many of the maggots which tunnel inside leaves, leaving pale, squiggly lines. Each fly has its own preference. One goes for ragwort, cineraria, chrysanthemum and sow thistle (puha). Another mines silver beet, fat hen, spinach and chickweed. But many specialise in one kind of plant only: e.g. māhoe, hebes, clematis or fern fronds. About 2500 species are known worldwide; almost 40 in New Zealand. (Note that similar squiggly lines are also left by the tiny caterpillars of **leafminer moths** – see page 41.)

Kākā Beak Leafminer
Liriomyza clianthi
Native   Kākā beak (*Clianthus puniceus*) is an attractive ornamental native shrub with showy red flowers; the tunnelling maggots of this pretty little fly make pale straight lines inside the leaves.

Litter Flies [Family: Lauxaniidae]

Found in moist forest and among shady vegetation in damp places. The tiny maggots live in compost and among leaf litter, where they are thought to feed on moulds. Some are known to mine inside dead leaves. About 1500 species are known worldwide; at least 15 in New Zealand.

Brownstriped Litter Fly
Sapromyza neozelandica
Native   A small red-eyed fly, very common in forest and scrub in the North Island and northern South Island. Often noticed on windows too.

Bat Flies

[Family: Calliphoridae. Subfamily: Mystacinobiinae]
Until recently, considered to be an ancient family with only one living member known and this found only in New Zealand. But, in spite of its unusual lifestyle and very odd looks, recent DNA analysis has shown that this hitch-hiking fly is closely related to **blowflies** (page 62).

New Zealand Bat Fly
Mystacinobia zelandica
Native   A strange fly, as it has no wings and cannot fly. Both the blind adult and its maggot get around instead by clinging to the fur of the native New Zealand short-tailed bat. They do not feed on the bat itself, as one might expect, but apparently enjoy only the bat's droppings, its mucous, and possibly also bat mites. When agitated, the males can make a high-pitched 'ziz', like the scream of a dentist's drill. Protected as a Category I Threatened Species.

Longlegged Flies [Family: Dolichopodidae]

Small, bristly, long-legged flies, often with a slender, tapered body. Many have metallic colours such as bronze, green or blue. Large numbers are seen resting or running on leaves in damp places, where they hunt small insects. Some feed on nectar. Many are good at running on the surface of water, so are also sometimes known as **running flies**. About 5500 species are known worldwide; over 130 in New Zealand.

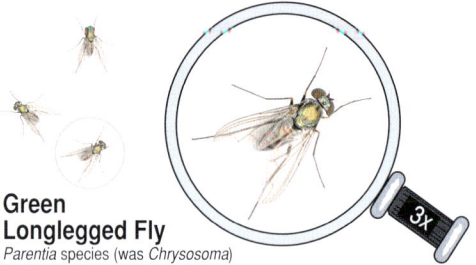

Green Longlegged Fly
Parentia species (was *Chrysosoma*)
Native   Common on windows.

Vinegar Flies [Family: Drosophilidae]

These tiny, red-eyed flies are attracted to the smell of fermenting fruit and other plants, as this is where their maggots feed. Also called **pomace flies** (from their importance in spreading the yeast to make cider). Not to be confused with **fruit flies** [Tephritidae], some exotic species of which attack *fresh* fruit, but fortunately these are not so far found in New Zealand. About 2900 species are known worldwide; at least 17 in New Zealand.

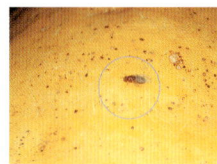
on a lemon
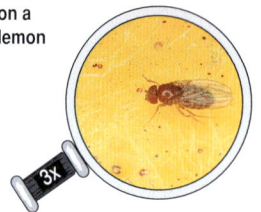

Vinegar Fly
Drosophila species
Found worldwide. Common. The tiny maggots are found in rotting fruit and other sweet foods, where they eat fungal yeasts. The flies are attracted to the same things, thus playing a useful role in spreading the yeasts used for making wine and cider. Breeding experiments with this fly have taught us most of what we know about genetics.

Ked Flies [Family: Hippoboscidae]

Sometimes known as **louse flies** for, like lice, they live on mammals and birds, using their clawed legs to cling to the fur or feathers to suck the animal's blood. Besides those living on farm animals, various species have been found on shags, gannets, herons and on the New Zealand robin. Some are wingless. About 200 species are known worldwide; five in New Zealand.

Sheep Ked
Melophagus ovinus
Found worldwide. It has no wings and clings to the wool of a sheep to suck its blood. The maggot is unusual in that it is kept inside the female fly and not born until the pupal stage.

Unless otherwise indicated, all photos are life-size

Bees, Wasps, Ants & Sawflies

[Order: Hymenoptera]

ADULT

PUPA

**HYMENOPTERA
LIFE CYCLE**

(Complete metamorphosis)

EGGS

LEGLESS GRUB
(Larva)

MOST ADVANCED INSECTS

MOST OF THIS GROUP [Hymenoptera] have a narrow waist. Those which can fly, all have four clear wings, with the front and back wings hooked together in flight. Their eggs are unusual in that all fertilised eggs produce females; only the unfertilised eggs produce males. Their maggot-like larvae all have well-developed heads and jaws.

A few Hymenoptera are pests, but many more are useful as flower pollinators or for pest control. One – the **honey bee** – is one of the world's most useful insects, both for the honey and beeswax it produces and for the pollination of crops and other flowers. Perhaps the most surprising use of honey bees however, is in war-ravaged countries where the insects are trained in the same way as sniffer dogs to locate by smell the explosives used in unexploded land mines. Many **ants** are as useful as earthworms in aerating the soil and recycling nutrients.

Although most Hymenoptera live solitary lives, several live in complex and fascinating social groups. Hence, Hymenoptera are regarded as the world's most advanced insects.

The females of some species have a 'stinger', which has evolved from an egg-laying tail spike (ovipositor). This stinger consists of a tube (sting canal) and two barbed, saw-like lancets which are rapidly sawn against each other to cut into an enemy's flesh, before the poison sac is contracted. The same apparatus is used by some species for both stinging and for laying eggs.

Overseas, some are used as food. For example, in Papua New Guinea, **wasp larvae** are baked and eaten, while **ants** are food items in Tasmania, Zimbabwe and South Africa. Ants of the large 'walking honey jar' type are popular too among the American Indians and Australian Aborigines. In Burma, India and Thailand, ants are mashed into a paste and served as a condiment with curry. Ants also feature on the menu in Colombia, where they are ground up and used as a spread on breads or exported in cans to the United States, covered in chocolate.

Worldwide, Hymenoptera range in size from giant, 8 cm-long, **spider hunting wasps** [Pompilidae] – half the width of this page – down to the smallest insects in the world: one kind of **fairyfly** [Mymaridae] which can be just 0.21 mm long. A dozen of these could sit on a metal pinhead with room to walk about. Such dust-like Hymenoptera can float on the wind so high that they have been collected from planes flying at altitudes of 4500 m.

This is one of the world's four largest insect Orders, with over 200,000 species known worldwide; over 1500 in New Zealand (600 described), most of them tiny parasites of other insects (or even parasites of parasites). At least 160 of the New Zealand total are **fairyflies** [Mymaridae] which are all small enough to develop inside the eggs of other insects. Indeed, up to fifty can develop inside the same egg. And yet such 'mere specks' can be powerful tools for pest control. Another interesting family of tiny, pinhead-sized wasps is the recently-discovered Maamingidae (from the Māori word for puzzling or mysterious) which crawl about in leaf litter. These tiny creatures are believed to be as ancient as the tuatara and are unique to New Zealand.

The main groups of Hymenoptera:

NARROW WAIST	Go to pages **69 – 73**
[Suborder: Apocrita]	

Includes all the **bees**, **wasps** and **ants**. All have a narrow waist. The bees can be further divided into social bees and solitary bees, while the wasps can be divided into social wasps, parasitic wasps and hunting wasps.

NO NARROW WAIST	Go to page **73**
[Suborder: Symphyta]	

Includes the **sawflies** and **wood wasps** (horntails). Unlike most Hymenoptera, these do not have a narrow waist, yet, unlike flies, they all have four wings (rather than two).

Social Bees

[Family: Apidae]

These bees live in colonies. Each group has an egg-laying female (queen), males (drones) and sterile worker females. Many social bees have a long tongue, allowing them to pollinate many flowers which *native* bees can't reach into and this is the reason they were introduced to New Zealand. They collect pollen (into small baskets on their legs) and nectar to feed their grubs (larvae). These grubs were cooked and eaten by the American Indians and stir-fried or added to curries in many parts of Asia. About 1000 species are known worldwide; five in New Zealand.

the beekeeper is pointing to the queen

Honey Bee / Pī Honi
Apis mellifera

Introduced from Australia in 1839. One of the world's most useful insects, bees gather nectar to make honey, collect pollen in 'baskets' on their hind legs and make beeswax. On a good day, one bee will visit about 1000 flowers, producing just two teaspoonfuls of honey. Each hive (or nest) has around 60,000 worker bees, several hundred male bees (drones), but only one female (queen). The queen can lay 3000 eggs a day. The temperature of the breeding chamber is critical and the worker bees keep this at 35 – 36°C. Cooling is achieved by bees fetching water and fanning it with their wings, while heating is provided by bees vibrating their flight muscles after first uncoupling their wings. Once the queen has mated, the drones are no longer useful, so are starved or stung to death and thrown out. On average, the workers live for about one month. Apart from the bees kept by beekeepers for honey, many more now live in the wild. The honey bee is New Zealand's most dangerous insect. Easily confused with a drone fly (page 63).

The Dance of the Bee: When a worker bee has found a good source of nectar, it performs a special dance. This dance tells the others exactly which way to go, how far the bees need to fly and how much nectar there is. The dances often take place outside the hive but, interestingly, when performed inside, the bee can turn the orientation of the dance on its side and the others will still understand.

Bee Stings: A worker bee will sting to defend its hive (or if it gets cornered), but stings only once. The smell of this sting then attracts more bees. When angry, a bee makes a special high-pitched war-cry. If stung, take care to scrape the barbed sting out without squeezing the poison sac on the end. Apply ice or vinegar.

Bumble Bee / Pī Rorohū
Bombus species

Introduced from England in the 1880s to help pollinate red clover flowers, as the shorter-tongued honey bees can't reach far enough inside. While not aggressive, the workers and queen can give a painful **sting** to defend themselves if they need to. Unlike the sting of the honey bee, this is not barbed. These fat, furry bees buzz loudly as they fly. The queen (pictured) is larger and hibernates on her own during winter. In spring, she makes a nest underground or in a tree and starts a new colony, feeding her young with pollen and honey. Her nest is much smaller than a honey bee hive, usually with only 200 – 300 bees. Bumble bees are often attracted to blue clothing and camping gear. Four species in New Zealand.

Solitary Bees

[Families: Colletidae & Halictidae]

Common in summer throughout New Zealand, around flowers or entering tunnels in the ground. Smaller than a honey bee, hairy and mostly black. Unlike honey bees, none of them live in groups. Instead, the females make narrow, branching tunnels in the ground, especially in roadside banks. These tunnels run 20 – 50 cm underground to individual cells, where the female lays her eggs and leaves pollen and nectar for the hatching larvae. They do not make honey, but are nevertheless important pollinators of native plants. These bees are not aggressive and can only give a little **sting**. The males live for a few weeks only. About 5500 species are known from these two families worldwide; about 40 of them in New Zealand, most of them unique to this country.

Wasp-Like Bee
Hyleoides concinna [Family: Colletidae]

Accidentally introduced from Australia about 1980, apparently on timber arriving in the ports of Napier and Gisborne. Flies November to March, feeding in various exotic ornamental flowers. The female makes a series of nest-cells inside existing tunnels in logs and sticks left by wood-boring beetle grubs. Although it looks like a large wasp, this bee is not aggressive and will sting only if pressed against the skin.

Native Bee
Leioproctus species [Family: Colletidae]

Native Its hairy back legs are often carrying a load of pollen. Also called **hairy colletid bee**. There are several similar species, most of which nest in branching tunnels which they dig in bare ground, such as in the clay banks along road cuttings. Often confused with soldier flies (page 64) or mason wasps (page 71).

Unless otherwise indicated, all photos are life-size

Social Wasps / Wāpi

[Family: Vespidae]

It has been estimated that in one wasp season, these wasps (especially *Vespula*) eat more insects in the beech forests of northern South Island than all the birds of these forests do in a whole year. Collectively, they have also become one of New Zealand's most serious threats to native insects. Living in social groups, these wasps build a nest out of 'wasp-paper' made from chewed-up plant fibre which they soften with saliva and then strip from wooden fences, telephone poles and weatherboards. Without them, you would probably not be reading this book for the Chinese inventor of paper, Tsa'ai Lun (50 – 121 AD), is believed to have learnt the art of paper-making from wasps. Both the adult females and the workers can give a painful sting – several times if need be. If stung, apply ice. Wasp larvae and pupae are eaten in Thailand and, in parts of Japan they are either fried or canned for sale. About 4000 species are known worldwide; four in New Zealand – all introduced.

German Wasp / Pī Waikato
Vespula germanica

Accidentally introduced to New Zealand in 1944 and now common in coastal and rural areas, particularly January to March. It eats meat and many other insects, also sweet foods, competing with native birds for nectar, fruit and honeydew (see page 91). The greyish nest is built from fresh, sound wood, usually underground, the temperature inside being carefully regulated with the use of insulating layers, while adult wasps warm the home by 'shivering'. Some colonies in the north of New Zealand survive through the winter, allowing the nests to keep on growing, sometimes reaching phenomenal sizes (2.5 – 3 m across). Māori named the wasp after the striped Waikato rugby colours. Can **sting**.

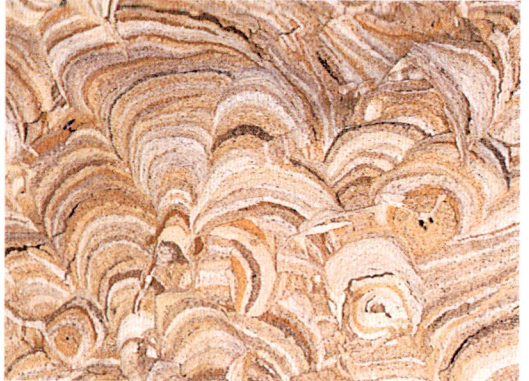

Common Wasp
Vespula vulgaris

Looks very similar to the German wasp, but usually *without separate black spots* on the back. Accidentally introduced to New Zealand in the early 1920s (when the first nest was found here) but didn't establish in New Zealand until the late 1970s. Now common in forest, often reaching plague proportions in the beech forests of the northern South Island from January to March. It eats other insects, but also competes with native birds for nectar, fruit and honeydew. Its brown nest is made from dead and rotten wood and is usually built underground; the temperature inside is carefully regulated with the use of insulating layers and 'shivering' adult wasps. The colony usually dies out in winter. Can **sting**.

Chinese Paper Wasp
Polistes chinensis

Accidentally introduced to New Zealand around 1979; found initially around Auckland but now common as far south as Nelson and Blenheim. It eats insects (mainly caterpillars) and some nectar, honeydew or fruit. The small nest is shaped like an upside-down mushroom – usually nearer the ground than the Australian paper wasp nest and can be found in a wide range of open habitats, including tidal estuaries. Over winter, these little nests are usually abandoned, the queen then often finding shelter under houses. Also called **Asian paper wasp**. Can give a painful **sting**.

Australian Paper Wasp / Pī Whero
Polistes humilis humilis

Arrived here in the 1800s but found only in the warmer parts of the North Island. It eats honeydew and insect larvae. In spring, the female builds a small nest, which hangs like an upside-down mushroom from branches and the eaves of house roofs. Inside, live male and female wasps (rather than castes of queens, workers and drones). These nests are usually abandoned in winter. Also called **Tasmanian paper wasp**. Can give a painful **sting**.

patterned outer surface of nest made by common wasp

nest of Chinese paper wasp

nest of Australian paper wasp

Unless otherwise indicated, all photos are life-size

Hunting Wasps (Solitary) [Families: Eumenidae, Pompilidae & Sphecidae]

Known collectively in Māori as **ngaro wiwī** (in reference to their hunting habit). Do not live in colonies. Female hunting wasps seek out spiders and caterpillars to feed to their young. They first sting their prey to paralyse or kill it, then either carry, or drag, their victim back to the nest, often over surprising distances – up to 100 m or more. One overseas species (*Pepsis*) – itself 8 cm long – will take on giant tropical bird spiders almost as large as one's hand and the wasp usually wins. To help with digging their nests, many have a comb of bristles on their front legs for flinging sand and loose earth back out of the way. About 12,000 species are known worldwide; about 30 in New Zealand.

Large Black Hunting Wasp
Priocnemis (Trichocurgus) monachus [Family: Pompilidae]

Native Found throughout, especially December to February. It nests in tunnels in sunny clay banks within forest. The female hunts tunnelweb and trapdoor spiders, which she drags backwards to her nest for the young to eat. The adult wasps feed mostly on ripe fruit and the nectar of flowers such as mānuka. It doesn't usually sting people, but its **sting is very painful**. Fortunately, the pain only lasts for a few seconds.

European Tube Wasp
Ancistrocerus gazella [Family: Eumenidae]

Arrived in Auckland in about 1987 but now found as far south as Otago. Common on windows, or searching out cracks and little holes to nest in. The female collects up to 20 caterpillars for each one-cell nest, as food for her larvae, then seals the cell with moulded mud. The adult wasp eats nectar and honeydew from aphids. Also known as **European potter wasp**. The female can **sting**, but this isn't painful.

Mason Wasp
Pison spinolae [Family: Sphecidae]

Native Found throughout New Zealand. The female makes a loud, high-pitched whine, while making cell-like nests out of white mud. These nests are often made in keyholes, musical instruments and folds in unused clothing or curtains. She stings an orbweb spider to paralyse it and flies the spider to her nest as food for the larvae. The adult wasp eats nectar. It doesn't usually sting people and the sting isn't painful. Sometimes confused with a soldier fly (page 64).

Golden Hunting Wasp
Cryptocheilus australis [Family: Pompilidae]

Australian. Arrived in New Zealand in about 1960. Seen in the northern North Island, mostly between January and March. It nests in cracks in compacted clay. The female hunts nurseryweb spiders, paralysing them with her sting, dragging the spider backwards into her nest to feed to the young larvae. The adult wasp feeds mostly on the nectar from flowers (e.g. mānuka). It doesn't usually sting people, but the **sting is painful**. (This photo was misidentified in early printings of *The Life-Size Guide to Insects* as one of several similar-looking species.)

golden hunting wasp dragging a paralysed nurseryweb spider back to her nest

Black Cockroach Hunter
Tachysphex nigerrimus [Family: Sphecidae]

Native Found throughout New Zealand. It nests in simple burrows in sand, silt or sand riverbanks, out of reach of floods. The female hunts and paralyses, then drags, small native cockroaches back to her nest for her larvae to eat. Typically, each wasp egg is given three cockroach nymphs.

Mammoth Wasps (Solitary) [Family Scoliidae]

Very large, dark, hairy wasps with fat bodies. Some overseas giants can be over 5 cm long. The males are much smaller and slimmer than the females, with longer, thinner antennae. The female finds scarab beetle grubs to sting and paralyse before attaching an egg. When the egg hatches, the wasp larva eats the beetle grub, then spins a cocoon in which to develop into an adult wasp. Found worldwide, but mostly in the tropics. About 350 species are known worldwide; one in New Zealand.

female   male

Yellow Flower Wasp
Radumeris tasmaniensis (was *Campsomeris*)

Australian. First found in New Zealand in the year 2000 at Te Paki in Northland. The adult wasps feed on nectar and honeydew, pollinating flowers. The female can burrow to depths of 1.2 m in search of a host on which to attach her egg. Its host in New Zealand is unknown, but is probably the grub of native sand scarabs and large chafer beetles. In Queensland, their eggs are often laid on canegrubs. Although it doesn't usually sting people, it is probably not a good idea to sit on one.

Ichneumonid Wasps (Solitary)

[Family: Ichneumonidae]

Known in Māori as **ngaro whiore** ('tailed fly'). Like hunting wasps, these **parasitic wasps** do not live in colonies. They are slender, usually with a long, thread-like waist and long antennae which quiver nervously all the time. Many of the females have a long spike at the back for laying eggs in the larvae of other insects, most specialising in just one species. Her antennae are so sensitive that she can use them to detect and identify a host larvae even when it is hidden deep in wood. Her egg-laying tail-spike (ovipositor) is so strong that she can use it to drill through hard wood to reach the host and inject her eggs. Others simply push their ovipositor down existing tunnels. When the eggs hatch, the wasp larvae eat their host, starting out with the non-vital bits. Though used primarily for egg-laying, some can also use their ovipositors to give **a weak sting**. Although many are native, several more species have been introduced for pest control. About 60,000 species are known worldwide; over 300 in New Zealand (about 80 of them named).

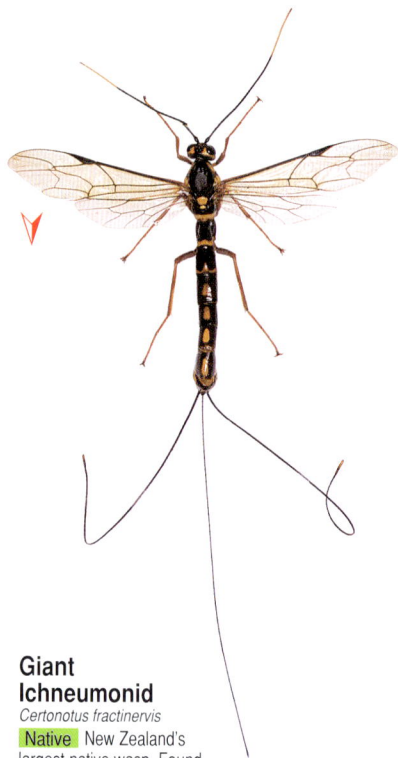

Whitespotted Ichneumonid
Echthromorpha intricatoria
Arrived from Australia about 1915. Very common. The spike at the back of the female is used for laying eggs inside the chrysalis of moths and butterflies (particularly red admiral butterflies), this chrysalis then providing food for the wasp larvae. The wasp has a strange smell.

Armyworm Parasite
Ichneumon promissorius (was *Pterocormus*)
Native Found also in Australia. The female wasp digs into the topsoil to find the chrysalis of **armyworm moths** (page 29) to lay an egg inside. When the egg hatches, the wasp larva eats the chrysalis, so this species is helpful for pest control.

Orange Ichneumonid Wasp
Netelia producta
Also found in Java and Australia. Children here sometimes call it the **red jacket** or **red soldier wasp** in reference to its sting. Found throughout most of the North and South Islands. Orange body. The female finds **armyworm caterpillars** (page 29) in which to lay her eggs.

Giant Ichneumonid
Certonotus fractinervis
Native New Zealand's largest native wasp. Found in native beech forest. The female lays her eggs in the grubs of **elephant weevils** (page 48). The egg-laying spike (ovipositor) is extraordinarily long in order to drill through wood down to the depths at which these grubs live. To aim this long 'drill spike' in the right direction, she raises her tail so high that she has to practically stand on her head. Another similar giant ichneumonid wasp, the **sirex wasp parasite** (*Rhyssa persuasoria*) is found in plantation forests, having been introduced from Britain in 1928 to control **sirex wood wasps** (page 73) in pines.

Lemon Tree Borer Parasite
Xanthocryptus novozealandicus
Native In March, the female searches for grubs of wood-boring beetles such as **lemon tree borer** (page 45). She pushes her egg-laying spike through the wood to lay her eggs inside the grub. In this way, the wasp helps to control the pest borer.

Yellowbanded Leafroller Parasite
Xanthopimpla rhopaloceros
Introduced for pest control; now found in the North Island. The spike at the back of the female pierces through rolled leaves to lay her eggs inside the chrysalis of a **leafroller moth** (page 36), hidden within. This chrysalis then provides food for the wasp larva.

Unless otherwise indicated, all photos are life-size

Ants / Pōpokorua

[Family: Formicidae]

Ants have a 'double waist' (or 'triple waist') and elbowed antennae (unlike termites) and live in social groups of about 100 to over one million. In summer, the winged males and young queens (females) fly in swarms, but the worker ants are wingless. Although some queens can live for thirty years, the workers live for about three years only. Some defend themselves by squirting formic acid. Many like sweet food; others prefer oily or fatty food. Ants follow smell trails but also navigate by using the sun. This can be tested by casting a shadow on a column of ants, then reflecting the sunlight from another angle with a mirror; the ants will change direction. They also communicate with each other by stroking, tapping and drumming on one another with their antennae. Some keep aphids, 'milking' them for a sweet sticky juice (honeydew). Others farm edible fungus. Ants have lived on Earth for at least 60 million years. Today, there are about one million ants for every human on Earth. Many play a useful role in loosening and aerating the soil. Some are used as human food (see pages 5 & 68). The biggest ants overseas can be up to 3 cm long; the smallest less than 1 mm long. Some tropical species can function at temperatures as high as 65°C. Alternative Māori names include **poko**, **pokorua**, **pokopokorua**, **upokorua**, **roro**, **rōroro** and **pōpokoriki**. About 20,000 species are known worldwide (most from tropical and subtropical countries). New Zealand is unusual in having just 40 or so species, less than a dozen of them native (compared to an estimated 3000 in Australia). Recently, two serious ant pests have arrived here: **Argentine ant** (*Linepithema humile*) which is now established here, and **fire ant** (*Solenopsis invicta*) which has so far been controlled. But individual species are often hard to distinguish without a microscope.

Large Native Ant
Amblyopone australis

Native Also native to Australia. New Zealand's largest ant is apparently restricted to the North Island and some off-shore islands, where it is usually found nesting in rotten logs in the forest. Slow-moving. It eats other insects and can give a painful **sting**. (Note that no native ant species is invasive; all household pest species are introduced.)

Whitefooted House Ant
Technomyrmex albipes

Worldwide. Very common in houses throughout the North Island and parts of Nelson. Nests in the ground, in rotting trees and house piles, behind weather boards and under house roofs. Attracted indoors by sweet food. Each colony can have several queens. In autumn, winged adults swarm in large numbers. (One of about six introduced ant species which normally come into houses.)

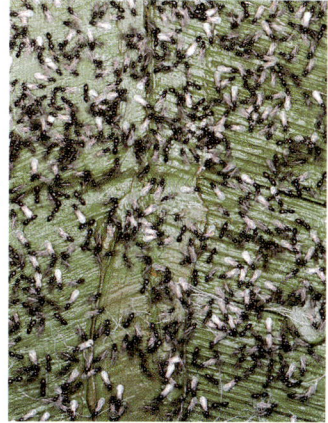

winged males (whitefooted house ants)

BEES, WASPS, ANTS

Sawflies & Wood Wasps

[Suborder: Symphyta]

Although these look similar to wasps, they have a cylindrical body with *no narrow waist*. They can be distinguished from flies [Diptera] by the fact that the adults all have four wings (not two). Named from the egg-laying spike at the back of many of the females which looks, and works, like a saw. They are primitive plant-eating insects which do not sting. The adults of many species are brightly coloured. About 7000 species are known worldwide; about 10 in New Zealand, most of them introduced.

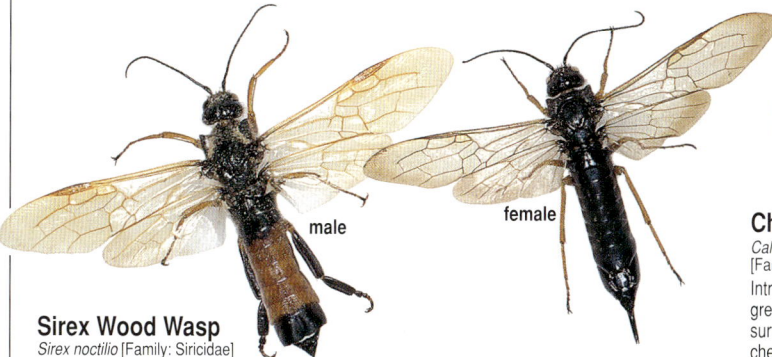

male

female

immature form
These larvae are the so-called slugs which give the insect its name.

Cherryslug
Caliroa cerasi
[Family: Tenthredinidae]

Introduced. In late summer, the shiny green-black slug-like larvae eat the top surface of the leaves of hawthorn, cherry, plum and pear trees, leaving a patchy leaf skeleton pattern. The adult sawfly is seen in early spring. The female has two saw blades which drop down out of her sheath to cut into these leaves for laying her eggs.

Sirex Wood Wasp
Sirex noctilio [Family: Siricidae]

Accidentally introduced from Europe before 1900. The blue females use the saw-like spike at the back for injecting fungus spores and eggs into unhealthy pine trees (occasionally also into larch or spruce). The fungus digests the wood which the grubs can then feed on over the next one or two years. The blue-and-orange males are usually smaller. Also called **sirex sawfly**, **steelblue sawfly** or **steelblue horntail borer**. The grubs are attacked by various parasitic wasps (see page 72).

Freshwater Insects

[Orders: Odonata, Megaloptera, Plecoptera, Trichoptera, Ephemeroptera]

DRAGONFLIES
& DAMSELFLIES

DOBSONFLIES

STONEFLIES

CADDISFLIES

MAYFLIES

AT HOME IN A WATERY WORLD

ONE OF THE CHALLENGES for freshwater insects is how to breathe underwater. Some obtain oxygen dissolved in water just as fish do. Some rise to the surface regularly like a snorkel diver to take a supply of fresh air down with them. Others can tap into the oxygen found within underwater plants.

Freshwater insects are found in an amazing range of habitats. Some, for example, specialise in the cold springs at the foot of glaciers, while others (certain fly and beetle larvae) are perfectly at home in hot springs bubbling away at 55°C. They can be found from stagnant swamps and crystal-clear lakes to the waters of rushing mountain streams. New Zealand is unusual in having species such as native **marine caddisflies** [Family: Chathamiidae] and a native **saltpool mosquito** (*Opifex fuscus*) which breed in saltwater rock pools.

And yet, many such insects are so particular about where they live that the water quality and temperature can be accurately measured by studying which species are found there. Another useful gauge of water quality is provided by the fact that the more species which thrive in a particular body of water, the 'healthier' that water is. In this way, such insects are useful pollution indicators. Many species also provide important food for fish and birds or are regularly harvested by people for food, particularly in South-East Asia and Papua New Guinea.

Freshwater insects include a few moths, beetles, flies and bugs – groups of insects which don't generally depend on ponds, lakes, rivers or streams. But the main freshwater insects are a group of specialised Orders, whose members *all* depend on having a body of water in which their young stage (larva or nymph) can live. As adults, many of these insects have wings, enabling them to fly much further afield to disperse their young. Such specialist freshwater insects include dragonflies, damselflies, mayflies, dobsonflies, caddisflies and stoneflies.

The main groups of freshwater insects (WINGED ADULTS):

INSECTS FOUND CLOSE TO WATER, RESTING WITH THEIR WINGS . . .		
HELD STRAIGHT UP (LIKE SAILS)	**Mayflies**	*Go to page 80*
OUT TO THE SIDE (LIKE AN AEROPLANE)	**Dragonflies**	*Go to page 76*
PRESSED TOGETHER CLOSE TO BODY	**Damselflies**	*Go to page 78*
FOLDED FLAT ON TOP OF BODY	**Stoneflies**	*Go to page 79*
FOLDED ROOF-LIKE OVER BODY	**Caddisflies**	*Go to page 80*
	& Dobsonflies	*Go to page 79*

The main groups of freshwater insects (IMMATURE FORM):

IMMATURE INSECTS LIVING ON OR UNDER THE WATER		
THREE 'TAILS' & HAS SIDE GILLS	**Mayflies**	*Go to page 80*
THREE 'TAILS' (NO SIDE GILLS)	**Damselflies**	*Go to page 78*
TWO 'TAILS' & LONG ANTENNAE	**Stoneflies**	*Go to page 79*
TWO 'TAILS' & SHORT ANTENNAE	**Diving Beetles**	*Go to page 81*
LOOK LIKE CENTIPEDES	**Dobsonflies**	*Go to page 79*
WITH PORTABLE CASE OR TAIL HOOKS	**Caddisflies**	*Go to page 80*
EXTENDABLE HINGED LOWER JAW	**Dragonflies etc**	*Go to page 76*
NO LEGS (MAGGOT- OR WORM-LIKE)	**Water Flies**	*Go to page 81*
MOUTH IS A PIERCING, SUCKING TUBE	**Water Bugs***	*Go to page 81*

*Adults or nymphs

FRESHWATER

DRAGONFLIES	*This page*	DAMSELFLIES	*Go to page 78*
• Rest with their wings *spread out* • Fly with *fast* and darting flight • Have a *thick* body • Eyes generally close together • Hind wings wider than front wings		• *Fold* their wings back over their body • Fly *slowly* and flutter like butterflies • Have a *thin* body • Eyes widely separated • All four wings a similar size	

Dragonflies

[Order: Odonata. Suborder: Anisoptera]

Flying at speeds of up to 58 km/ h, these dragon-like insect-hunters are among the fastest fliers in the insect world. They can fly backwards, rise vertically like a helicopter, shoot forward like a rocket or screech to a sudden halt as if they had just hit a brick wall. Their eyes cover most of their face, each eye being made up of 10,000 – 30,000 facets. Rotating their head sideways 180°, backward 70° and downward 40°, their vision – night or day – is exceptional. Also known as '**horse-stingers**' or '**devil's darning needles**' (although they have no sting). Many are territorial. To mate, dragonflies form a 'mating wheel' (described and illustrated under damselflies – page 78). The insect-eating nymphs (see photo) feed in water or mud. When mature, these clamber up onto a plant to emerge soon after sunset as an adult dragonfly. In Papua New Guinea and the Philippines, these nymphs are eaten, while on Lombok and Bali and in Thailand, it is the adults (minus the wings) which are eaten. Dragonflies have been around for over 250 million years. Indeed, the biggest insect ever to have lived on Earth was a seagull-sized dragonfly from this period, with a 70 cm wingspan. Over 3000 species of dragonflies are known worldwide; 11 in New Zealand. Overseas species are also sometimes blown here from Australia or from islands in the south-western Pacific.

Life Cycle (Incomplete metamorphosis): Egg > Nymph > Adult Dragonfly

Baron Dragonfly

Hemianax papuensis [Family: Aeshnidae]

Native Also found throughout Australia, this dragonfly is a relatively recent immigrant to New Zealand, first seen in Warkworth in 1918. At 64 – 68 mm long, it is New Zealand's third largest dragonfly. (Second largest is the **mountain giant dragonfly**, *Uropetala chiltoni*.) The baron dragonfly has so far been seen here only in the North Island, more commonly in Northland, flying from late December to April. Although breeding in ponds, adults can be found in sheltered scrub and bush areas several kilometres away. The baron dragonfly is a fast-flying hunter, capable of catching cicadas, flies and bees.

immature form

Shed skin of baron dragonfly nymph. Such nymphs are found on well-lit pond vegetation. Here the nymph actively hunts, striking out with its lower jaw to catch anything smaller than its own head.

Unless otherwise indicated, all photos are life-size

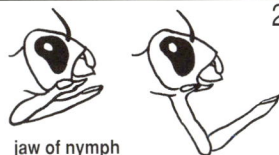

jaw of nymph
Dragonfly nymphs have a hinged, extendable, mask-like lower jaw (here shown at twice life-size).

2x

Bush Giant Dragonfly / Kapokapowai

Uropetala carovei [Family: Petaluridae]

Native The male has broad claspers at the back. Seen early summer to autumn, near the edges of native forest. With a wingspan often reaching 13 cm and a body length 79 – 86 mm, this is New Zealand's largest dragonfly. Clattering flight. Large eyes, far apart. It can eat 20 house flies in one hour and has been seen catching insects as large as cicadas. Yet the adults themselves are often eaten by rats, wild cats, kingfishers and even wasps. The Māori name (in its various forms: **kākapowai**, **kapowai**) has been used for all large dragonflies and means 'water snatcher'.

immature form (nymph)
The nymph lives for up to six years in a U-shaped tunnel in wet mud and uses its extendable, mask-like lower jaw to snatch passing insects at night.

Red Percher Dragonfly

Diplacodes bipunctata [Family: Libellulidae]

Native Also found from Australia right across to the south-eastern Pacific. It perches on clay banks, November to May, often holding its wings slightly forward. It is most common in Northland, particularly at the Kaiiwi Lakes north of Dargaville, but has been found as far south as Haast. Many of these have probably been blown over from Australia. Body length 29 – 34 mm. Easily recognised by its small size and red colouring.

Unless otherwise indicated, all photos are life-size

Damselflies

[Order: Odonata. Suborder: Zygoptera]

Damselflies are generally smaller and more slender than dragonflies and hold their wings back, close to their body. (See table, page 76, for other differences.) Damselflies are otherwise similar to dragonflies, with a similarly impressive flying ability and vision. About 80 percent of their total brain power is devoted to processing visual images. As with dragonflies, pairs are often seen flying while joined together, the male holding the female behind the head with its 'tail' claspers. To mate, the female reaches her body forward to form a 'mating wheel' (see photo). The adults eat other flying insects, chasing off any other damselflies which enter their hunting territory (which is usually about 15 sq m). Unlike the immature form (nymphs) of dragonflies, damselfly nymphs swim by wriggling and have three 'tail whiskers' (see photo). Over 1000 species of damselflies are known worldwide; six in New Zealand.
Life Cycle (Incomplete metamorphosis): Egg > Nymph > Adult Damselfly

damselflies in the first step of forming a 'mating wheel'

Blue Damselfly / Kēkēwai
Austrolestes colensonis [Family: Lestidae]
Native New Zealand's largest damselfly is seen perching in the sun near still water, rushes and reeds and flies from October to May. The male is brilliant blue and black; the female greener. To regulate body temperature, it can change colour, turning brighter in hot weather or darker (to absorb more heat) in cold weather. The males tend to bob up and down, a behaviour described in an alternative Māori name: **tīemiemi**.

immature form of red damselfly
Damselfly nymphs have three 'tail whiskers'.

Red Damselfly / Kihitara
Xanthocnemis zealandica [Family: Coenagrionidae]
Native Found from brackish coastal water to high alpine tarns, usually near plants along the edges of ponds, lakes and some rivers, flying close to the ground November to March. The male is red with black markings; the female sometimes more orange-brown. During drought, the nymphs can survive for several months by burying themselves in damp mud.

Unless otherwise indicated, all photos are life-size

Dobsonflies

[Order: Megaloptera]

Dobsonflies have two pairs of large, similar wings usually held roof-like over the body when at rest. The body is very soft. (Distinguished from lacewings – page 109 – by their larger wingspan and broader base to the back wings.) The adults do not eat, are not good fliers and stay close to water. The immature form (larva) lives in water, where it hunts other water creatures. The Yukpa people of South America eat the larvae as well as adult dobsonflies. (The head, wings and legs are first removed.) This is the most primitive Order of insects to go through a complete change (metamorphosis) from egg to larva to pupa to adult. About 300 species are known worldwide; only one in New Zealand. Also known as **alderflies**.

Life Cycle (Complete metamorphosis): Egg > Larva (toebiter) > Pupa > Adult Dobsonfly

Dobsonfly
Archichauliodes diversus [Family: Corydalidae]

Native Common in stony streams throughout New Zealand. The adult lives for just 6 – 10 days, usually noticed when it flies into lights near streams on summer evenings. The large larva (**toebiter**, **black-creeper**, **puene** or **pūeneene**) has powerful jaws, hence the angler's name. This can be up to 4 cm long and looks like a centipede, but most of its 'legs' are really gills. During the day, this creeping creature hides under stones in, or near, clean, fast-flowing streams, coming out at night to eat underwater insects.

adult dobsonfly
Rests with its wings held roof-like over its body.

immature form
The dobsonfly larva looks like a centipede.

Stoneflies

[Order: Plecoptera]

Usually found near streams and rivers. Adults and nymphs (immature form) both have two 'tail whiskers'. Adult stoneflies have long, soft bodies with parallel sides, their wings neatly folded back over their bodies when at rest. They fly with a clumsy, fluttering flight, have a short life and never eat. To attract females, the males of many species drum their bodies on the ground. The flat nymphs live for up to four years, crawling on or under stones, in clean, oxygen-rich water, such as in cold fast-flowing rivers and clear lakes. Some nymphs are hunters; others vegetarian. In parts of Japan, both the adults and the nymphs are eaten. About 2000 species are known worldwide; over 100 in New Zealand, all unique to this country, most of them dark coloured. High in the South Island mountains, a few wingless species have even been found hiding under stones, well away from water.

Life Cycle (Incomplete metamorphosis): Egg > Nymph > Adult Stonefly

adult stonefly
Rests with wings held flat over its body.

Large Green Stonefly
Stenoperla species [Family: Eustheniidae]

Native There are four similar species. Usually green but sometimes yellow. Common in spring and summer throughout (even high in the mountains), hiding during the day among streamside plants, but attracted to lights at night. The grass-green nymphs are common in very clean, cool water in stony streams, so are a useful sign of pollution-free water. Here they eat mostly mayfly nymphs (or get eaten by trout).

immature form
Stonefly nymphs are flat, with gills. Their long antennae are about the same length as their two 'tail whiskers'.

at rest

Black Stonefly
Austroperla cyrene
[Family: Austroperlidae]

Native The slow-moving adults are seen among streamside plants. The nymphs are found on wood submerged in streams, feeding on leaves and twigs.

a large green stonefly (*S. maclellani*) on Mt Burns, circa 1600 m

Unless otherwise indicated, all photos are life-size

79

Caddisflies / Pūrerehua

[Order: Trichoptera]

Adult caddisflies are always found near water. They have long, forward-pointing, whip-like antennae and large compound eyes. With their hairy wings, held roof-like over their body when resting, they look like moths, explaining why Māori traditionally grouped them together (pūrerehua), as some modern moth specialists also do. The caterpillar-like larvae live in water, many using silk to weave fascinating tubes or snail-like cases for protection; some spin nets; others are free-living. New Zealand and Australia are unusual in having some that even live at sea, between the tides. Because the larvae need plenty of dissolved oxygen, the purity of water can be gauged by which species are found there. The adults often swarm in the evening over lakes and rivers and are attracted to lighted windows on summer nights. Most adults feed on nectar (though some don't eat at all); the diet of the larvae varies with the species. Adults, larvae and pupae are all eaten by trout. In parts of Japan, they provide human food too. About 8000 species are known worldwide; over 200 in New Zealand, all but one unique to this country. Several are listed as Protected Threatened Species.

Life Cycle (Complete metamorphosis): Egg > Larva (**caddis**) > Pupa > Adult Caddisfly (**sedge**)

adult caddisfly
Rests with wings held roof-like over its body and easily mistaken for a moth.

free-living larva and pupal cases of a
Netbuilding Caddis
[Family: Hydropsychidae]
Native The larva uses small pebbles and pieces of plant in which to spin a cone-shaped net attached to larger rocks. This net is used as a retreat and food-catching filter. Found in streams throughout.

larval cases of a
Spiral Caddis
[Family: Helicopsychidae]
Native The larva builds a low spiral case (like a snail shell) out of grains of sand and grit. Found in crevices and under stones in streams throughout. An excellent indicator of pollution-free water.

larvae inside cases
Hornycased Caddis
Olinga feredayi [Family: Conoesucidae]
Native The larva carries around a hard, smooth, curved tube for protection. Common in clean stony streams throughout New Zealand.

larval cases of a
Stoneycased Caddis
Pycnocentrodes species
[Family: Conoesucidae]
Native The larva builds a curved tube-shaped case out of tiny stones. Common in streams and the edges of lakes throughout New Zealand.

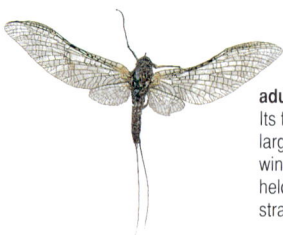

larvae in cases
Stick Caddis
Triplectides species [Family: Leptoceridae]
Native The larva builds its case out of small pieces of stick or leaves. Common throughout New Zealand along the edges of clean, slow-flowing streams. (The larva of a similar species actually lives *inside* a stick.)

Mayflies / Piriwai

[Order: Ephemeroptera]

Named after the month in which many northern hemisphere adults appear. At rest, a mayfly's delicate wings point straight up like sails, their back wings dwarfed by the much larger front wings. Nymphs have three tail whiskers (cerci); adults have either two or three. Adult mayflies have no mouth and never eat, some living for a few days; others for just one hour. And yet mayflies can appear in such large swarms that they will make roads slippery or clog gutters. When found in such swarms in Papua New Guinea, they are skimmed off the water, eaten raw or fried in sago pancakes. Both the adults and the nymphs are also an important food for many birds, freshwater fish and other insects. The males of many species perform a flying dance to attract the females, and mate while flying. The nymphs cling to rocks and pebbles in clean water, living for up to four years eating plants. Mayflies are the most ancient and primitive Order of living, winged insects, with fossilised wing impressions showing that they have lived on Earth for some 300 million years. About 2500 species are known worldwide; about 40 in New Zealand, all unique to this country (including one Threatened Species).

Life Cycle (Incomplete metamorphosis): Egg > Nymph > Subadult (**dun**) > Adult Mayfly (**spinner**; **drake**)

adult mayfly
Its front wings are much larger than the back wings. At rest, these are held together, pointing straight up like a sail.

immature form
Mayfly nymphs have side gills and three 'tails'.

80

Unless otherwise indicated, all photos are life-size

Water Bugs [Order: Hemiptera]

Water bugs – as shown below – live only in *still* water, not in fast running water. For more information, see page 86.

WALKING ON TOP OF THE WATER

Water Measurers
[Family: Hydrometridae]
See page 86.

Pond Skaters
[Family: Veliidae]
See page 86.

SWIMMING UNDERWATER

Water Boatmen
[Family: Corixidae]
See page 86.

Backswimmers
[Family: Notonectidae]
See page 86.

Water Flies [Order: Diptera]

The most common and conspicuous families of water flies in New Zealand are shown. Other less conspicuous New Zealand water flies include **dance flies** [Empidae] and **moth midges** [Psychodidae].

Non-Biting Midges
[Family: Chironomidae]
See page 61.

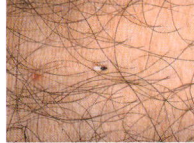

Biting Midges
[Family: Ceratopogonidae]
See page 61.

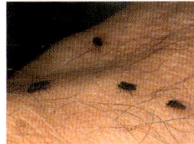

Sand Flies
[Family: Simuliidae]
Breed only in *running* water.
See page 61.

Mosquitoes
[Family: Culicidae]
Breed only in *still* water.
See page 60.

Crane Flies
[Family: Tipulidae]
A few species breed only in water. See page 58.

FRESHWATER

Water Beetles [Order: Coleoptera]

Diving beetles [Dytiscidae] are the most conspicuous water beetles in New Zealand. Of the smaller water beetles, **riffle beetles** [Elmidae] are the most common. Other small species include whirling **whirligig beetles** [Gyrinidae], **marsh beetles** [Scirtidae], **scavenging water beetles** [Hydrophilidae] and **cascade beetles** [Hydraenidae].

Diving Beetles
[Family: Dytiscidae]
See page 54.

immature form
The underwater larva of diving beetles have short antennae and two 'tail whiskers'.

Water Moths [Order: Lepidoptera]

The caterpillars of these moths live underwater, breathing through hair-like gills which cover much of the body. Only one such species is known in New Zealand.

Pond Moth
Hygraula nitens [Family: Pyralidae]
See page 35.

Unless otherwise indicated, all photos are life-size

Bugs

[Order: Hemiptera]

ADULT BUG

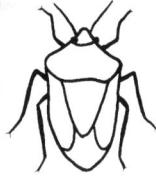

BUG
LIFE CYCLE
(Incomplete
metamorphosis)

NYMPH

EGGS

ALL BUGS ARE SUCKERS

WHAT IS A BUG? This word is so often loosely used to cover all insects and other invertebrates, but, technically speaking, bugs are a special group (Order) of insects, all of which have a straw-like mouth. This fine 'straw' is used for piercing holes in plants or animals to suck out liquid food. Within this piercing tube are two inner pipes which are unimaginably fine: typically, the sucking pipe at the front has a diameter of about one thousandth of a millimetre. The blowing one at the back (for injecting the bug's saliva) is finer still.

New Zealand bugs are found from the seashore up to mountain tops at almost 2000 m, some species remaining in the mountains all year, surviving up there in the most extreme winter conditions. Many of these alpine bugs are black to absorb what little heat from the sun there is at that altitude. The most intriguing of these are probably the black alpine cicadas, for – so far as is known – New Zealand is the only place in the world where cicadas have evolved to live close to the summer snowline. At similar altitudes a black alpine shield bug also lives – a native relative of the common introduced green shield bug found in the vegetable garden.

Some bugs live only in freshwater, either diving for food or doing that most mesmerising trick of walking across the surface of the water.

In many countries, cicadas and their nymphs are an important human food, as are the excretions of several bug species, which provide honeydew and manna (the 'manna from heaven'). The **lac bug** (*Laccifer lacca*) of South-East Asia supplies us with shellac for use in varnish and hair sprays, while other bugs give us the crimson dye 'kermes', the cochineal dye of the Aztecs (still used in lipsticks and food) and (from the **Chinese wax scale insect**) a kind of wax for making candles.

Worldwide, bugs range in size from the tiniest scale insects, several of which would fit on a pinhead, right up to **giant water bugs**, 10 cm long.

About 82,000 species are known worldwide; over 800 in New Zealand.

There are three main groups of bugs:

WINGS OVERLAP TO FORM A CROSS	*Go to page 84*
[Suborder: Heteroptera]	

With flat bodies and much of their front wings hardened, these bugs are often mistaken for beetles. Many have stink glands. Some feed on animals, while others suck plant sap. Their 'sucking tube' is attached at the front of the lower side of the face, rather than further back. (When not in use, this tube is often folded back against their 'chest', so can be hard to see.) Also sometimes known as the 'true bugs'.
Examples: **shield bugs**, **bed bugs**, **damsel bugs**, **water bugs**, **flat bugs**, **seed bugs**, **mirids**, **shore bugs**

WINGS ANGLED LIKE THE ROOF OF A HOUSE	*Go to page 87*
[Suborder: Auchenorrhyncha (sometimes included with Sternorrhyncha in Homoptera)]	

At rest, the wings of most of these are held on an angle like the roof of a house. All are plant feeders, sucking on sap. The males of most of these bugs can sing, although their song is, in many cases (except for cicadas), outside the hearing range of humans.
Examples: **cicadas**, **spittle bugs**, **planthoppers**

APHID RELATIVES (ALL SMALL INSECTS)	*Go to page 90*
[Suborder: Sternorrhyncha (sometimes included with Auchenorrhyncha in Homoptera)]	

On these small insects, the sucking tube is attached between their front legs (or even further back). All are plant feeders, sucking on sap.
Examples: **aphids**, **scale insects**, **mealybugs**, **whiteflies**, **psyllids**

BUGS

Shield Bugs
[Superfamily: Pentatomoidea]

These shield-shaped bugs are also known as **stink bugs** because they can make a strong defensive smell when touched. Most are green or brown, although some overseas species are brightly coloured. In winter, the adults hide under bark, rocks, leaves etc, coming out in spring to mate. The females lay neat clusters of barrel-shaped eggs on the underside of leaves. Some can make sounds. In India, shield bugs are eaten with rice. They are also eaten in Zimbabwe, South Africa and Mexico. In New Zealand, the green vegetable bug is usually eaten only by accident on home-grown vegetables. Over 6000 species are known worldwide; about 18 in New Zealand, including two Threatened Species from the South Island mountains.

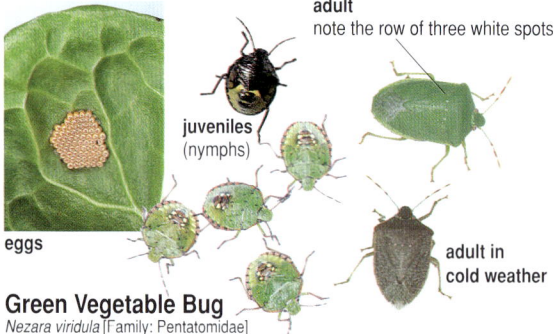

adult
note the row of three white spots

juveniles
(nymphs)

eggs

adult in cold weather

Green Vegetable Bug
Nezara viridula [Family: Pentatomidae]
Arrived from Europe before 1944 and now found throughout New Zealand. It sucks the sap of many summer vegetables, sometimes making short, buzzing flights in the evening. In cool weather, they are often more brown-coloured. Odd ones can even be turquoise or yellow. The young ones (nymphs) have quite different colour patterns again (see photos).

Brown Soldier Bug
Cermatulus nasalis [Family: Pentatomidae]
Native Common in October, again in February and March, throughout up to 2000 m in the North Island and 1200 m in the South Island. It feeds by sucking the juice out of caterpillars (see photo). Can fly. (Three subspecies.)

New Zealand Vegetable Bug
Glaucias amyoti [Family: Pentatomidae]
Native Found all year, throughout. This native bug can be distinguished from the similar introduced green vegetable bug by its very shiny body and the fact that it *doesn't have a row of three white spots on its back*. It is usually green but sometimes yellow. The common name is misleading, for this bug feeds on karamū (*Coprosma*) and other native plants and is not a pest. It can fly.

Black Alpine Shield Bug
Hypsithocus hudsonae [Family: Pentatomidae]
Native Dark brown or black. Flightless. Females have short 'wing-covers'. Seen November to February, in the South Island mountains at 1200 – 1800 m on *Celmisia* and *Hebe odora* etc in tussock grassland. Only six scattered populations are known: Eyre Mountains, Harris Mountains, The Remarkables, Old Man Range, Ben Lomond and Rock & Pillar Range. Protected as a Category I Threatened Species.

Pittosporum Shield Bug
Monteithiella humeralis [Family: Pentatomidae]
Probably introduced from Australia in the early 1900s. Brown with a pale stripe on its shoulders. Found all year, but most common in November (when it is seen flying) and again in March. Feeds mostly on the unripe fruits of *Pittosporum* shrubs, particularly on karo (*Pittosporum crassifolium*). Found throughout both main islands, from sea level to about 900 m.

Schellenberg's Soldier Bug
Oechalia schellenbergii [Family: Pentatomidae]
Native Also found in Australia. Brown. Common in places throughout New Zealand. Found all year but mostly in summer. This is one of New Zealand's most useful bugs, as it attacks many pest caterpillars as well as the Eucalyptus tortoise beetle (page 54). Note the pointed shoulders. It can fly. (The name is often misspelt *schellembergii*.)

Forest Shield Bug
Oncacontias vittatus [Family: Acanthosomatidae]
Native New Zealand's only true forest-dwelling shield bug, found on trees and shrubs throughout, from the coast to subalpine altitudes, often near water, where it sucks the sap of these trees. Common in October and again in January (or November and February in cooler parts). It can fly.

Sedge Shield Bug
Rhopalimorpha obscura [Family: Acanthosomatidae]
Native Feeds on the sap of sedges, flax, rushes and grasses. Common throughout New Zealand in summer in open places along the edges of streams, swamps and marshes, especially near forest. Also found in farmland, scrub and sometimes in vegetable gardens. It can fly. A related shield bug from the South Island mountains (*R. alpina*) is on the Threatened Species List.

Bed Bugs [Family: Cimicidae]

Very flat bugs with small eyes and no wings. At night, they suck the blood of reptiles, mammals and birds, finding their host partly by sensing body heat. During the day, they hide in cracks nearby. About 90 species are known worldwide; only two of which attack humans. One species in New Zealand.

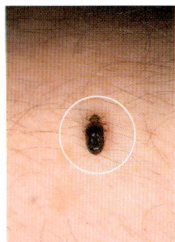

bed bug full of fresh blood

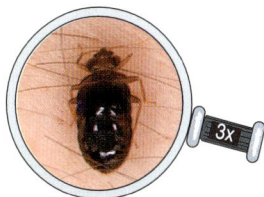

`3x`

Bed Bug
Cimex lectularius
Not common in New Zealand nowadays, but sometimes brought in by tourists on baggage and clothing and found in some backpackers' hostels and hotels. It feeds at night on the blood of warm-blooded animals, including people, chickens, rats, pigeons and domestic pets. Can also survive for up to 15 months without food. Eaten by cockroaches. Flightless.

Seed Bugs [Family: Lygaeidae]

Narrow, flat-bodied bugs, common on plants. Most feed on sap or seeds, but some hunt mites and other small insects. Also called **chinch bugs**, after a notorious American crop pest from this family. Over 4000 species are known worldwide; over 75 in New Zealand, most of them native (including several species found only on mountain daisies).

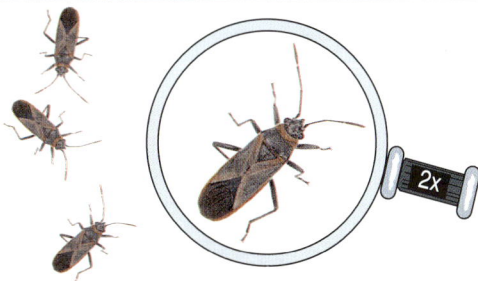

`2x`

Swan Plant Seed Bug
Arocatus rusticus (was *ruficollis*)
Australian. Now common here in gardens, orchards and scenic reserves on New Zealand jasmine (*Parsonsia*), swan plant seed pods, tweedia and under bark. Often hibernates under the old leaves of cabbage trees. Its grey colouring and red collar is distinctive.

Flat Bugs [Family: Aradidae]

Extremely flat, oval bugs with black or dark red-brown camouflage and a rough, bark-like top surface. Most live under the loose bark of rotting trees or in leaf litter, so are also known as **bark bugs**. Here, they lay their eggs and suck the juices of moulds and other fungi. The sucking tube that they use to suck this juice can be more than six times as long as the insect's body. When not in use, this is coiled like a watch spring inside the bug's head. About 1800 species are known worldwide; about 28 in New Zealand, most of them unique to this country.

Bark Bug
Ctenoneurus hochstetteri
Native Common under loose flakes of bark. It has a peculiar bug smell. Also sometimes known as **flat fungus bug**.

Mirids [Family: Miridae]

Small bugs with a long or oval body. They can run or jump. Most are sap-suckers, though a few suck the juices out of aphids and scale insects. Many are crop pests. Most inject their eggs into plants. Also sometimes known as **plant bugs**. About 10,000 species are known worldwide; about 100 in New Zealand.

Slender Crop Mirid
Stenotus binotatus
Introduced. Common on grasses, feeding on flower-heads of cocksfoot along roadsides or on seed crops. Flies December to January. Also common is the similar-looking introduced **potato mirid** (*Clisterotomus norvegicus* – was *Calocoris*), which feeds on a range of garden vegetables, cereal crops and roadside vegetation.

Damsel Bugs [Family: Nabidae]

Delicate, long-bodied bugs, narrow at the front and back, with strong front legs for hunting soft-bodied insects. Easily found by sweeping a fine net through long grass. Some can make sounds by scraping their back legs against their body. About 500 species are known worldwide; about five in New Zealand.

A Native Damsel Bug
Nabis biformis
Native Sometimes found under stones and logs, where they burrow into loose soil.

Pacific Damsel Bug
Nabis kinbergii (formerly thought to be *capsiformis*)
Very common in Australia and New Zealand. Helpful in the control of agricultural pests, feeding, for example, on aphids, mirids, seed bugs and small caterpillars, particularly among lucerne and lotus crops.

Shore Bugs [Family: Saldidae]

Small, brown or black, oval-shaped bugs with long legs, found on the seashore among plants and seaweeds, but also along the muddy edges of salt marshes, streams and ponds. A few can hide underwater when the tide comes in, living in bubbles of air trapped between rocks. They feed on other insects and can run fast or jump to escape predators. About 300 species are known worldwide; about seven in New Zealand, all unique to this country.

Shore Bug
Saldula species
Native These can run fast on water and jump from the water surface, but can also take short, fast flights. Seven *Saldula* species are known in New Zealand, one specialising in living in the water in North Island hot springs.

Unless otherwise indicated, all photos are life-size

Water Bugs

[Families: Corixidae, Hydrometridae, Notonectidae, Veliidae]

A few adults of each species have wings, enabling populations to spread from one pond to another. All live only in *still* water, never in fast running water. Overseas, many species (including their eggs) are collected or are 'farmed' for human food. In these four families, about 1600 species are known worldwide; about 11 in New Zealand.

SWIMMING UNDERWATER

Backswimmer /
Hoe Tuarā

Anisops assimilis [Family: Notonectidae]

Native Common in freshwater lakes, ponds, drinking troughs and weed-clogged streams. This large-eyed bug swims jerkily along on its back, often resting just under the surface with its legs spread out. It dives and breathes underwater in the same way as the water boatman, eating other insects, including mosquito larvae. Some adults have wings enabling them to fly between ponds. Adult males can 'sing' underwater by rubbing their front legs over their 'beak'. In an aquarium, this chirping is easily audible. There are two similar species.

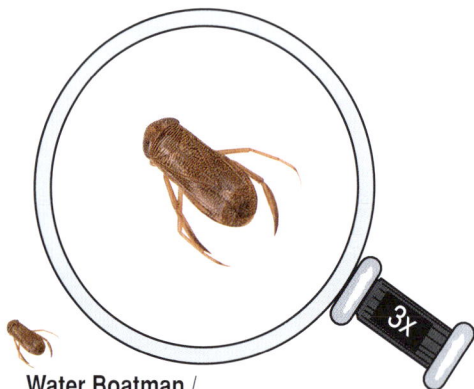

Water Boatman /
Hoehoe Tuarā

Sigara arguta [Family: Corixidae]

Native Common in lakes, ponds, drinking troughs and weed-clogged streams. The adult uses its hairy back legs to row and to drag air under its body before diving. This air gets caught in tiny hairs under its body. By breathing from this stored air supply, it can stay underwater for 15 minutes, feeding on algae at the bottom of ponds. It swims on its front and can fly between ponds. The males 'sing' by rubbing their legs together. This is the most common of six species.

WALKING ON WATER

Pond Skater

Microvelia species [Family: Veliidae]

Native Very common throughout in still water on the edge of ponds, lakes, ditches and weed-clogged streams, where they walk or run quickly over the surface of still water, eating other tiny insects trapped on the water surface. Some adults have wings; some don't. Also called **waterskater**. There are two similar species.

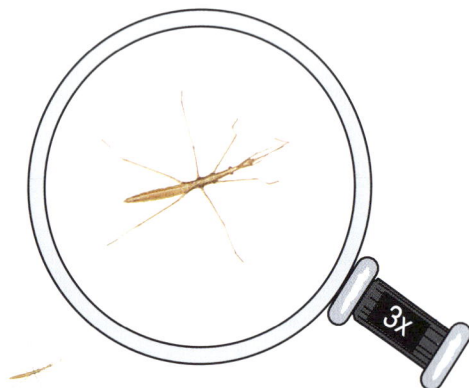

Water Measurer

Hydrometra risbeci [Family: Hydrometridae]

Native These long-legged insects are seen walking slowly across the water surface of lakes and ponds. Also seen on plants and stones. They eat other insects, such as mosquito larvae. Some adults have wings; some don't. (The name is often misspelt *ribesci*.)

86

Unless otherwise indicated, all photos are life-size

Planthoppers

[Superfamily: Fulgoroidea]

These hopping bugs suck the sap of plants. With the aid of special amplifying equipment, it has been discovered that many of these sing to one another. Native ones are found on flax, bracken and black tree fern (mamaku). Some species carry plant diseases, such as the phytoplasma (*Phytoplasma australiense*) disease in cabbage trees (sudden decline), flax (yellow leaf), karamū (coprosma lethal decline). Over 8000 species of planthoppers are known worldwide; over 40 in New Zealand (most of them native).

nymphs (fluffy bums)

egg-laying sites on a twig

Passionvine Hopper

Scolypopa australis [Family: Ricaniidae]

Arrived from Australia about 1876. A suspected carrier of the 'Sudden Decline' disease in cabbage trees. A common garden pest in summer and autumn, from Nelson north. Also common in regrowth forest. The moth-like adult walks like a ballerina. The wingless nymphs (**fluffy bums**) and adults both leap off with a 'snap' when disturbed and suck the sap of plants, leaving a sweet honeydew collected by bees. On the tutu shrub (*Coriaria*) this can be a problem for, although tutu sap is harmless to the hoppers and tutu honeydew is safe for the bees, the honey which the bees make from this is very poisonous to people.

adult

Cixid Planthopper

Cixius species [Family: Cixiidae]

Native   One of about 25 known cixid planthoppers in New Zealand, all native (including five Threatened Species). They look rather like miniature cicadas, most of them just 4 – 8 mm long. They can be bright green, yellowish brown, greyish or dark brown and feed on a wide range of plants, including native flax, grass tree, *Hebe*, karamū, kiokio, māhoe and cabbage tree.

Green Planthopper

Siphanta acuta [Family: Flatidae]

From Australia. The adults are very well camouflaged, looking like large thorns on green stems. The female lays flat clusters of eggs on leaves, her fluffy-tailed nymphs hatching in spring. When disturbed, both adults and nymphs hop away. Adults can also fly short distances. The odd adult can be pale yellow or blue-green.

Grey Planthopper

Anzora unicolor (was *Sephena cinerea*) [Family: Flatidae]

From Australia. The adults are very well camouflaged on grey-brown twigs. Both the adults and the fluffy-tailed nymphs hop away when disturbed. They carry 'fire blight', a bacterial disease of apple and pears.

Longheaded Bracken Hopper

Thanatodictya tillyardi [Family: Dictyopharidae]

Native   Sucks the sap of various plants including bracken fern (rārahu). It has very long front wings (longer than the body) and an unusually long 'nose'.

Red Fingernail Bug

Achilus flammeus [Family: Achilidae]

From Australia, where it is commonly known as the **red fungus bug**. The nymphs of this family of bugs live under loose bark or in holes in dead wood. In Australia this species has also been found in termite nests. Here it is rare, but occasionally found in Auckland.

BUGS

Spittle Bugs

[Family: Cercopidae]

Adult spittle bugs look rather like miniature cicadas. Because of their frog-like faces and habit of jumping, these adults are also known as **froghoppers**. But the more usual common name comes from the young (nymphs) which hide inside a kind of waxy froth which they make by mixing a special fluid with air and squirting it out their anus, a new bubble appearing about one every second. From inside this foam, they can safely suck sap from the host plant. The insect can breathe only by taking air from one of the larger bubbles or by drawing in air from the surface of the foam. The foam protection isn't perfect for **damsel bugs** (page 85) can still penetrate it and suck on the nymphs; some wasps even drag the nymphs out altogether. About 2400 species are known worldwide; about 15 in New Zealand, all but one of them native.

typical 'spittle' blown by the nymphs

Meadow Spittle Bug

Philaenus spumarius

Accidentally introduced from England in about 1960 and now found throughout most of the country. It has so far been found feeding on almost 400 different species of plants. The froth-covered nymphs are seen October to March (see photo).

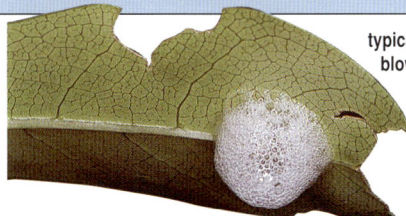

adults

Unless otherwise indicated, all photos are life-size

Cicadas / Kihikihi, Tātarakihi
[Family: Cicadidae]

Cicadas have a blunt head and tapered body; cannot jump but can fly. They are often noticed because of the male's loud summer mating call which he makes by buckling two lid-like plates (tymbals) on top of his body near the back legs. Below these (just behind the back legs) are the conspicuous amplifier plates (opercula). Some (*Amphipsalta*) species clap their wings too, by banging the hard front edge against a branch. (Try imitating this by snapping your fingers to lure the males to land on your hand.) The song of each species is so distinctive that each can be identified by this alone. When captured, they make 'dying yells'. Adult cicadas live for one or two months, sucking plant sap. The males can suck and sing at the same time, but usually stop singing when you get close. The females (which are generally larger than the males) have no song. In between the usual two compound eyes, cicadas have an extra three simple eyes (ocelli) on top of the head, which glow red like tiny rubies. Where do cicadas come from? The wingless cicada nymph (**matua kihikihi**) lives in darkness underground for at least three years, sucking roots. (Several North American species are known to spend 17 years underground.) When ready to hatch, it crawls out onto a tree trunk at dawn; the winged adult breaks out of its old nymph skin (**ngengeti**) and flies away. The largest cicadas, from Borneo and Java, can be 8 cm long with a wingspan of 20 cm (almost the height of this page). Both the adult cicadas and their nymphs have long been used as human food by the American Indians, in South-East Asia, Australia and by Māori in New Zealand. Here, live adult cicadas are also thrown onto water as bait for fly fishing. The underground nymphs of some New Zealand cicadas are sometimes attacked by a fungus, called **vegetable cicada** (*Cordyceps sinclairii*) and the adults by the **sugar icing fungus** (*Beauvieria bassiana*). Some New Zealand cicadas live only in forest; some in coastal sand dunes; others in the mountain tops. Nowhere else in the world are cicadas known to live close to the summer snowline. About 2500 species are known worldwide; about 40 in New Zealand, all unique to this country, including one Threatened Species from the Orongorongo Valley (*Maoricicada myersi*).

underground nymph

old nymph skin

cicada egg-laying
Female cicadas lay their eggs in the stems of plants. This photo shows the herring-bone damage to a twig made by the egg-laying of a clapping cicada (below).

cicada nymph
The immature form of a cicada is a wingless nymph (**matua kihikihi**) which lives underground for at least three years, sucking the sap from tree roots. At dawn, it then crawls out onto a tree trunk, breaks out of its old nymph skin (**ngengeti**) and flies away. These empty nymph skins are often seen still attached to the tree.

Chorus Cicada / Kihikihi Wawā
Amphipsalta zealandica

Native New Zealand's largest, best-known and most widespread cicada, with a *green* patch on top and extra-long wings. Found in tall forest throughout. It begins calling *after* Christmas, this timing noted by Māori as marking the eighth month of the traditional calendar. Wawā means roaring like heavy rain, referring to the male's particularly noisy chorus call (especially in mid-summer) — a call which ends with two or three claps: 'trrrrrrreeeeeee—drurp-snip, snip'. The female answers with wing clicks. She forces her eggs into branches, leaving herring-bone scars (see photo). Also known as **kihikihi tara** or **chorus clapper**.

Clapping Cicada
Amphipsalta cingulata

Native Very similar to the chorus cicada, but has an *olive* patch on top and yellow markings among the black underneath; it begins calling *before* Christmas (from about Labour Day onwards). The male calls: 'Drrrreeeeeeeeeam n' keep a meter sweeter', often with one click of the wings included. Also called **solo clapper** as it rarely sings in chorus. The female can answer with wing clicks. She forces her eggs into branches, leaving herring-bone scars – see photo. Found in the North Island only, in scrub and exposed forest.

Chirping Cicada
Amphipsalta strepitans

Native Found November to February, around rocks and tree trunks in open places in the South Island and southern North Island, particularly on coastal cliffs. The male makes a loud chattering or chirping song, interspersed with wing clapping. The female answers with wing clicks. As with other **clapping cicadas**, *Amphipsalta* species (this page), you can sometimes attract the male by snapping your fingers in imitation of the female. Also called **shingle cicada** or **chirping clapper**.

Murihiku Cicada
Kikihia species [unnamed]

Native Common in subalpine scrub and grassland in southern South Island and Stewart Island. The male has a song similar to the little grass cicada. Named from the Māori name for the southern part of the South Island (a name also given to a geological region in Southland).

Unless otherwise indicated, all photos are life-size

Tussock Cicada
Kikihia angusta

Native Can be either green or brownish. A favourite food of trout. The male of this species has a rather monotonous song: 'zit, zit, zit, zit ...'. Found in tussock grassland in eastern South Island (not on the West Coast) and on Stewart Island. In the northern part of its range it lives only in the mountains (up to 1500 m), but comes down to near sea level in the south.

Snoring Cicada
Kikihia cutora

Native Found from the North Island and its off-shore islands right up to the Kermadecs, from sea level to the highest subalpine scrub on the Central Plateau and Mt Taranaki (Egmont), feeding and singing from a wide range of trees and shrubs. The male call sounds like someone snoring: 'didididididi dambo dambo dambo'. It can be heard in every month of the year. Although most are very bright green (with a prominent yellow stripe and orange markings), a few of the males and females can be orange or yellow, or even red. At higher altitudes it can also be much darker coloured.

Clock Cicada
Kikihia horologium

Native The common and scientific names refer to the male's very simple song, like the ticking of a cheap alarm clock, with the occasional 'tick' missing. Found January to March in the South Island mountains from the Kaikoura Ranges to Aoraki (Mt Cook), mostly at subalpine altitudes. It lays its eggs on *Hebe* and similar shrubs.

Little Grass Cicada / Kihikihi Kai
Kikihia muta

Native Also called **variable cicada** as it can be green to almost black. A few females can even be brown, yellow or orange. Common, but not found on Stewart Island. Kai means 'food', for the adults were mashed into a paste by Māori and eaten (as were the mature nymphs of most cicadas). The male call is: 'zee zit zit zit' (with no wing-clicks). The female lays her eggs in a straight line in flax, cabbage tree leaves and grass stems. The nymphs spend at least three years underground before emerging as an adult.

April Green Cicada
Kikihia ochrina

Native Found only in the North Island. The male has a penetrating, rapidly repeated, monotonous call ('dididididididididi') which begins about Christmas, continuing until April, May or even June. Usually recognised by its unusually vivid shade of green. However, a few of the males and females can be bright orange or yellow, or even red.

Campbell's Cicada
Maoricicada campbelli

Native Found along riverbeds in the South Island and in subalpine areas of central North Island. The male's call has been described as 'tut-tut-tut ... who-ō-ose dik? who-ō-ose dik?' with the '*whose*' part sounding at 220 – 330 clicks per second. (This is one of about 20 *Maoricicada* species, all of them black, each with a different distribution, many of them alpine.)

High Alpine Cicada
Maoricicada nigra

Native Lives among alpine herbs in the South Island mountains at 1200 – 1830 m, where this cicada and *M. oromelaena* often call within a few metres of summer snow patches. Only in New Zealand are cicadas known to live in such extreme alpine conditions. The male makes a rustling song: 'er-chit-er-chit-er-chit-er-chit ...' The 'er' part of this call is sounded at about 540 clicks per second; the 'chit' is made at a higher frequency.

North Island Clay Bank Cicada
Notopsalta sericea

Native Found throughout the North Island on clay banks and coastal cliffs, also on pumice soils of the Central Plateau, also on the walls of houses, garden walls and drive-ways. The male often sings on clay banks, making a long, penetrating entry note followed by a sequence of shorter notes. It will happily sing if caged and in the sun. This cicada is similar to one found in Australia, so may be the most recent cicada to have arrived in New Zealand.

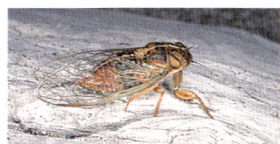

Redtailed Cicada
Rhodopsalta cruentata

Native Found singing in shrubland and the edges of forest from Canterbury north and common near the coast and along riverbanks. A very distinctive small cicada, its green-veined wings contrasting with a red and black body. The male makes a shrill, weak and rather monotonous song, like a small cricket and can be difficult to locate, often singing from inside low shrubs: 'tiktack tiktack tiktack'.

BUGS

Unless otherwise indicated, all photos are life-size

Aphids / Kuturiki
[Family: Aphidae]

In modern Māori, aphids are known as **weo** (to stab or spear), **kuturiki** (little louse) or **peperiki**. These small, soft-bodied insects (usually green, pink, black or brown) can reproduce without fertilisation. Some have wings; some don't. They suck the sap of many fruit trees, vegetables and flowers. Most species specialise in just one kind of foodplant, many of them pests capable of spreading diseases from one plant to another. On the plant, they leave a sugary honeydew which is often collected by bees and **ants**. Some ants have even learnt to milk the aphids like cows. Such ants can go to great lengths to protect the aphids' food source, building access ramps for them or carrying the aphids to the best plants. They are also known to protect their aphid herd from the cold and from predators. Aphids are eaten by ladybirds, praying mantids and birds, which is just as well, for, with unlimited food and no predators, a single **cabbage aphid** could have sufficient descendants in one year for its extended family to weigh 822 million tonnes, or more than three times the weight of the world's total human population. Many have been collected from high-flying aeroplanes. About 2250 species are known worldwide; over 80 in New Zealand, including several native ones found only on native plants.

Oleander Aphid
Aphis nerii
Introduced. These orange aphids feed on the sap of *Oleander* and swan plants (*Gomphocarpus*).

Rose Aphid
Macrosiphum rosae
Introduced. Green aphids often tinged with red. These are the most common aphids found on roses in New Zealand. Silvereyes and goldfinches feed on them.

Whiteflies
[Family: Aleyrodidae]

Tiny, moth-like flying insects similar to aphids, covered with a waxy white powder. They sit on the underside of leaves, sucking sap and do not jump. About 1200 species are known worldwide; about 13 in New Zealand, of which two introduced ones are common pests in gardens and greenhouses.

Greenhouse Whitefly
Trialeurodes vaporariorum
Accidentally introduced. A common pest in greenhouses, but also common outdoors during the summer and autumn in northern New Zealand. The adults hide on the underside of leaves, feeding on plant sap. A black mould often grows on the honeydew excreted by both adults and nymphs.

Psyllids
[Superfamily: Psylloidea]

Also known as **jumping plant lice** or **lerp insects**. Except for their longer antennae, these look like *really tiny* planthoppers and have strong jumping legs. The females lay stalked eggs on, or in, plants. When the nymph hatches out, it feeds on the leaf, often creating little bumps on the leaf surface. In New Zealand, common ones specialise in blue gum, wattle, kōwhai, broom, pittosporum, native fuchsia, tree fern, lancewood and pōhutukawa trees. About 1500 species are known worldwide; over 50 in New Zealand (most of them native).

bumps on pōhutukawa leaf
left by pōhutukawa psyllids

Pōhutukawa Psyllid
Trioza curta [Family: Triozidae]
Native These bumps (see photo) are common on the leaves of young pōhutukawa trees. Each bump shows where the tiny pōhutukawa psyllid has laid its eggs. The same insect is also found on the kiekie vine (*Freycinetia*).

Unless otherwise indicated, all photos are life-size

Scale Insects & Mealybugs / Kutu Papa
[Superfamily: Coccoidea]

Both the nymphs and adults suck plant sap. The flat, wingless females stay in one place, protected by a covering of wax, which can be either soft or scale-like. They can reproduce without fertilisation. The males are much rarer, some with wings, some without. When the eggs hatch, the first stage (known as **crawlers**) can move about. The honeydew of many overseas species provides important human food, e.g. the manna found on larch and tamarisk trees in the Sinai Desert. The secretion of one species provides shellac; another produces a wax used for making candles in Asia; others are a source of red dyes used in food and cosmetics. Elsewhere, the scale insects themselves are used in medicine or are even worn as jewellery. About 7000 species are known worldwide; about 250 in New Zealand. Introduced ones are pests on fruit trees and other cultivated plants, but most New Zealand species are native and found only on native plants.

wasp (see page 70) **feeding on honeydew** from the sooty beech scale (below)

Longtailed Mealybug
Pseudococcus longispinus
[Family: Pseudococcidae]
From Australia, but now a worldwide pest in greenhouses and on grapes and citrus. In New Zealand, it is also found outdoors in the North Island and northern South Island, mostly from December to July. Sooty mould often grows on the honeydew they excrete.

Hemispherical Scale
Saissetia coffeae [Family: Coccidae]
Introduced. A common pest on pot plants and ferns. They are also common on citrus trees but are rarely harmful here. The photo shows the mature female. (No males have ever been found.) Unlike most introduced soft scale insects, this one has found its way into native forest. Indeed, it has so far been recorded feeding on 18 introduced plants and 14 native species. Found from the Otago Lakes north.

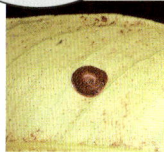

Sooty Beech Scale
Ultracoelostoma species [Family: Margarodidae]
Native Common in the northern South Island, living in a waxy capsule beneath the bark of native beech trees, especially black beech (*Nothofagus solandri*). Here, it feeds on sap, excreting honeydew through a long, slender wax tube. These sweet drops provide food for lizards, birds and insects (including wasps). Honey bees also produce honeydew honey from it, a popular export to Germany. Drops of honeydew landing on the trunk of the tree feed a kind of black sooty mould – hence the name.

Cottony Cushion Scale
Icerya purchasi [Family: Margarodidae]
From Australia. Found from about Christchurch north on many plants, including citrus trees. The photo shows the mature female with its corrugated egg sac, which protects 500 – 800 eggs. Eaten by the cardinal ladybird (page 47).

BUGS

Unless otherwise indicated, all photos are life-size

Wētā, Crickets & Grasshoppers

[Order: Orthoptera]

ADULT

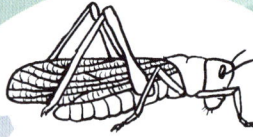

ORTHOPTERA
LIFE CYCLE
(Incomplete metamorphosis)

NYMPH

EGGS

BIG BACK LEGS

INSECTS IN THIS GROUP [Orthoptera] can be recognised by their unusually big back legs, which are generally used by the insect for making big leaps to escape danger. Most are plant eaters, with strong jaws for chewing. Those which can fly have toughened, straight front wings protecting their larger, more delicate, back wings. Many can 'sing', these 'songs' being sung mostly by the males wanting to attract a female for mating. In most cases these songs are made by rubbing a row of fine pegs inside their back legs against a ridge on the side of their body, or by rubbing their front wings together.

New Zealand is unusual for its high altitude species. Elsewhere in the world, grasshoppers are creatures of warm places, but most New Zealand grasshoppers live only in the South Island mountains. One kind, the **skiing grasshopper** (*Sigaus villosus*), has even learnt to use its legs as ski poles, 'skiing' about on its smooth belly on snow slopes at altitudes over 2000 m.

For its wētā, too, New Zealand is famous. For although these cricket-like creatures are found throughout much of the world, no other country has so many different kinds or as many giants. Like grasshoppers, some live at very high altitudes. While most insects this far up into the mountains contain antifreeze to survive low temperatures, the **mountain stone wētā** (*Hemideina maori*) is known to freeze solid in cold weather, thaw out and carry on as if nothing had happened. It is the largest insect in the world known to be able to do this. And near the glaciers of Mt Cook, at altitudes of more than 3100 m lives the **giant scree wētā** (*Deinacrida connectens*). Here, it survives by hiding under stones heated by the sun. And then higher still – up to 3400 m – lives a cave wētā known as the **Mount Cook flea** (*Pharmacus montanus*) at altitudes where few plants and other animals can survive.

Worldwide, insects in this group [Orthoptera] are popular as food. Indeed, many larger species – especially locusts, grasshoppers and crickets – provide an important source of protein for much of the world's population. Modern recipes (see page 5) include 'cricket crisps' and 'tempura cricket with vegetables', 'stir fried cricket curry' and 'chocolate covered crickets'. When roasted, most species are said to taste like nuts, that is after the wings and legs have first been removed. While here in New Zealand, **wētā** were eaten by Northland Māori, mashed with kūmara.

A few Orthoptera are important pests, the worst being tropical locusts, single swarms of which in some tropical countries can darken the sky for a week, completely stripping all vegetation for thousands of square kilometres.

Although a few species are small (some crickets are just 5 mm long), this group includes many of the world's largest insects. Indeed, one grasshopper from the border between Malaysia and Thailand measured a remarkable 254 mm long (including legs and antennae); it could leap 4.6 m in a single leap. Longer still, though, is New Zealand's **giant cave wētā** (*Gymnoplectron giganteum*) from the Poor Knights Islands, which can be 45 cm long (about twice the height of this page).

Worldwide, about 20,000 species are known; over 130 in New Zealand.

To tell wētā from cave wētā, check where the bases of the antennae meet on the face:

CAVE WĒTĀ	*Go to page 96*	WĒTĀ	*This page*
• Antennae almost touching at the base		• Separated by the width of an antennae base	

Wētā

[Family: Anostostomatidae (was included in Stenopelmatidae)]

Active at night. Some overseas wētā can fly but New Zealand species are all wingless. Their antennae are often twice as long as their body. The females have a long egg-laying spike at the back. Wētā are more ancient than the tuatara, for fossils have been found in Queensland dating back 190 million years, from the period when New Zealand was still joined to Australia. Even today, wētā are found not just in New Zealand, but also in New Guinea, New Caledonia, Australia, India, Malaysia, Vietnam, southern China, Madagascar, throughout southern Africa and from Chile, Argentina, Brazil, Venezuela and Central America to California, where they are known as **king crickets**. In New Zealand, wētā were eaten by early Māori, presumably after removing the spiny legs. Nowadays, rats are a major predator. Worldwide, over 260 species are known (about 160 named). Not counting cave wētā (which are in a different family – page 96), about 50 species are known (22 named) in New Zealand, all unique to this country.

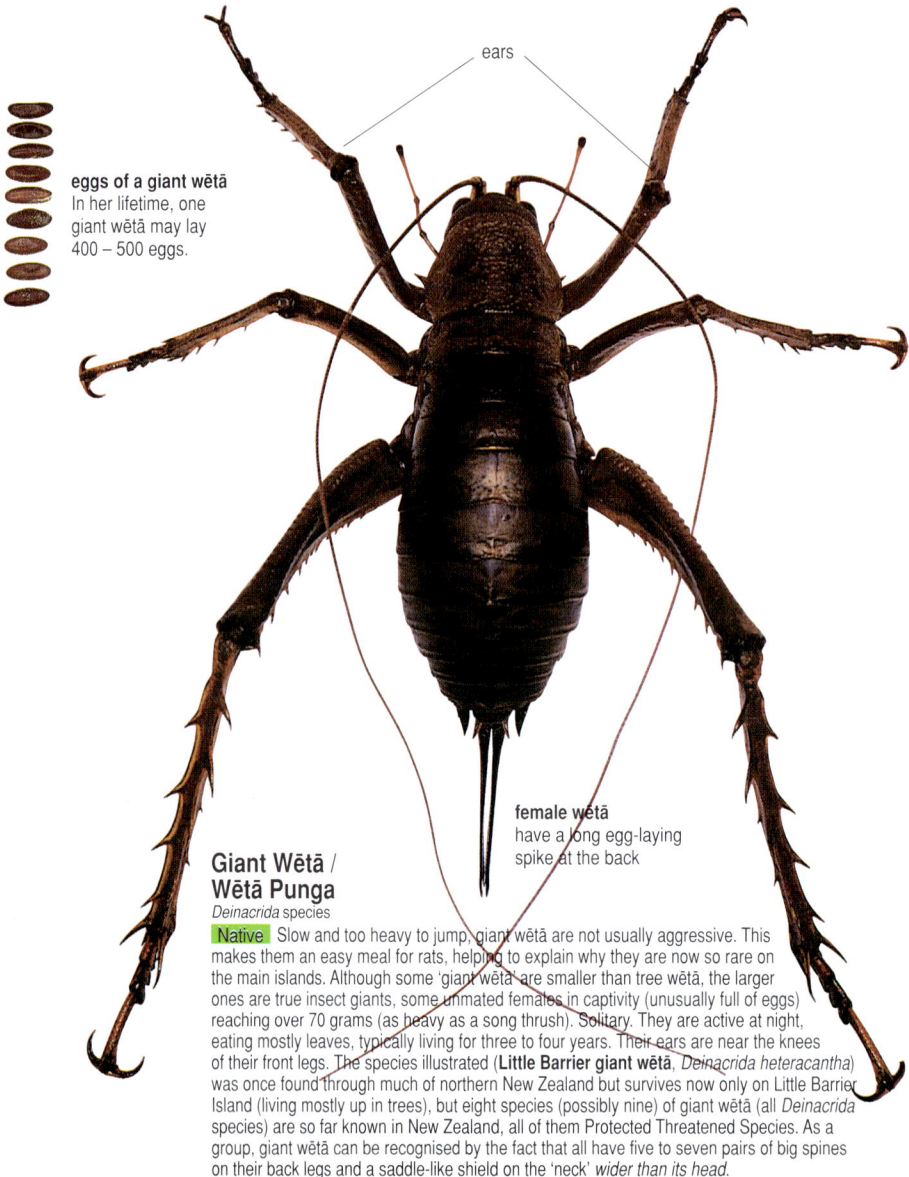

ears

eggs of a giant wētā
In her lifetime, one giant wētā may lay 400 – 500 eggs.

female wētā
have a long egg-laying spike at the back

Giant Wētā /
Wētā Punga
Deinacrida species

Native Slow and too heavy to jump, giant wētā are not usually aggressive. This makes them an easy meal for rats, helping to explain why they are now so rare on the main islands. Although some 'giant wētā' are smaller than tree wētā, the larger ones are true insect giants, some unmated females in captivity (unusually full of eggs) reaching over 70 grams (as heavy as a song thrush). Solitary. They are active at night, eating mostly leaves, typically living for three to four years. Their ears are near the knees of their front legs. The species illustrated (**Little Barrier giant wētā**, *Deinacrida heteracantha*) was once found through much of northern New Zealand but survives now only on Little Barrier Island (living mostly up in trees), but eight species (possibly nine) of giant wētā (all *Deinacrida* species) are so far known in New Zealand, all of them Protected Threatened Species. As a group, giant wētā can be recognised by the fact that all have five to seven pairs of big spines on their back legs and a saddle-like shield on the 'neck' *wider than its head*.

Unless otherwise indicated, all photos are life-size

Tusked Wētā

Motuweta isolata (& other tusked wētā)

Native   Very rare Protected Threatened Species. The first New Zealand tusked wētā was only discovered in 1970. Tusked wētā are similar to ground weta except for the tusks on the mature males which are used for fighting and for rubbing together to make sounds. The ears of these wētā are near their front knees. They are excellent jumpers. Tusked wētā eat more animal food than other wētā, taking mostly dead moths, beetles and caterpillars. So far, three species are known: a very small one from Northland (**Northland tusked wētā**, *Anisoura nicobarica*), one locally common one from the East Cape (**Raukūmara tusked wētā**, *Motuweta* species) and the one illustrated here from the Mercury Islands off the Coromandel Peninsula (**Mercury Island tusked wētā**, *Motuweta isolata*). Other species of tusked wētā are found in Africa and Australia.

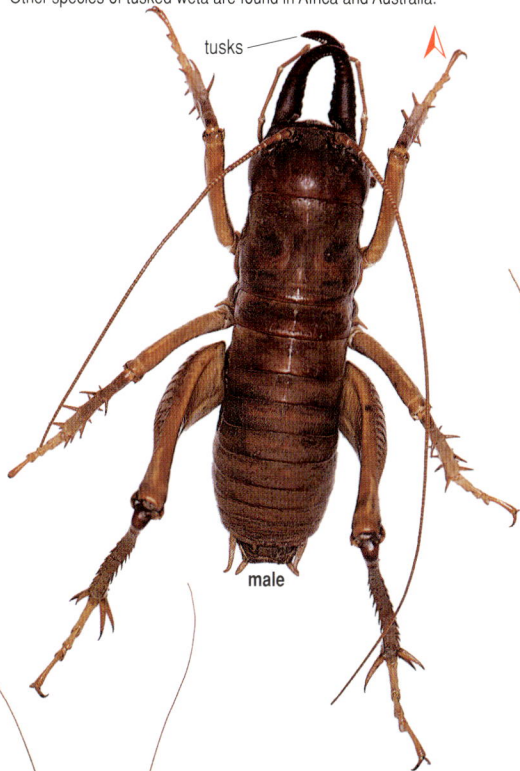

tusks

male

Tree Wētā / Pūtangatanga

Hemideina species

Native   Common in forest, orchards and gardens, especially in firewood sheds. They hide during the day in holes in trees, coming out at night to eat mostly fresh leaves, but also small insects. If handled roughly, they can inflict a painful **bite**, kick or scratch with their legs. To Māori and early Pākeha, the large masked horse-head of many of the males represented a goblin (**taipo** or **taepo**). The males can often be heard at night on trees and shrubs, rubbing their back legs against their body to make a sound like a fingernail running over the teeth of a comb. Their 'ears' are just below the knee of their front legs. If not eaten by birds, cats or rats, they can live for at least eight years. All tree wētā have five to seven pairs of big spines on their back legs; the saddle-like shield behind their head is the *same width as the head*. Seven species of tree wētā (all *Hemideina* species) are so far known in New Zealand, including a Protected Threatened Species (**Banks Peninsula Tree Wētā**, *Hemideina ricta*). The species illustrated is the **Wellington tree wētā** (*Hemideina crassidens*) which is found from Mt Ruapehu to Haast. One unusual 'tree wētā', the **mountain stone wētā** (*Hemideina maori*), has nothing to do with trees and lives only among tussock in the South Island mountains where it freezes solid in cold weather and later thaws out to walk off unharmed.

Ground Wētā

Hemiandrus species

Native   These soft-bodied wētā live in holes in the ground (retreating backwards), but climb trees and shrubs at night to eat leaves and insects. Various species are found from coastal sand dunes to mountain tops. Some look like crickets. The female's egg-laying spike is long on some ground wētā; short and blunt on others. Ground wētā do not kick but are impressive jumpers. They are only able to make soft calls (by rubbing their back legs against their body) and have no 'ears'. Often eaten by rats, mice, cats and stoats. Over 30 species of ground wētā (all *Hemiandrus* species) are so far known in New Zealand (including several Protected Threatened Species) but only seven are so far named. As a group, ground wētā can be recognised by the fact that their back legs have no heavy spines, but *more than 10 pairs of short spines and a cluster of longer ones on the ankle*. Other species are found in eastern Australia.

BIG BACK LEGS

Cave Wētā / Tokoriro

[Family: Rhaphidophoridae]

Active at night. Cave wētā have no wings, but are impressive jumpers, some species covering up to 3 m in one jump. They are not aggressive. They are silent and have no 'ears'. Most have small bodies, very long antennae and long spindly legs. They can be recognised by the fact that their antennae almost touch at the base and are up to four times as long as the insect's body. The smallest have a body not much bigger than an ant. The largest in New Zealand (and also one of the largest in the world) is the **giant cave wētā** (*Gymnoplectron giganteum*) from the Poor Knights Islands, which can be 45 cm from the tip of its antennae to its back toes (about twice the height of this page). Cave wētā are found from sea coast caves, under stones, in hollow tree trunks, in tunnels, water tanks and under houses right up to the mountain tops among the highest flowering plants at heights of up to 3400 m (e.g. the so-called **Mount Cook flea**, *Pharmacus montanus*). Cave wētā eat mostly live and dead plants and fungi, but also insects. Cave wētā are found not just in New Zealand but also in Australia, New Guinea, Chile, South Africa, Europe, Asia and North America, where they are known as **cave crickets** or **camel crickets**. About 500 species are known worldwide; over 50 in New Zealand (although many more await discovery), all unique to this country.

SEEN IN FOREST & CAVES – some examples

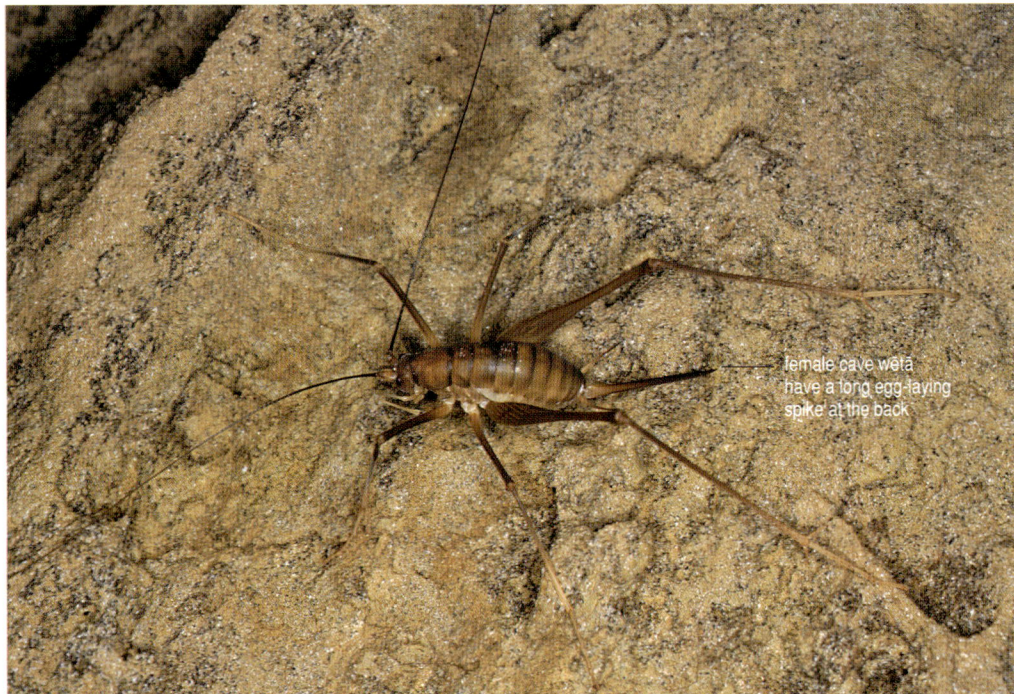

female cave wētā have a long egg-laying spike at the back

Oparara Cave Wētā
Gymnoplectron species

Native This species is apparently found only in caves in the Oparara region north of Westport. (Photographed in caves near Oparara, 16 March 2001. One of 12 newly discovered, unnamed cave-dwelling species from the North-West Nelson area.)

Painted Cave Wētā
Neonetus species

Native (Photographed at night from the forest floor near Waikawau Bay, Coromandel Peninsula, February 1998. One of four new species from this area or possibly the described one.)

Unless otherwise indicated, all photos are life-size

Auckland Cave Wētā
Gymnoplectron acanthocera

Native This cream-banded cave
wētā is common in caves, forest and
firewood in west Auckland. During the
day it can often be found hiding under
vegetation. It has not so far been
found south of Auckland. Measured
from the tips of its antennae to its
back toes, it can reach 355 mm.

BIG BACK LEGS

Unless otherwise indicated, all photos are life-size

Goldmine Cave Wētā
Gymnoplectron uncata
Native This attractively chequered cave wētā is often seen in large groups on the ceilings of caves and old goldmine tunnels on the Coromandel Peninsula. Also found in West Auckland.

Remarkables Cave Wētā
[Undescribed species]

Native One of several mountain cave wētā which live in the snow and scree among the highest flowering plants. Here, they survive sub-zero temperatures, often hiding in large numbers in cracks between the rocks. (A previously unrecorded species photographed at 1800 m, above the ski-fields on The Remarkables, 18 February 2001.)

Black Tumbling Cave Wētā
[Undescribed species]

Native This stocky cave wētā is jet black with daubs of gold and lives in the South Island mountains in scree, near patches of snow. To escape danger, it leaps, then rolls down the scree to tumble into a gap between the stones, its black colouring helping it to absorb radiated heat from the sun. (A previously unrecorded species photographed at Gertrude Saddle, near Homer Tunnel, 22 February 2001.)

BIG BACK LEGS

Unless otherwise indicated, all photos are life-size

Short-Horned Grasshoppers

[Family: Acrididae]

Named after their *short antennae* and the fact that they are good jumpers, most of them active during the day, eating plants, especially fresh grass. The flightless species are generally known in Māori as **kōwhitiwhiti** (also **kauwhitiwhiti**, **whitiwhiti** or **māwhitiwhiti**), meaning to jump or hop. When handled, most regurgitate a toxic brown fluid from their mouth as a defence (see photo – facing page). The females are larger than the males and (unlike wētā and crickets) have no obvious egg-laying spike at the back. Many (especially the males) make chirping sounds by rubbing a file-like row of fine pegs on the inside of their back legs against a scraper on the side of their body (or by rubbing their front two wings together). Their ears are on either side of the body, just above the back legs. Many are brightly coloured, a feature which some species use when signalling elaborate messages to one another with their wings and legs, using a sign language which differs from species to species. Many have served as food for humans (see page 5). About 10,000 species are known worldwide; about 15 in New Zealand, each with a different song. Most of these are flightless and unique to the South Island mountains, with many rarer species being limited to just one area – in effect, on an archipelago of alpine islands separated by uninhabitable river valleys. The easiest way to tell them apart is by their distribution and size, and the shape of their 'neck shield' (pronotum).

SEEN IN BOTH THE NORTH AND SOUTH ISLANDS

adult
with wings spread, showing the large, delicate back wings

adult at rest

'neck shield' (pronotum)

juvenile

Migratory Locust / Kapakapa
Locusta migratoria

Native Found throughout most of the world, except in North and South America. Thought to have arrived in New Zealand in the last 10,000 years and now found in rough grassland and sand dunes from about Christchurch north. When disturbed, it makes a clattering flight, crash-landing a few metres away. Few survive the winter. This is New Zealand's largest grasshopper with a body length of 30 – 55 mm. These insects are an important food for many people overseas, where, during periods of drought and food shortage, they sometimes fly in huge swarms. A single swarm can cover over 5000 sq km, darkening the skies for up to a week with some 250,000 million insects eating over 120,000 tonnes of plants a day, leaving a virtual desert behind them. The temperatures in New Zealand are not high enough to trigger the insects into flying in large swarms here, so it fortunately causes no serious damage. (With climate warming, this could of course change.) The Māori name, kapakapa, refers to the insect's clattering flight; also known as **rangataua**.

New Zealand Grasshopper
Phaulacridium marginale

Native Common at low altitudes in grassland throughout, but rarely found above 900 m. Individuals can be brown, grey or green, even pinkish or orange, depending on the colour of the background vegetation. This is believed to be because those individuals which stand out are more readily spotted and picked off by birds. Body length: 10 – 20 mm. The females never have wings and only a few of the males can fly.

New Zealand grasshopper
(showing another colour form)

Unless otherwise indicated, all photos are life-size

North Island Grasshopper
Sigaus piliferus

Native Large, angular body; length: 15 – 40 mm. Found only in the North Island, mostly in the mountains (e.g. Tongariro National Park and the Ruahine Ranges), but also at much lower altitudes on the East Cape, Coromandel Peninsula and at Rotorua. Flightless. Protected as a Category I Threatened Species. (This photo from the Coromandel was misidentified in early printings of *The Life-Size Guide to Insects* as the smaller New Zealand-wide *Phaulacridium*.)

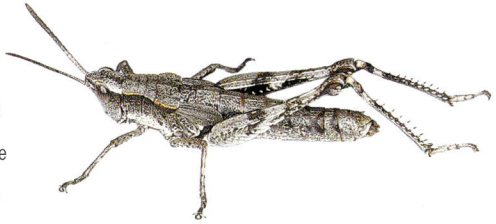

SEEN ONLY IN THE SOUTH ISLAND

northern tussock grasshopper
(showing another colour form)

Northern Tussock Grasshopper
Paprides nitidus

Native Green to olive green or grey-green, always with pale stripes along its back. Body length: 14 – 30 mm. Found only in the northern half of the South Island (from near Lake Tekapo north), above 900 m (to 1500 m), always in or near tussock. Flightless.

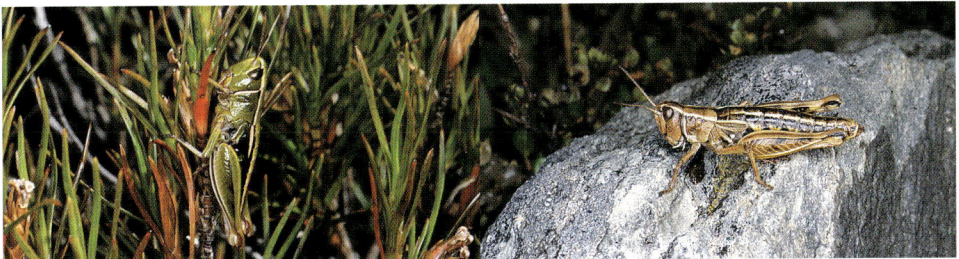

southern tussock grasshopper
(showing another colour form)

Southern Tussock Grasshopper
Sigaus australis

Native Various colours from dark brown or grey to light olive green, often with a pale vertical line behind its head. Body length: 12 – 40 mm. Very common at South Island ski resorts from about Arthur's Pass to near Queenstown, mostly in tussock at 1000 – 1500 m. Flightless.

southern tussock grasshopper
(from underneath, showing the toxic defence fluid typical of short-horned grasshoppers)

Notched Grasshopper
Sigaus campestris

Native Not common. Found in South Island grassland only, from Hanmer Springs to Southland, usually at 300 – 1000 m. Recognised by a series of notches along the back edge of its square-angled neck shield. Various colours. Body length: 13 – 32 mm. Flightless.

BIG BACK LEGS

Unless otherwise indicated, all photos are life-size

101

Long-Horned Grasshoppers

[Family: Tettigoniidae]

Named after their *long, hair-like antennae*. The males of many species make loud mating calls by rubbing tiny pegs on one front wing against the edge of the other front wing. Their ears are beneath the 'knees' of their front legs. They feed on plants, where most are very well camouflaged. The females have a long spike (ovipositor) at the tail end for laying eggs in plants or soil. Fossil remains have been found from about 200 million years ago. Also known as **katydids** or **bush crickets**. About 6000 species are known worldwide; four of them in New Zealand (plus one on the Kermadec Islands), each with a different song.

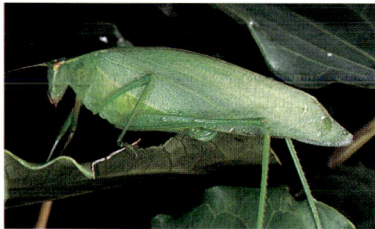

Katydid / Kiki Pounamu
Caedicia simplex

May be native. Also found in Australia. Common on garden shrubs, well-camouflaged by its leaf-like shape and the leaf-vein patterns on its wings. On still summer evenings, it (especially the male) makes a quiet 'zip-zip' or 'scissor snip' sound. It can jump or fly. At night, it eats fresh leaves, flower buds and young fruit, these sometimes changing the insect's colour from the usual green to a pinkish red. Named after the call of the American katydid: 'Katy did! Katy didn't!' Alternative Māori names include **tititi pounamu** and **kikiki pounamu**.

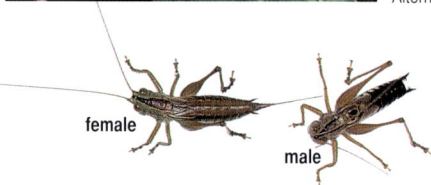

Field Grasshoppers
Conocephalus species

Native Also found in Australia. These little jumping grasshoppers eat long grass and call with a shrill high-pitched buzz which is outside the hearing range of some older people. They can be green or brown, with either short or long wings. So far, three species are known. Also known as **tussock katydids**.

female

male

Crickets

[Family: Gryllidae]

Māori names for crickets include **areinga**, **pihareinga**, **piharenga**, **pīrenga** and **rirerire**. Flattish brown or black insects, active at night. The males make loud, high-pitched chirping songs by rubbing their front two wings together. The species can be distinguished by their tune alone (although some species do require the use of a frequency analyser). The speed of their song also changes with temperature. With one overseas species, one only needs to count the chirps in 15 seconds and add 39 to find the temperature in degrees Fahrenheit. The ears of crickets (as in their cousins, the wētā) are in their front legs, beneath their 'knees'. They have two, long sensory spikes at the back (cerci). The female has a third, extra long spike (ovipositor) between these for laying her eggs in damp soil. For centuries in Asia, crickets have been kept as caged pets. They are also widely eaten (see pages 5 & 93 for recipes). Crickets have lived on Earth for more than 200 million years. About 4000 species are known worldwide; eight in New Zealand.

Black Field Cricket / Pihareinga
Teleogryllus commodus

Native Also found in Australia. Along with the cicada, it was seen by Māori as one of the 'singing birds of Rehua'; that is, its call signals the reappearance on the horizon of the summer star, Antares. Its place in traditional lore suggests that it is a true native of New Zealand. Common from Kaikoura north in grassland, hiding in cracks in the ground or under stones or wood; they will also come into houses. The male makes long, loud, shrill calls on autumn evenings but stops when you get close. They eat grass leaves, flowers and seeds. During dry summers, they can become a serious pest on farms. They are often seen jumping or running, but on late summer evenings will sometimes fly. Swarms have even been seen 50 km offshore.

Small Field Cricket / Rirerire
Bobilla species

Native Small crickets often heard (and sometimes seen) during the day in long grass, making a faint tinkling call on sunny days throughout most of the year. At around 8 kHz, this is lower pitched than the call of the field grasshoppers (above). Four similar species are so far known.

Mole Crickets

[Family: Gryllotalpidae]

Underground, burrowing crickets with short antennae. They look like miniature moles with their small eyes and wide, splayed, shovel-like front legs used for digging. They live in tunnels, in damp sand or soil near freshwater, where they feed on plant roots and stems, insects and worms. They come to the surface to mate. Unlike other members of this Order [Orthoptera], they *don't* have particularly big back legs. The males of some overseas species construct an acoustic cone at the entrance to their tunnel from which to broadcast their chirping – which they do by rubbing their front wings together. Their ears are in their front legs. In the Philippines, they are eaten fried, broiled or sautéed with vegetables and, in times of famine, they are also eaten by the Shona people of Zimbabwe. About 60 species are known worldwide; only one in New Zealand.

Mole Cricket / Honi
Triamescaptor aotea

Native Previously common in both undisturbed and cultivated ground, but nowadays very rarely seen, with recent sightings only from coastal and inland Hawke's Bay, near Wanganui, Manawatu (Levin), around Lake Wairarapa and on D'Urville Island.

It has no wings (and is therefore silent) but is a *very* fast runner. While underground, it moves like a little bulldozer, feeding on roots, grass grubs and porina caterpillars. It lives about 10 – 15 cm underground, in circular galleries (about 10 cm diameter), with side chambers dug as nurseries for its young. They are known to be eaten by eels and, no doubt, also by rats.

Unless otherwise indicated, all photos are life-size

Other Insects

[The smaller Orders]

STICK INSECTS

COCKROACHES

PRAYING MANTIDS

EARWIGS

TERMITES

LACEWINGS

FLEAS

LICE

BOOKLICE

THRIPS

SILVERFISH

SPRINGTAILS

Stick Insects / Rō, Whē

[Order: Phasmatodea]

Traditionally grouped by Māori along with praying mantids as rō, whē or **wairaka** – a similarity recognised by many scientists. Although all the species found in New Zealand have long, stick-like bodies, some tropical species (known as **leaf insects** [Family: Phylliidae]) look more like leaves. Most live among trees and shrubs, but New Zealand also has one alpine species which lives in tussock up to 1500 m. Stick insects walk rather awkwardly, often swaying in the wind. At night, they eat leaves. Males of many overseas species can fly, but in New Zealand all are flightless, depending for survival on their camouflage. Resting with their front legs stretched forward, they look very much like the plants that they eat. Although they do look more dull coloured with age, adults cannot change colour at will. If a leg is grabbed by a predator, the stick insect will detach it, the younger ones often regrowing it later. The males are usually smaller than the females. Some can reproduce without being fertilised by a male. The females lay eggs in autumn and have usually died by winter. The young hatch in early spring. Many are attacked by wasps. Overseas, several species are used as human food. The record for the world's longest insect is held by a giant stick insect from Borneo (*Pharnacia kirbi*) with a body length of 328 mm (or 546 mm including its legs). It would almost extend across two open copies of this book laid side by side. Fossil records show that stick insects lived alongside the dinosaurs, some 150 million years ago. About 2500 species are known worldwide; 16 in New Zealand (plus about five varieties), all native.

Life Cycle (Incomplete metamorphosis): Egg > Nymph > Adult Stick Insect

brown form (female with smaller male)

green form (female)

Common Stick Insect

Clitarchus hookeri [Family: Phasmatidae]

Native New Zealand's commonest stick insect, found throughout the country. By 1944, it had even established itself in England. Its smooth body can be either bright green or light brown. Some females can live for up to fourteen months, surviving one winter. They eat mānuka, kānuka and pōhutukawa leaves. Also called **smooth stick insect**. Female body length: 81 – 106 mm; male: 67 – 74 mm.

Unless otherwise indicated, all photos are life-size

female with smaller male

Rough-Skinned Stick Insect
Mimarchus salebrosus [Family: Phasmatidae]

Native   Grey or brown with black markings. Found on bush lawyer and roses from Otago Peninsula, Bank's Peninsula and southern Wairarapa. Female body length: 46 – 56 mm; male: 39 – 43 mm.

female
(no males of this species have ever been seen)

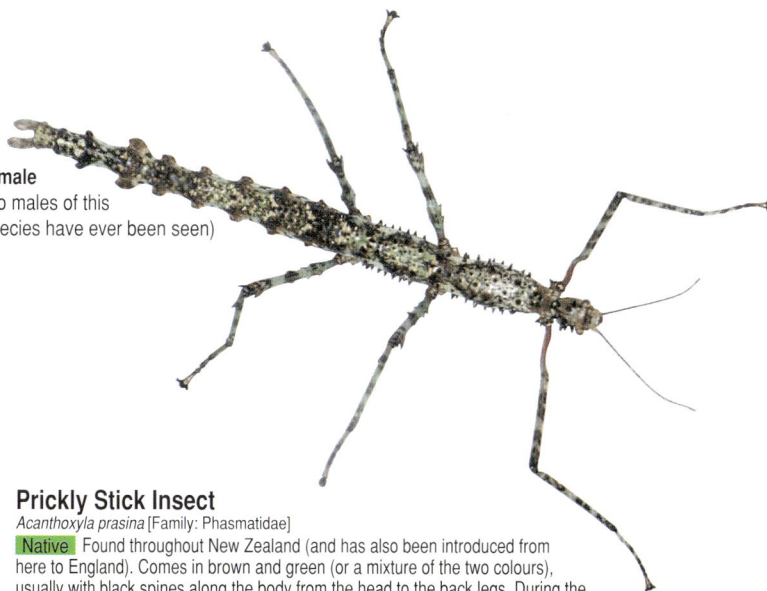

Prickly Stick Insect
Acanthoxyla prasina [Family: Phasmatidae]

Native   Found throughout New Zealand (and has also been introduced from here to England). Comes in brown and green (or a mixture of the two colours), usually with black spines along the body from the head to the back legs. During the insect's lifetime, these colours do not change. Strangely, the female can produce eggs without being fertilised by a male; indeed no males of this species have ever been seen. Female body length: 75 – 108 mm. Also called **black-spined stick insect**.

OTHER INSECTS

male

female

Large Spiny Stick Insect
Argosarchus spiniger [Family: Phasmatidae]
Native Found throughout New Zealand but not common. It has a long,
light brown to greenish brown body with two rows of prickly spines along the
sides. It chews mānuka and kānuka leaves, but also needs some ramarama
(*Lophomyrtus*) and white rātā leaves to remain healthy. It has been raised on
a diet of pōhutukawa leaves too, but has rarely been found naturally here.
Female body length: 120 – 145 mm; male up to 100 mm.

Cockroaches / Kokoroihe

Broad, flat, greasy, fast-running insects with spiky legs, active at night, hiding by day in dark corners. Most have stink glands for protection. Some are wingless, but even those which can fly, can't fly far. Two spikes (cerci) at the back are used for detecting air movement and as rigid feelers when the cockroach is backing up into tight spaces. Native species eat some rotting wood, but mostly feed on fungus in leaf litter. Introduced ones eat food scraps and sewage, spreading diseases. But note that less than one percent of the world's cockroach species are pests. Indeed, cockroaches have been widely used for food and medicine in China, Thailand, Australia and French Guiana, and in Indonesia roasted cockroaches are eaten as a cure for asthma. The female of many species carries its purse-like egg case (see photo) around until the young (up to 40 of them) are ready to hatch from it. When hatched (and after each moult), the young are white for the first few hours. The common name comes from the Spanish, cucaracha. Traditionally, Māori grouped cockroaches along with beetles (**pāpapa** or **papata**) because of the similarity of their shape and scurrying habits. The more recent name, kokoroihe, comes from English. Fossil records show that cockroaches were common over 300 million years ago, long before the first dinosaurs. About 4000 species are known worldwide; over 30 in New Zealand, most of them native, including one Threatened Species.

Life Cycle (Incomplete metamorphosis): Egg > Nymph > Adult Cockroach

INTRODUCED COCKROACHES

Giant Cockroach
Blaberus giganteus [Family: Blaberidae]
Often found alive in banana crates entering New Zealand from Equador but, fortunately, too large and tropical to survive in the wild here. This species can be over 88 mm long and 38 mm wide, is a fast runner and can fly. It occurs naturally from the West Indies to northern South America but is kept elsewhere in glass tanks as a pet. It even has its own internet site (page 114). Thirty to forty of them will eat a hamburger in less than an hour.

egg case (purse-like)

American Cockroach
Periplaneta americana [Family: Blattidae]
From tropical America. Even here, it needs the heat of the tropics, so is found mostly in bakeries and hospitals. This cockroach is believed to be the world's fastest-running insect, reaching speeds of up to 5.4 km/h or fifty body-lengths per second. The adults have wings yet seldom fly. Up to 4 cm long.

German Cockroach
Blattella germanica [Family: Blatellidae]
Thought to have arrived in New Zealand with Captain Cook in 1769. In spite of its common name, it comes from North Africa and is now very common in heated buildings all over the world, including in hotels, hospitals, restaurants and homes. The adults have wings but seldom fly. Less than 2 cm long.

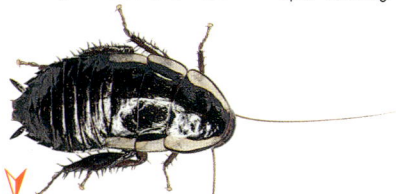

Gisborne Cockroach
Drymaplaneta semivitta [Family: Blattidae]
Common in timber arriving from western Australia. First seen in Gisborne but now found from Auckland to Nelson. It often comes indoors, sheltering in warm, dry ceilings and garages. It has been found both live and cooked on car engines and is thought to get around the country mostly by car. Easily recognised by the broad cream stripes down the sides. It has no wings.

Australian Cockroach
Periplaneta australasiae [Family: Blattidae]
From India and Australia. Here, it is usually found only on ships. It needs warm conditions to survive. Has a yellow strip along the outer edge of wings and a dark spot near the front. Looks similar to the American cockroach, but is smaller (3 cm).

NATIVE COCKROACHES

Black Cockroach / Kēkerengū
Platyzosteria novaeseelandiae [Family: Blattidae]
Native Found in the North Island and northern South Island. Also known as **stinkroach** as it makes a strong smell when disturbed. It lives in native forest under the bark of trees, in rotting logs and even (in some areas) on coastal rocks. It is sometimes brought into houses with firewood, but is not a pest. It has no wings. Tribal variations include: **kekeriru, kekereru, kēkereū, keriru** and **kikararu**.

A Native Bush Cockroach
Celatoblatta species [Family: Blattidae]
Native Lives in logs and under loose bark, but is sometimes brought into houses with firewood. It has no wings and is not a pest. There are about 15 similar native *Celatoblatta* species, some of which are found only under stones among scree in the South Island mountains.

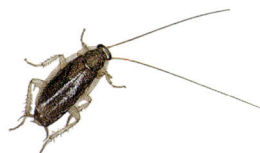

Winged Bush Cockroach
Parellipsidion latipennis [Family: Blatellidae]
Native Lives in native forest under the loose bark of trees, but is often brought into houses with mānuka firewood. The adults have lacy wings yet seldom fly. Not a pest. (In all, there are six or seven species of winged bush cockroaches.)

OTHER INSECTS

Unless otherwise indicated, all photos are life-size

Praying Mantids / Rō, Whē
[Order: Mantodea]

Uncannily like 'space aliens', praying mantids stare with huge, bulging eyes, turning their triangular heads from side to side. In between these huge eyes are three more eyes. Under their body (between their back legs) is a single ultrasonic ear. Their wings are held flat over their body. Mantids are best known however for the way they hold their large, powerful, front legs together as if praying. With these, they snatch flies, cicadas, crickets, wasps and moths. This 'grabbing moment' takes about one twentieth of a second. Young mantids eat smaller insects like aphids. At the other end of the scale, larger adults overseas can snatch at lizards and small birds. In Papua New Guinea, China, Japan and in Thailand, they are sometimes used as food. Praying mantids and stick insects were traditionally grouped together by Māori, who called both kinds of creatures rō, whē or **wairaka**, just as scientists sometimes include both in the grasshopper Order: Orthoptera. The oldest fossil records of mantids so far found are about 40 million years old. About 2000 species are known worldwide; only two so far seen in New Zealand.

Life Cycle (Incomplete metamorphosis): Egg > Nymph > Adult Praying Mantis

foamy egg case

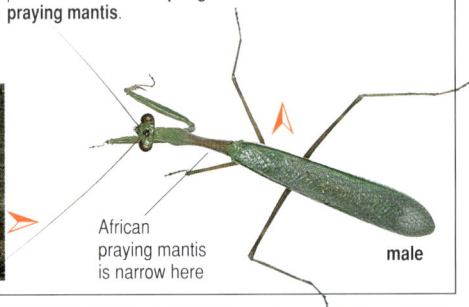

note blue patch near front knee of NZ praying mantis

egg case

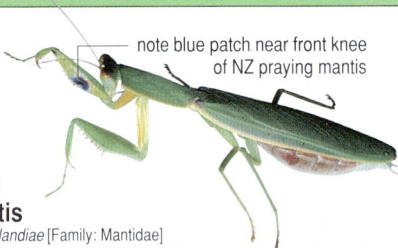

New Zealand Praying Mantis
Orthodera novaezealandiae [Family: Mantidae]

Native Very similar to one of Australia's 100 or so praying mantis species, but this one is found only in New Zealand. *Usually green* (rarely yellow), it sits on *top of leaves*. The bright *blue and purple patch* on the inside of its front legs clearly distinguishes it from the South African species. The females *can fly* and rarely eat the males. One individual can eat 25 flies a day. The adults don't usually survive the winter. This native species makes a neater, more compact egg case than the introduced African mantis (see photos).

African Praying Mantis
Miomantis caffra [Family: Mantidae]

Arrived here from South Africa in about 1978 and now very common in northern New Zealand and spreading. It is *green to pale brown* and often *larger* than the native New Zealand mantis. The body section between the first two pairs of legs is *narrower than the head*. This species usually hides *underneath leaves* or in long grass. The females *cannot fly*, are much larger than the males and often eat the males during or after mating. This mantis often survives the winter, giving it an advantage over the New Zealand species. It leaves a foamy egg case – see photo. Also known as **springbok mantis** or **South African praying mantis**.

African female laying eggs

African praying mantis is narrow here

male

Earwigs / Hiore Kakati
[Order: Dermaptera]

Long, thin insects, usually brown, with a flat, flexible, leathery body. For defence, they have stink glands and tail nippers, often curling their tail forward over their head, like a scorpion. They hide during the day – usually in groups – in damp places: under rocks, bark or leaves, or inside fruit or flowers (where they are useful pollinators). Fast runners, active at night, eating plant and animal matter. Introduced ones have short, leathery front wings and large, tightly folded, ear-shaped back wings; native ones have no wings. The Māori name means 'nipping tail'. The English name is thought to come from an old belief that earwigs wiggled into ears (they rarely do), or (less likely) from the ear-shape of their wings (ear-wing > ear-wig). In England, at the turn of the sixteenth century, a paste made from ground up earwigs was poured into the ears as a cure for deafness. Earwigs have unusual social lives, choosing their mates while living together in communities. After mating, the female drives the male away. She is very protective of her eggs and young, but once her mothering duties are over, things change: the children eat her. Or, if she is still strong, she may eat them. About 1900 species are known worldwide; over 20 in New Zealand, most of them unique to this country.

Life Cycle (Incomplete metamorphosis): Egg > Nymph > Adult Earwig

Seashore Earwig / Matā
Anisolabis littorea [Family: Labiduridae]

Native Named in Māori for its shiny black appearance, like obsidian (matā). Common throughout, above the high-tide mark on pebble beaches, hiding under stones and driftwood, near seaweed and other plants. Here they eat seaweed, millipedes, hoppers and slaters. The female's tail nippers are relatively straight and symmetrical; on the male, these are shorter and more curved, the right one more tightly incurved. Wingless. The female licks her eggs to cover them with a protective coating of fungicide. New Zealand's other native earwigs are all much smaller (6 – 15 mm long) and found mainly in southern South Island forest.

European Earwig
Forficula auricularia [Family: Forficulidae]

Introduced. Common in summer in gardens, particularly inside apricots and peaches, eating around the stones. They also hunt other insects. In winter, they burrow into the ground. Although they rarely fly, they do have tightly folded wings which are hidden under hard wing-covers (rather like the hidden wings of a beetle). An up-turned flowerpot stuffed with crumpled damp paper will attract them. The male's tail nippers are more tightly curved than the female's.

Unless otherwise indicated, all photos are life-size

Termites

Termites live in communities of up to two million: a king and queen, soldiers and workers. The soldiers and workers have no eyes or wings and, although the king and queen do initially have wings, they lose these after mating. In some overseas species, the queen's body may swell to make a huge bag – up to 10 cm long – while laying up to 10,000 eggs a day. The traditional Polynesian termite name '**ane**' has not been recorded here, although it survives in the Māori names for rotten (wood): hane or hanehane. Sometimes known as 'white ants', a name later translated into Māori as **pōpokorua mā** or **pōpokorua tea**. Many are indeed white, but they are not related to ants, for they have straight antennae and no narrow waist. They are, in effect, socialised cockroaches. Termites feed on wood, dry grass, fungi and animal dung. In the tropics, the damage they do to timber rates them among the world's most serious pests. Yet termite swarms also provide an important source of human food in these countries, eaten fresh and raw, or sun-dried and sold commercially. About 2750 species are known worldwide; New Zealand has three native species, plus four introduced Australian ones which have arrived here in shipments of timber.
Life Cycle (Incomplete metamorphosis): Egg > Nymph > Adult Termite

New Zealand Drywood Termite
Kalotermes brouni [Family: Kalotermitidae]
Native Found in dead trees, rotten logs, fence posts, power poles and untreated timber. They generally feed only on dead, dry wood, but will sometimes enter living trees via wounds in the bark to feed on heartwood. Found from about Christchurch north.

Lacewings

Lacewings have four, delicate, similar-sized, net-veined wings, which are held roof-like over their slender body when at rest. These short-legged adults have ears on their wings and eat insects at night. The larvae have five to seven eyes on each side of their head with which to spot their prey. They bite their victim, inject poison to paralyse and dissolve the unfortunate creature, then suck up a liquid meal. Many can even pierce human skin to give a 'sting' rather like a wasp. About 4000 species are known worldwide; about 16 in New Zealand.
Life Cycle (Complete metamorphosis): Egg > Larva > Pupa > Adult Lacewing

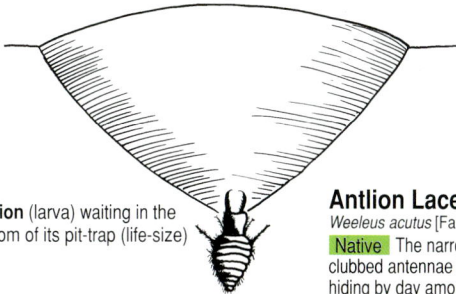

antlion (larva) waiting in the bottom of its pit-trap (life-size)

Antlion Lacewing
Weeleus acutus [Family: Myrmeleontidae]
Native The narrow-winged adult has clubbed antennae (unlike a damselfly), hiding by day among leaves and flying only at dusk. The larva (known as an **antlion**) makes a cone-shaped pit (5 cm across) in loose or sandy dry soil, and waits in a hole at the bottom to eat insects which stumble in. If the prey looks like getting away, the larva pelts sand at it.

adult at rest

adult at rest

Tasmanian Lacewing
Micromus tasmaniae [Family: Hemerobiidae]
From Australia. At night, both the larva and the adult eat mostly aphids (but also mealybugs), so are useful in the garden and on farms. Found all year, but most common in autumn. The larva looks like a flat caterpillar and sucks its food, while the adult chews.

OTHER INSECTS

Fleas / Keha

[Order: Siphonaptera]

Also known in Māori as **puruhi**, **mōrorohū** or **tuiau**. Tiny, jumping, wingless insects which look as if they have been flattened sideways. After a jump, they land facing backwards (the way they have just come from). Both the males and females suck blood. Only after their first meal, can fleas reproduce. In New Zealand, dogs, cats, rats, chickens and people (and many other animals) are attacked, but each kind of flea prefers the blood of only one of these animals. Fleas are important disease carriers, **rat fleas** being the main carrier of the Black Death (bubonic plague) which, from 1347 to 1350, killed one quarter of the population of Europe. The larvae do not eat blood but live instead on debris found in the host's dwelling. Continued exposure to sunlight kills all stages. Since ancient times, people have been entertained by harnessing fleas as 'coach horses' onto little carriages to perform in flea circuses. About 2500 species are known worldwide; 35 in New Zealand including native ones on long-tailed bats, weka, kea, fernbirds and many seabirds.

Life Cycle (Complete metamorphosis): Egg > Larva > Pupa > Adult Flea

Cat Flea
Ctenocephalides felis [Family: Pulicidae]

Introduced. Common in summer on cats. They do prefer the blood of cats, but often bite people too. For its size, this is the world's best insect jumper, one reaching a height of 34 cm in one jump, with an acceleration over 20 times that of a space rocket (with a G force of up to 140). In terms of acceleration, the human equivalent would be an athlete doing a high jump of 31 m. But, unlike the athlete, the flea will happily keep on jumping 600 times per hour for up to three days. One flea can lay 500 tiny white eggs, which hatch into bristly, whitish, thread-like 'maggots', about 2 mm long. These live in and under carpets etc, not on the cat.

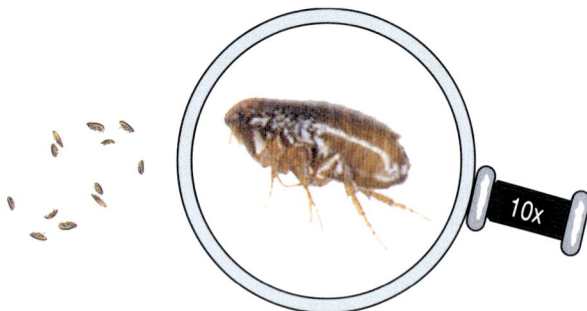

10x

Parasitic Lice / Kutu

[Order: Phthiraptera]

Tiny, flattened, wingless insects, living on birds and mammals. Males are usually smaller than females. There are two main kinds: **sucking lice** which suck blood; and **chewing** or **biting lice** which chew feathers, hair, scales etc; each species usually feeding on just one kind of animal. They can spread diseases. Found on all domestic animals, but not on possums or hedgehogs. Native lice are found on fur seals, sea lions and birds, with specific species known from kiwi, kea, kererū, tūī, bellbird, kingfisher, takahē, whio, New Zealand dotterel and many others. In many countries, human head lice are eaten but probably more as a convenience during mutual de-lousing rituals than for nutrition. About 5000 species are known worldwide; about 350 in New Zealand.

Life Cycle (Incomplete metamorphosis): Egg > Nymph > Adult Louse

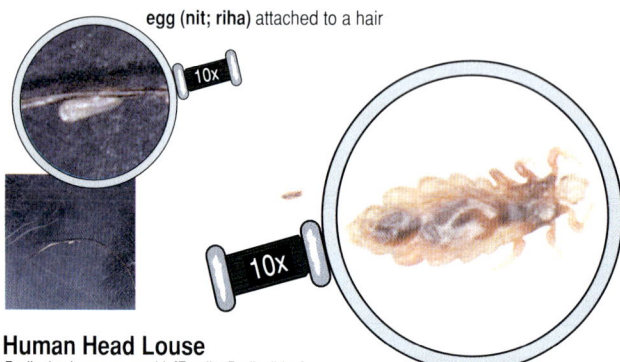

egg (nit; riha) attached to a hair

10x

10x

female   male
albatross louse

adult on an albatross feather

Human Head Louse
Pediculus humanus capitis [Family: Pediculidae]

Introduced to New Zealand before Europeans arrived. Widely known both here and overseas as **cooties** from the Polynesian and Malay name: **kutu**. These sucking lice live in people's hair, where the female lays 80 – 100 eggs (known in English as **nits**; in Māori as **riha** or **rihariha**) during her one-month life. She attaches the eggs to individual hairs using a quick-setting water-insoluble cement. Some people have been found with as many as 16,000 adult lice on them. Two other kinds of lice can trouble people in New Zealand: the **human body louse** (usually found on clothing) and the **crab louse** (mostly on pubic hair).

adult (cootie; kutu) full of blood

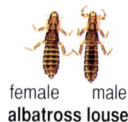

Albatross Louse
Harrisoniella hopkinsi [Family: Philopteridae]

Native A chewing louse found clinging to the wing feathers of the wandering and royal albatrosses. The male has longer antennae which he uses to grip the female when mating. First collected in 1772 on Cook's second voyage. This is New Zealand's largest louse and ranks among the largest lice known worldwide.

Unless otherwise indicated, all photos are life-size

Booklice
[Order: Psocoptera]

Small, soft-bodied insects, found mostly on the leaves and branches of trees and shrubs, under bark and in leaf litter, eating algae, fungi and lichens. However, it is the species which come into houses which are usually noticed. Although some are wingless, many species can fly. The females of some have amplifiers and rows of teeth on their legs, so are believed to be able to 'make music'. About 3000 species are known worldwide; over 50 in New Zealand.

Life Cycle (Incomplete metamorphosis):
Egg > Nymph > Adult Booklouse

A Booklouse
Trogium pulsatorium [Family: Trogiidae]

Introduced. So tiny that they are often overlooked, as they run quickly across the furniture, then suddenly stop. They feed on moulds growing on the glue in bindings of damp old books and wallpaper, but rarely do any damage. The female is sometimes heard at night signalling to the male by beating a hard lump on her tail-end on whatever she is standing on. This tapping sounds like the ticking of a watch and is loudest when she is standing on paper; it can go on for as much as an hour at a time. Wingless. Another common household species, *Liposcelis divinatorius*, behaves in the same way.

Silverfish
[Order: Thysanura]

Flat, wingless insects with three, long, widely-spread tail bristles. Most are active at night. The males leave their sperm on the ground on silken threads for the females to pick up. Silverfish have lived on Earth for over 300 million years – since before the first dinosaurs. About 370 species are known worldwide; at least three in New Zealand (although several more native species are thought to live in forest leaf litter). One small, yellowish, native species (a so-called 'goldfish') lives in ants' nests in the northern half of the North Island.

Life Cycle (Primitive): Eggs hatch as little silverfish

paper with silverfish damage

Silverfish
[Family: Lepismatidae]

Found worldwide and accidentally introduced to New Zealand by early settlers. These insects are shaped like a small, flat fish, covered with silvery scales. Originally, they would have lived in caves, but have since found that the damp, dark areas of homes are just as good. Here, they are common, often damaging books and wallpaper, attracted to flour and paper with glue in it. They are active at night, moving quickly like a tiny lizard. (Surprisingly, the common species in New Zealand is from South Africa.)

Thrips
[Order: Thysanoptera]

Tiny (1 – 3.5 mm long), slender, flattened, sucking insects with two pairs of narrow, feather-like wings. Most feed on plants, especially in flowers; a few feed on small insects. Common ones in New Zealand include **gorse soft shoot thrips** (introduced to help control gorse), **onion thrips**, **greenhouse thrips** and **New Zealand flower thrips**. (Note that the word 'thrips' is both singular and plural.) About 5000 species are known worldwide; about 34 in New Zealand, many of them native.

Life Cycle (Incomplete metamorphosis):
Egg > Larva > Pupa > Adult Thrips

Greenhouse Thrips
Heliothrips haemorrhoidalis [Family: Thripidae]

Introduced. Arrived in New Zealand about 1930. Now found from Christchurch north. Seen all year but especially in autumn. It is so tiny that it is usually spotted only by a silver pattern left where the nymphs and adults have been sucking on the top surface of leaves or fruit.

Springtails
[Superclass: Hexapoda. Class: Collembola. Order: Collembola]

Tiny, wingless, soft-bodied creatures, very common in damp leaf litter and compost, where they eat mostly rotting leaves. Found from Antarctica to the Himalayan peaks. Most are just 1 – 3 mm long, but New Zealand is home to two of the world's largest known species (about 14 mm long). In spite of having six legs, springtails are **not true insects**, for they have a different kind of mouth. Many are blind, although they can still sense light and dark. With a forked spring under their tail, many can leap into the air to escape predators. Fossil records show they have lived on Earth for about 370 million years. About 6500 species are known worldwide; about 400 in New Zealand, most of them unique to this country.

Life Cycle (Primitive): Eggs hatch as little springtails

Springtails
[Order: Collembola]

Many species found in leaf litter. They often fall into swimming pools, where they can lie so thick on the water as to look like piles of soot.

Unless otherwise indicated, all photos are life-size

Troubleshooting

Does it have six legs? If not, check:

(1) Does it have eight legs? If so, it is a spider or a spider relative (**Arachnid***). For example:

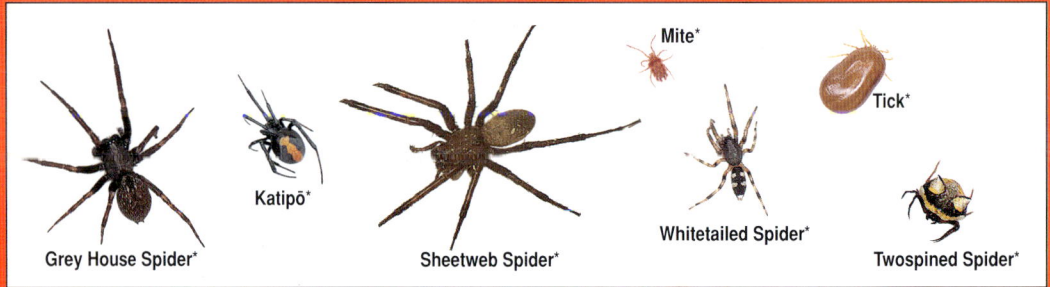

Mite*

Tick*

Katipō*

Grey House Spider*

Sheetweb Spider*

Whitetailed Spider*

Twospined Spider*

(2) Does it have ten legs or more? If so, it is **another kind of Arthropod***. For example:

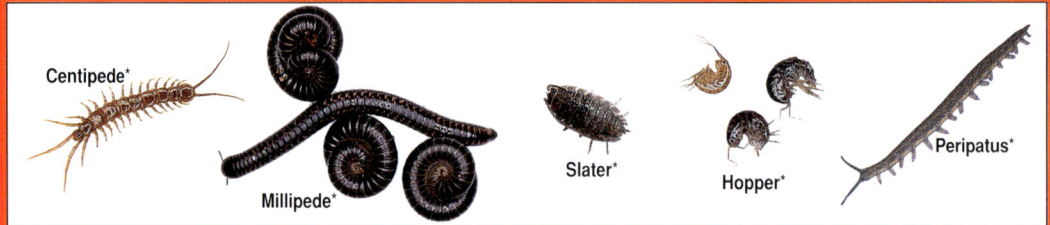

Centipede*

Millipede*

Slater*

Hopper*

Peripatus*

(3) If it has no legs and is slimy, it may be **another kind of invertebrate***. For example:

Flatworm*

Snail*

Worm*

Slug*

(4) If it has no legs, it may be a **larva** (young form) of an insect. For example:

Maggots (page 62)

Wireworm (page 51)

Rat-Tailed Maggot (page 63)

(5) If it has six ordinary jointed legs at the front and a set of stubby 'false legs' further back, it is a **caterpillar** (a larva of a butterfly or moth). For example:

Monarch Caterpillar
(page 10)

* For such non-insect invertebrates, see *The Life-Size Guide to Insects and Other Land Invertebrates of New Zealand* by Andrew Crowe (Penguin, 1999).

Jargonbuster

Unless explained within the text itself, technical terms have been avoided.
The most useful of these terms are here explained in more detail.

abdomen: An insect's abdomen is the back section of its body (the part with no legs or wings attached).

antennae: An insect's 'feelers'. These are often used as much for smelling as for feeling.

arthropod: A group of **invertebrates** with jointed legs and a 'skeleton' on the outside. Includes insects, but also spiders, slaters, hoppers, centipedes and millipedes.

biodiversity: Variety of life.

complete metamorphosis: The development of an insect which begins life as a **larva**, then rests as a **pupa** to transform into a very different-looking adult. For example: a caterpillar resting as a chrysalis before changing into a butterfly. See page 6.

ecosystem: A community of living things and the environment they live in.

elytra: The hard wing-covers on a beetle.

endemic: An endemic New Zealand insect is a species found only in this country.

habitat: The place where something lives.

halteres: The little wing-like 'drum-stick' shapes that flies have in place of back wings. These are used to help the fly to keep good balance while flying. See page 58.

hexapod: A group (Superclass) of **arthropods**, all of which have six legs. Hexapods include both insects and springtails (page 111).

incomplete metamorphosis: The development of an insect which changes gradually in several stages (**instars**) from its young form (**nymph**) into an adult. Such insects do not go through a **pupal** resting stage. For example: a cockroach is born from its egg looking like a little cockroach. See page 6.

insect: The main group of six-legged creatures (**hexapods**). Does not include springtails.

instar: One of the moulting stages in an insect's life.

introduced: Brought to a particular country by people (often by accident).

invertebrate: An animal without a backbone. Includes **arthropods** but also soft-bodied creatures such as slugs, snails and worms.

larva (plural: **larvae**): The young form of an insect, where it is completely different from the adult. Includes caterpillars (from a butterfly or moth), grubs (from a beetle) and maggots (from a fly).

native: Lives and breeds in a particular country or region (e.g. New Zealand) but not introduced by people. (Note that most native insects are also **endemic**.)

nymph: The young form of an insect, where it looks similar to a small adult. (Note however that some modern scientists don't differentiate between a 'larva' and a 'nymph'.)

ovipositor: The egg-laying organ of a female insect. On some insects, like wētā, this is a very conspicuous spike at the tail end.

pupa (plural: **pupae**): The resting stage of those kinds of insects which transform from being a **larva** into a very different-looking adult.

thorax: An insect's thorax is the mid-section of its body, the part between its head and its **abdomen**, where all its legs are attached – and its wings, too, if it has these. The thorax can be further divided into three parts (one for each pair of legs): front legs (prothorax), middle legs (mesothorax) and back legs (metathorax).

Threatened Species: On the Department of Conservation's official List of Threatened Species. An **endemic** species in trouble because its **habitat** is being damaged or because it is being eaten by an **introduced** animal.

undescribed species: A species which no one has yet studied in enough detail to give it a scientific name.

Useful Books

The following titles have been selected as useful books for the beginner.
This list does not include the more technical insect catalogues published by Landcare.

Bigelow, R. S. *The Grasshoppers of New Zealand.* University of Canterbury, Christchurch, 1967.

Chapman, Bruce. *Backyard Bugs: A Guide to Pest Control in the Home and Garden.* Lincoln University Press, 1998.

Child, John. *New Zealand Insects.* Fontana Periwinkle, 1974.

Dale, Patrick. *A Houseful of Strangers: Living with the common creatures of the New Zealand house and garden.* HarperCollins, 1992.

Foord, Malcolm. *The New Zealand Descriptive Animal Dictionary.* Malcolm Foord, Dunedin, 1990.

Forster, R. R. & L. M. *Small Land Animals of New Zealand.* John McIndoe, Dunedin, 1970.

Forster, Ray & Lyn. *Spiders of New Zealand and their Worldwide Kin.* University of Otago Press, 1999.

Gaskin, D. E. *The Butterflies and Common Moths of New Zealand.* Whitcombe & Tombs, 1966.

Gibbs, George. *The Monarch Butterfly.* Reed Books, 1994.

Gibbs, George. *New Zealand Butterflies: Identification and Natural History.* Collins, Auckland, 1980.

Gibbs, George. *New Zealand Weta.* Reed Books, 1998.

Grant, Elizabeth A. *An Illustrated Guide to some New Zealand Insect Families.* Manaaki Whenua Press, Lincoln, 1999.

Hudson, G. V. *The Butterflies and Moths of New Zealand.* Ferguson & Osborne, Wellington, 1928. (And *Supplement*, 1939.)

Hudson, G. V. *New Zealand Beetles and their Larvae.* Ferguson & Osborne, Wellington, 1934.

Meads, Mike. *Forgotten Fauna.* DSIR Publishing, 1990.

Parkinson, Brian & Brian Patrick. *Butterflies and Moths of New Zealand.* Reed Books, 2000.

Powell, A. W. B. (ed. B. J. Gill.) *Powell's Native Animals of New Zealand.* Bateman, 1998.

Rowe, Richard. *The Dragonflies of New Zealand.* Auckland University Press, 1987.

Salmon, J. T. *The Stick Insects of New Zealand.* Reed Books, Auckland, 1991.

Scott, R. R. (Ed.) *New Zealand Pest and Beneficial Insects.* Lincoln University College of Agriculture, 1984.

Scott, R. R. & R. M. Emberson. *Handbook of New Zealand Insect Names.* Entomological Society of New Zealand, 1999.

Sharell, Richard. *New Zealand Insects and their Story.* Collins, Auckland, 1971.

Taylor, Ronald L. & Barbara J. Carter. *Entertaining with Insects.* Woodbridge Press, USA, 1976.

Taylor, Ronald L. *Butterflies in My Stomach.* Woodbridge Press, USA, 1975.

Films

Microcosmos Directed by Claude Nuridsany & Marie Perennou. (Available on video.)

Websites

For information on specific insects, simply type the scientific name (e.g. *Blaberus giganteus*) into a search engine. At present, this works best for insects introduced from overseas.

Bay Area Bug Eating Society, USA	www.planetscott. com
Butterfly & Orchid Garden, Victoria Street, Tararu, Thames	www.butterfly.co.nz
Edible Insects	www.eatbug.com
Manaaki Whenua Press (for technical publications)	www.mwpress.co.nz

Clubs

The Entomological Society of New Zealand, P.O. Box 498, Ashburton.
(Auckland Branch: c/o Landcare, Private Bag 92170, Auckland.)
(Dunedin Branch: c/o Otago Museum, P.O. Box 6202, Dunedin.)

Index

Where there are several page numbers,
the main entry is shown in **bold type**.

116

117

119

124

Māori names

Unlike the modern Western evolutionary model of insect classification, the traditional Māori (and Polynesian) classification system is based primarily on observations about their behaviour. Names also vary from tribe to tribe. It is easy, then, to see how many of the 400 or so recorded Māori insect names have been wrongly applied in Māori dictionaries (and other insect name lists) to a particular species (or Order of insects) when they in fact represent tribal or regional variations of names for the wider historical category in which the insect was placed. Such errors can often be identified through a comparative study of Polynesian languages.

As the Māori language evolves, there is a trend, however, toward the use of more specific names, some of which are derived from English, e.g. pī (bee), wāpi (wasp) or kokoroihe (cockroach).

Such recent names have now entered popular usage. Hence, the Māori names used in this book embrace both approaches to the language: traditional and Western.

Common names

Internationally, common names for most of the insect families in this book are already well established. Common alternatives have also been included. When it comes to individual species, the common names used here are, wherever practicable, those published by the Entomological Society of New Zealand, or CSIRO (Australia). Where no such name has been established, this book generally follows those names already published elsewhere (as summarised in Malcolm Foord's *Descriptive Animal Dictionary*). Where no common name has been published before (or the published common name is confusing), leading entomologists in those fields, or I, in consultation with them, have coined a new name. In addition, several common colloquial names in particularly wide usage are also included, e.g. sandfly, mozzie, nit, cootie, crawler, gnat, sedge, dun, skipjack and stink bug. Hopefully, the inclusion of these names will help to make conservation and natural science more accessible.

Scientific names

Scientific names follow Landcare's *Fauna of New Zealand* series, except where published names supersede these. To help with cross-referencing to other books, simplified synonyms have been included in an abbreviated form, e.g. (was *Hydriomena*).

Acknowledgements

The field of insect study is so huge, complex and time consuming that it is certainly a big ask to seek help from experts in this field. I have been, then, all the more impressed, while researching for this book, to have met so many remarkably generous, helpful and patient people ready to share their hard-earned knowledge.

I would especially like to thank John Early, Rosemary Gilbert and Stephen Thorpe (all of Auckland Museum) for good humouredly answering so many questions and requests; likewise a **big** thank you to John Dugdale (Landcare, Nelson – retired) and Brian Patrick (Otago Museum) both of whom offered considerable help with common names for native moths and hitherto unpublished information on their foodplants. (That's John Early's blood on page 85.)

Ricardo Palma (Te Papa), Brian Patrick (Otago Museum) Trevor Crosby (Landcare), and Roger Crabtree (FRI, Rotorua) all provided valuable advice and access to their collections. Thanks also to Olwyn Green (MAF, Lynfield), Chris Morrison (Biosecurity, MAF), Grace Hall and Leonie Clunie (Landcare, Mt Albert) all of whom kindly fielded many of my enquiries.

For further specialist input I am indebted also to Andre Larochelle, Robert Hoare, Richard Leschen, Jo Berry, Trevor Crosby, Marie-Claude Larivière, Graeme Ramsay, Willy Kuschel, Thomas Buckley and Rosa Henderson (all of Landcare, Mt Albert), Alan Flynn (MAF, Lynfield), John Bain (FRI, Rotorua), Qiao Wang and Ian Andrew (both of Massey University), Mary McIntyre (Victoria University), Carl McGuinness (DoC, Wellington), Richard Toft (Landcare, Nelson), Rowan Emberson (Lincoln University), Barry Donovan (Crop & Food Research, Lincoln), Peter Johns and Bob Pilgrim (University of Canterbury), Anthony Harris (Otago Museum), Alan Eyles (consultant), Kate Senner (consultant), Hugh Oliver (consultant), Rod Morris, Stuart Chambers and David Lane.

Carol Muir offered a useful South Island perspective from public enquiries to MAF, Lincoln. Based on extensive field research, Wendy Pond provided valuable guidance on Māori and Pacific languages. For help with internet research, my thanks to Tania Norfolk (Auckland City Library) and David Skilton.

And to all those sharp-eyed kids and fun-loving adults who helped in the grand chase for moths and butterflies, mountain grasshoppers and cicadas, fleas, flies etc: thank you for coming along.

For moral support: Kia ora, katoa! To each and all of you: I greatly appreciate your generosity and enthusiasm; I am well aware that, without it, this book could never have been written.

Andrew Crowe

About the Author

Andrew Crowe has been short-listed eleven times for various New Zealand Book Awards, receiving the AIM Children's Book Award for non-fiction in 1995 (*Which Native Forest Plant?*), and the New Zealand Library Information Association Children's Book Award for non-fiction in 1998 (*The Life-Size Guide to Native Trees*). For the design contribution to his books, he was a finalist in 1998 in GP Print Book Design Awards (*The Life-Size Guide to Native Trees*). He works full-time researching, designing, illustrating, photographing and writing on nature and travel subjects, and has had over 30 books published in New Zealand and overseas.

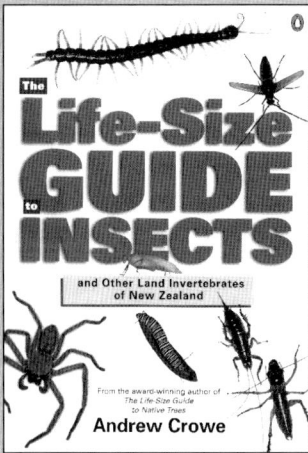

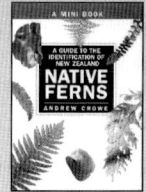

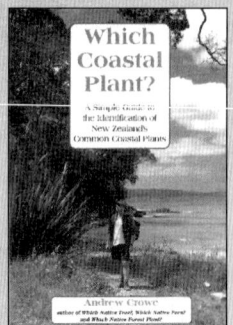

also available by
Andrew Crowe:

The Life-Size Guides

Mini Guide series

Which? identification series

Nature Flip Guides
(laminated fold-out charts)

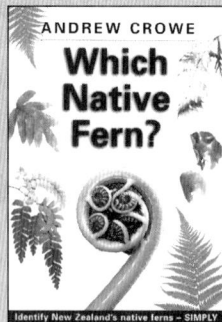

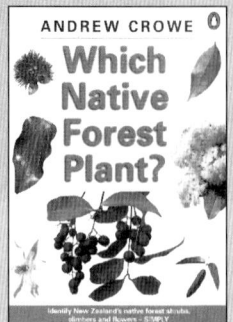